Algorithms

P9-ECQ-502

INTERNATIONAL COMPUTER SCIENCE SERIES

Consulting Editor: **A D McGettrick** *University of Strathclyde*

SELECTED TITLES IN THE SERIES

Algorithms: a functional programming approach

Second edition

Fethi Rabhi
Guy Lapalme

Addison-Wesley

Harlow, England ● Reading, Massachusetts ● Menlo Park, California ● New York
Don Mills, Ontario ● Amsterdam ● Bonn ● Sydney ● Singapore
Tokyo ● Madrid ● San Juan ● Milan ● Mexico City ● Seoul ● Taipei

© Pearson Education Limited 1999

Pearson Education Limited
Edinburgh Gate
Harlow
Essex CM20 2JE
England

and Associated Companies throughout the world.

The rights of Fethi Rabhi and Guy Lapalme to be identified as authors of this Work have been asserted by them in accordance with the Copyright, Designs and Patents Act 1988.

All rights reserved. No part of this publication may be reproduced, stored in a retrieval system, or transmitted in any form or by any means, electronic, mechanical, photocopying, recording or otherwise, without either the prior written permission of the publisher or a licence permitting restricted copying in the United Kingdom issued by the Copyright Licensing Agency Ltd, 90 Tottenham Court Road, London W1P 9HE.

The programs in this book have been included for their instructional value. They have been tested with care but are not guaranteed for any particular purpose. The publisher does not offer any warranties or representations nor does it accept any liabilities with respect to the programs.

Many of the designations used by manufacturers and sellers to distinguish their products are claimed as trademarks. Pearson Educaiton Limited has made every attempt to supply trademark information about manufacturers and their products mentioned in this book. A list of the trademark designations and their owners appears on this page.

Cover designed by Designers & Partners, Oxford
Typeset in 10/12 pt Times by 56
Printed and bound in Great Britain by Biddles Ltd, Guildford and King's Lynn.

First published 1999

ISBN 0201-59604-0

British Library Cataloguing-in-Publication Data
A catalogue record for this book is available from the British Library

Library of Congress Cataloguing-in-Publication Data
Rabhi, Fethi
Algorithms : a functional approach / Fethi Rabhi, Guy Lapalme.
        p.   cm.
Includes bibliographical references and index.
ISBN 0-201-59604-0
1. Computer algorithms. 2. Functional programming languages. I. Lapalme, Guy. II. Title.
QA76.9.A43R34   1999
005.1–dc21   99-10106
                                                                                                   CIP

Trademark notice
The following are trademarks or registered trademarks of their respective companies.

Miranda is a trademark of Research Software Limited.

UNIX is licensed through X/Open Company Ltd.

Windows is a trademark of Microsoft Corporation.

AUGUSTANA LIBRARY
UNIVERSITY OF ALBERTA

Contents

Preface

....

Purpose/goals

This book is primarily an introduction to the design of algorithms for problem solving. Its prominent feature is to use a *functional language* as an implementation language. Because of the high level of abstraction provided, functional programs tend to be shorter, clearer and faster to develop than their imperative counterparts. This contributes to a better understanding of the algorithm being implemented and makes it possible to explore alternative solutions more rapidly. Although we believe that this is true for a wide range of algorithms, the book also discusses the limitations of functional style in dealing with certain problems.

This book is not about a particular functional language. The material is arranged in the same way as in a classic algorithms book: it is a succession of chapters on 'traditional' topics such as sorting and searching algorithms. In addition, the choice of a functional language permits the introduction of algorithm design strategies such as divide-and-conquer and dynamic programming by means of higher-order functions. New concepts such as process networks and parallel algorithms can also be introduced in a non-conventional way. Due to this extra material, topics such as lower bound proofs and N-P completeness theory are not covered.

The emphasis of the book is on intuitive and pragmatic program development techniques. This is only a small step forward, as we believe that functional programming provides a link between the study of algorithms and the study of correctness proofs and systematic derivation from formal specifications. We are hoping that more publications covering this area will emerge in the near future.

Another aim of this book is to provide a useful reference of functional programs related to a variety of problems. Programmers will be able to choose (or adapt) a functional program that is relevant to their problem as they already do with other languages such as Fortran, Pascal or C. We are also hoping that this book will contribute towards making functional languages more viable as a programming tool.

Approach

Each chapter addresses a specific problem area by describing the associated algorithms. Each algorithm is specified using a trivial (but sometimes inefficient) functional program. In some cases, a more efficient (and often more obscure) version can be derived. Sections containing non-essential material are marked with a (†) symbol and can be safely skipped. Exercises are included at the end of each chapter. For an excellent companion book which provides further details about most of the algorithms presented in this book, we recommend Brassard and Bratley's *Fundamentals of Algorithmics* [19].

Another feature of the book is the use of Haskell, a newly proposed functional language standard, named after the logician Haskell B. Curry. Haskell is purely functional, uses lazy evaluation and incorporates most of the features of modern functional languages. It is free to use, has numerous implementations on almost all platforms, and is available from sites worldwide. Appendix A provides some information about these implementations.

The Haskell source code of the programs given in this book and the answers to selected exercises are available from the following WWW site:

```
http://www.iro.umontreal.ca/~lapalme/Algorithms-functional.html
```

Target audience

This book is primarily targeted at undergraduate students in computer science studying algorithms. Within a traditional course that uses imperative languages, only a fraction of the known algorithms can be completely implemented. By adopting a functional language, more prototypes can be developed; this contributes to a better understanding of the techniques involved, since implementing a particular algorithm requires a complete understanding of all the details related to this algorithm. This approach also allows experimentation with certain types of algorithms (such as process networks) which would be too difficult to program in an imperative language.

The prerequisites are:

- Students must have had some programming experience in any language, preferably a functional language. Some notion of how functional languages are implemented is also desirable.

- A minimum mathematical background (mostly summations) is required for the analysis of algorithms although these sections can safely be omitted by those who are not interested in complexity or efficiency analysis.

The book can also be used to support an advanced functional programming course in a variety of ways: (1) by presenting examples of implementing and using data structures such as queues, trees and graphs, (2) by introducing program design techniques, (3) by increasing the awareness concerning time and space efficiency, and (4) by presenting some advanced topics such as process networks and parallel algorithms.

As mentioned previously, the book is also a useful source of functional programs which can be regarded as executable specifications of the algorithms concerned.

Overview

The book is roughly divided into three parts. The first part contains all the background information needed before embarking on the main body of the book. Chapter 1 presents the basic concept of an algorithm and highlights key features of functional languages with a brief history of their evolution and role in recent years. Chapter 2 contains an introduction to the functional language Haskell. Chapter 3 is a review of evaluation mechanisms such as strict and lazy evaluation, with an overview of the graph reduction model. It defines what is meant by 'efficiency' and presents some simple transformations that increase the efficiency of programs. Chapter 4 examines simple concrete data structures (lists, trees, and arrays) and the efficiency of the operations used to manipulate these data structures.

The second part of the book considers some basic algorithms for a variety of purposes. Chapter 5 examines abstract data types (ADTs), using them to represent for example priority queues and binary search trees. Chapter 6 presents sorting techniques such as quicksort and heapsort and Chapter 7 discusses graphs and associated algorithms such as computing the minimum spanning tree and depth-first search.

The last part addresses some high-level methodologies used in the design of algorithms. Chapter 8 describes top-down design techniques such as divide-and-conquer and backtracking search. Chapter 9 explains some inefficiencies in top-down algorithms and how they can be solved by adopting a bottom-up approach, namely dynamic programming. Finally, Chapter 10 examines some advanced topics such as process networks, monads, and parallel algorithms through some extensions to the Haskell language.

Acknowledgements

The idea of the book came while the first author was a visiting lecturer at Allegheny College so our special thanks are due to Mike Holcombe, Bob Cupper and Ben Haytock for making it possible. We would like to thank Aster Thien, Marina Mahmood, Chris Meen, Len Bottaci and Rob Turner for their contribution to some of the programs presented in this book. We also thank Guy St-Denis for his many constructive suggestions on a preliminary version of this book, our editor Michael Strang for his continued support, and the anonymous reviewers who found many inaccuracies and gave constructive ideas on presentation. Finally, we are grateful to the (enthusiastic!) Haskell community for their efforts in designing a standard functional language and for providing the scientific community with free implementations.

Fethi Rabhi (F.A.Rabhi@dcs.hull.ac.uk)
Guy Lapalme (lapalme@iro.umontreal.ca)

Introduction

....

This chapter provides some background information for reading and assimilating the material presented in the rest of the book. It introduces some basic mathematical and algorithmic concepts and the essential features of functional programming languages.

1.1 Algorithms

First, we give a brief introduction to the concept of an algorithm, how algorithms are implemented, and what is meant by analyzing an algorithm.

1.1.1 What is an algorithm?

The word algorithm comes from the name of the famous Persian mathematician Mohammed al-Khowarizmi who is credited for inventing the rules for adding, subtracting, multiplying and dividing decimal numbers. An informal definition of an algorithm would state that it is 'a step by step procedure for solving a problem or accomplishing some end'. Harel [49] defines it as 'an abstract recipe, prescribing a process which may be carried out by a human, a computer or by other means'. Although this can mean that algorithms may be applied in any context, our main interest is in how algorithms are implemented on a computer.

Euclid's algorithm for finding the greatest common divisor (gcd) of two numbers is probably one of the oldest and most frequently used examples of an algorithm. Given two positive integers m and n, the gcd, which is defined as the largest positive integer that evenly divides both m and n, is obtained as follows:

1. Use two counters x and y. Initialize the value of x with m and the value of y with n.

2. If $x > y$, then the new value of x becomes $x - y$.

3. If $x < y$, then the new value of y becomes $y - x$.

4. Repeat the operations 2 and 3 until the value of x equals the value of y.

The final value of x (or y since it is the same) is the gcd of the two original numbers m and n. This algorithm, which can be traced back to well before the time of the ancient Greeks, can also be expressed using division and modulus operations to avoid repeated subtractions.

Since this book is dedicated to the study of algorithms, it contains several examples of algorithms classified either according to the problem they are solving or according to the design strategy that produced them in the first place.

1.1.2 Implementing algorithms

An algorithm is only useful if it can be translated into instructions that are executable. In other words, algorithms need to be implemented using a computer language. Several language paradigms, such as imperative, functional, and logic paradigms, are available to the algorithm implementor. The best-known one is the imperative (or procedural) paradigm which forms the basis for most common languages such as Pascal and C. Translating an algorithm into an imperative language involves building the solution using data structures such as variables and arrays and joining them with control structures such as conditional and loop statements. The main advantage of using imperative languages is that they have been designed with the computer architecture in mind, so the way the algorithm is executed by the computer is fairly straightforward.

If another language paradigm is used, then the algorithm must be formulated using the constructs offered by this new paradigm. These constructs are then turned into machine code by the compiler for this language. For example, the functional language paradigm offers recursion as the main control structure, and non-updatable lists as one of the main data structures. The use of these higher level constructs eases the implementation of an algorithm but can make it harder to reason about the efficiency of the program.

1.1.3 The analysis of algorithms

The main motivation for using computers to implement algorithms is that of speed. As millions of instructions can be executed in only a few seconds, some problems that are too large to be solved by hand can be easily tackled. Then, an important question arises: given several algorithms for solving the same problem, which one should be selected for implementation? The answer is that the most efficient one should be used, that is, the one that takes less time to execute. Given that algorithms would have to work on large problems, the payoff for designing a 'good' algorithm can be significant at execution time.

At this stage, we must decide on the criteria that should be used to measure the efficiency of an algorithm. The exact execution time could constitute one possible measure but this approach suffers from several serious defects. First, this time varies according to the computer being used. Secondly, it depends on how various language constructs are translated into machine code by the compiler. In addition, it is often desirable to compare different algorithms before implementing them so as to avoid developing code unnecessarily. The usual technique used in analyzing an algorithm is to isolate an operation fundamental to the problem under study. This is called the *complexity measure*. Then, a walk through the algorithm reveals how many times the operation that corresponds to our measure is invoked. The result of the analysis is often expressed as a function of the size of the input. The size of the input is often related to the size of the data structure used in the algorithm.

For example, consider computing the maximum value in a list of n numbers. We assume that the complexity measure is a comparison operation between two numbers. A simple algorithm for this problem initializes the maximum value with the value of the first number in the list, and compares this maximum with every remaining number, replacing the current maximum value with any value found to be greater. The number of comparisons made by this algorithm is equal to the length of the list minus one since the first number is not compared. Therefore, the time complexity of this algorithm can be described by a function that takes the size n of the input list as an argument. This function is defined as:

$$T_{\texttt{maximum}}(n) = n - 1$$

Chapter 3 is devoted to explaining in more detail the mechanics of analyzing algorithms expressed in a functional language.

Worst-case, best-case, and average-case analysis

Even with the same input size, an algorithm might perform a different amount of work, particularly if the work performed is dependent on data values. For example, consider the problem of searching for an item sequentially in a list of n items. We assume that the complexity measure is a comparison operation between two items. The solution might take from one step (if the item is found at the beginning of the list) to n steps (if the item is found at the end of the list).

The *worst-case complexity* is defined as the maximum work performed by an algorithm. Similarly the *best-case complexity* represents the minimum amount of work and the *average-case complexity* represents the work done on average. For the sequential search example, the worst-case and the best-case complexities are respectively:

$$T_{\texttt{search}_{WC}}(n) = n$$
$$T_{\texttt{search}_{BC}}(n) = 1$$

In the average-case, the complexity is measured in terms of probabilities. It is defined as the sum of the work performed times the probability for all possible situations. In the previous example, if we assume that the searched item can be in any position in the list with an equal probability of $1/n$, the average-case complexity is:

$$T_{\texttt{search}_{AC}}(n) = \sum_{i=1}^{n} \frac{1}{n} \times i = \frac{1}{n} \sum_{i=1}^{n} i = \frac{1}{n} \times \frac{n(n+1)}{2} = \frac{n+1}{2}$$

The average-case complexity is harder to carry out since we need to know the probability of success or failure of all the tests in the algorithm. The worst-case analysis is usually easier to perform so it is the one carried out in most of the algorithms in the book.

Besides choosing measures that provide an idea about time complexity, we could also choose measures that give other information concerning the behavior of the program such as the *space complexity*. Given a suitable measure, such as the number of list cells used during the execution, the space analysis can proceed in exactly the same way as the time analysis.

Asymptotic growth of complexity functions

We have just seen that the analysis of algorithms only provides an approximation of the run-time behavior of a program after it has been implemented on a computer. This approximation can be used to determine which algorithm is more efficient.

Supposing that two algorithms which solve a problem of size n are found to have the following complexities:

$$T_1(n) = 2n$$

$$T_2(n) = 4n$$

It is tempting to say that the first algorithm is more efficient than the second one. However, remember that we are only counting the occurrences of a specific operation while ignoring the rest of the program so a closer approximation would be $T_1(n) = 2cn$ where c is a constant that represents the remaining operations. Similarly, the second algorithm's equation is better approximated by $T_2(n) = 4c'n$ where c' is another constant. In this case, it is no longer possible to take it for granted that the first algorithm is better than the second, since it all depends on the constants c and c'.

Consider now the complexity of a third algorithm:

$$T_3(n) = 0.001n^2$$

We can see that for small values of n, the third algorithm is more efficient than the previous two and that for large values of n, it is less efficient. If we add a constant as in the previous two cases, we can see that this algorithm will still be less efficient than the previous two for large values of n.

Since the main motivation for comparing algorithms is to test their behavior on large problems, the comparison between algorithms is going to be on *the asymptotic rate of growth* of the complexity function.

The growth of functions is therefore determined by ignoring constant factors and small input sizes. What matters most in algorithms 1 and 2 is the factor n so it is said that they belong to the same class, namely $O(n)$. The notation $g(n) \in O(f(n))$, read 'g is in big Oh of f', provides an upper limit on the growth of $g(n)$ which is no more than the growth of $f(n)$. Formally, $g(n) \in O(f(n))$ means that there exists a positive integer n_0 and some positive real constant c such that $g(n) \leq cf(n)$ for all $n > n_0$.

The three algorithms described previously can now be classified according to their asymptotic growth rate:

$$T_1(n) \in O(n)$$

Table 1.1 Examples of functions and their growth rates.

Function	Growth rate	Example	Time for $n = 1000$ (assuming 1 step = 1 microsecond)
$O(1)$	Constant	10	10 microseconds
$O(\log n)$	Logarithmic	$2\log n + 3$	23 microseconds
$O(n)$	Linear	$\frac{n}{2} + 50$	0.55 milliseconds
$O(n^2)$	Quadratic	$2n^2 - 3n$	2 seconds
$O(n^3)$	Cubic	$n^3 - n^2 + 2n$	16 minutes
$O(2^n)$	Exponential	2^n	10^{86} centuries
$O(n!)$	Factorial	$n!$	10^{2552} centuries

$$T_2(n) \in O(n)$$
$$T_3(n) \in O(n^2)$$

According to our definition, we also have $T_1(n) \in O(n^2)$ and $T_2(n) \in O(n^2)$. Other more precise notations (such as θ) exist but the 'big Oh' notation is sufficient for our purposes.

Table 1.1 shows the most common asymptotic functions in increasing growth rate, with an example and how much it would take to run on a hypothetical computer. It can be seen that the exponential and factorial growth rates for a large input size are well beyond the capacity of any computer and even beyond the age of the universe!

Various mathematical concepts and formulas for analyzing the complexity of algorithms are listed in Appendix B.

1.2 Functional languages

This section introduces the basic concepts behind functional languages, most of which will be considered in more detail in the next chapter. It also presents a brief overview of the theoretical foundations and evolution history of functional languages.

1.2.1 Functions, λ-calculus and induction

A function can be loosely described as a way of computing an output value from an input value. Functions have already been used earlier for example to define complexity growth rates but it is important to look closer at the mathematical foundations of the notion of a function.

A function can be represented by a graph depicting its input–output relation. For example, a function for computing the double of a natural number would be described 'extensionally' by pairs where the first element is the input value and the second element the corresponding result:

$(0, 0), (1, 2), (2, 4), (3, 6) \ldots$

But from the algorithmic point of view, this representation of a function is not very useful because we are often more interested in determining *how* to compute the output value from a given input than in looking up an output value in a set of precomputed pairs. Some ways of computing an output are more efficient than others. For example, we could (at least conceptually) sort a list of numbers in increasing order by permuting these numbers and then checking that every number in the new list is less or equal than the preceding one. Unfortunately, this algorithm is not very efficient and is not of any practical value. Programming seeks to define efficient means for finding the output value and functional programming is no different in this respect.

We are more interested in an 'intensional' definition of a function. Mathematicians have defined the λ-*calculus* to express rules of correspondence between input and output values. The λ-calculus gives a notation for defining a function by $\lambda x.M$ where M is an expression involving x. The value computed by such a function using an input value is given by the 'application' of that function on that value. For example, $(\lambda x.M)Y$ will compute the expression M after having replaced all occurrences of x in M by Y. For example, in the following equations we can see the results of some applications.

$$(\lambda x.x * x)(4 + 2) \rightarrow (4 + 2) * (4 + 2)$$
$$(\lambda x.xx)(\lambda y.y) \rightarrow (\lambda y.y)(\lambda y.y) \rightarrow (\lambda y.y)$$

More details about this formalism can be found in [7, 48]. This seemingly simple idea is very powerful and it has been shown that every computable function can be defined using the λ-calculus.

This model has long been used by computer scientists as a theoretical basis for computer languages. Unfortunately, as λ-calculus models mathematical functions, it does not take into account the modifications of variables. Allowing such modifications was one of the fundamental ideas used by the von Neumann model for computers. It was not until the mid-1970s that efficient implementations of purely functional languages were developed so that they could then show their usefulness on real problems.

Mathematical induction is another powerful tool that is at the root of functional programming. It is used in mathematics for proving properties by building upon a simple case, the *base case*, for which the property is easily proved. The next step is proving that if the property holds for some n, then it is also true for $n + 1$. For example, for proving the first summation formulation of Appendix B.3 (the sum of the n first integers is $\frac{n(n+1)}{2}$), we can check that the property is true for $n = 1$ because $\frac{1 \times 2}{2} = 1$. We then assume that the property is true for some $n > 1$, that is

$$1 + 2 + \ldots + n = \frac{n(n + 1)}{2} \qquad (*)$$

We now try to prove that the property is true for $n + 1$, which corresponds to the following sum:

$$1 + 2 + \ldots + n + (n + 1)$$

Since the sum of the first n terms is given by our assumption $(*)$, the expression becomes:

$$1 + 2 + \ldots + n + (n + 1) = \frac{n(n + 1)}{2} + (n + 1)$$
$$= \frac{n^2 + n + 2n + 2}{2}$$

$$= \frac{n^2 + 3n + 2}{2}$$

$$= \frac{(n+1)(n+2)}{2}$$

which is the formula to be proved for $n + 1$. As this property is true for 1 and any $n + 1$ given that it is true for n, then it is true for any $n \geq 1$. This is the simplest and least powerful form of mathematical induction.

In computer science, algorithms are often defined recursively: starting with a problem dealing with n values, we solve the problem using the solution for $n - 1$ and so on until we arrive at a simple case for which it is not necessary to subdivide further. We can see that this process is quite similar to induction which is often used for proving properties of algorithms such as the memory space used and the time it takes to execute.

1.2.2   Why functional languages?

Functional languages draw their names from the fact that their basic operations are defined using functions which are invoked using function applications and 'glued' together using function composition. Another interesting characteristic is that functions are 'first-class' objects, that is, they can be used as any other object: given as parameters, returned as results of other functions and stored in data structures.

Using functions in this way gives a lot of flexibility to the programmer because of the fundamental properties of functions that make it possible to abstract or easily modularize the processing of data. Functions can also be composed to give rise to new functions.

For example, the three following functions define respectively the factorial of n, the sum of integers up to n and the sum of the squares of the integers up to n:

```
fact n    | n==0  = 1
          | n>0   = n * fact(n-1)

sumInt n | n==0  = 0
         | n>0   = n + sumInt(n-1)

sumSqr n | n==0  = 0
         | n>0   = n*n + sumSqr(n-1)
```

These functions are written in Haskell, the functional language we will use in this book, using *recurrence equations* (see Appendix B.4). As we will see later, these functions can also be defined in a simpler way but here we choose to stay close to the standard mathematical definitions.

If we look closely at these definitions, we can see they all rely on the same recursion principle: that is, define the base case and then define the value of the function for n in terms of a combination of n and the value of the function for $n - 1$. It would be interesting to abstract the recursion principle in terms of the base case and a function for combining values. It can be defined as follows:

```
induction base comb n | n==0 = base
                       | n>0  = comb n (induction base comb (n-1))
```

The first equation indicates that the base value is returned if $n = 0$ and the second equation states that the combination of values is done using a function having two parameters, the first one being the current value of n and the second being the value of the induction for $n - 1$. In our notation, function application is indicated by juxtaposition.

With this framework we can unify our previous examples: fact uses 1 as a base case and multiplication for combining values while sumInt uses 0 as base case and addition for combination. In Haskell, (*) denotes the standard multiplication function and (+), the addition function; we can thus define these functions using our induction framework like this:

```
fact    n = induction 1 (*) n
sumInt  n = induction 0 (+) n
```

For the third function sumSqr, we need a function to add the square of the first argument with the second one; as this function is not predefined we can define one; we use the usual infix form for the addition and multiplication.

```
f x y = x*x + y
```

and define sumSqr with

```
sumSqr n = induction 0 f n
```

But as f would probably be needed only in this definition we can use an anonymous function notation resembling the lambda calculus notation $(\lambda\ x\ y\ .\ x * x + y)$ which is written in Haskell as (\x y -> x*x + y). So sumSqr can be defined as

```
sumSqr n = induction 0 (\x y -> x*x + y) n
```

This simple example has shown the power of expression of a functional language whose kernel language only consists of the definition and application of functions. Control structures like loops are defined using function application. In the rest of the book, we will show many examples of the power of abstraction of small functions which are combined and composed in order to build flexible modules.

1.2.3 History and evolution

The first functional languages date from the 1960s, for example, Lisp [80, 81] and Iswim [78], but these languages allowed features such as assignments that made them less 'pure'. The interest in purely functional languages was renewed in 1978 by the Turing lecture of Backus [6], the father of Fortran. Functional languages are most often characterized by the features they lack, that is, no assignment and no explicit sequencing, rather than by the features they possess: functions as first class objects and referential transparency. We will come back to these points later.

Much of the important work in purely functional languages originated in the United Kingdom: in 1976 David Turner introduced SASL (St-Andrews Static Language) [118]

followed in 1982 by KRC (Kent Recursive Calculator) [117] by which programs were defined by recursive equations. As expressions were evaluated only when necessary (dubbed *lazy evaluation*), it was possible to specify infinite lists. He also introduced a new implementation method based on combinatory logic.

Another 'thread' was developed in Edinburgh by Milner and his group who defined a new typed functional language ML (Meta Language) [45, 85]. The typing was polymorphic in the sense that it was possible to define statically typed functions for many different types of arguments provided that they used the same algorithm, for example, it was possible to define a typed function for counting the number of elements in a list of any type of elements. Moreover, the types of the functions were being inferred by the system. The user did not have to explicitly specify the types of functions; in fact, in the first versions, it was not even possible to do so. ML used an applicative style of evaluation as in Lisp, that is, parameters are fully evaluated before the function call is executed; this is in contrast with the normal order of evaluation which evaluates a parameter only when needed in a function call. There were other similar languages which used the same kind of ideas but with a slightly different point of view: Hope [23] used polymorphic typing but the types were not inferred by the system, they had to be specified by the user.

In 1986, David Turner defined Miranda [105, 119] which merged these two trends into a 'polymorphically typed lazy evaluated language with recursive equations'. Following this development, other languages appeared in the same 'vein' but with slightly different features (such as Orwell [125]). In 1990, an international committee was formed to define a new language that was finally called Haskell in honour of Haskell B. Curry, a logician whose work forms the logical basis of much of the theory behind functional programming.

Haskell mainly differs from Miranda in the following points (to which we will return later):

- it permits the overloading of function names which is often called 'ad-hoc polymorphism';
- it presents a 'monadic' view of the input–output mechanism;
- it defines a notion of functional arrays that can be implemented efficiently while keeping the notion of referential transparency.

In February 1999, Haskell 98 was defined, which is the dialect we use in this book. In Appendix A, we give some indications on how to get hold of a Haskell implementation as well as the programs used in this book.

1.2.4   Advantages and disadvantages of functional languages

The main advantages of functional languages are summarized as follows:

- **declarativeness** of the expressions which have unique values. The order of execution is not specified by the programmer but rather it is left up to the system how to compute the values given the relations to be satisfied between the values. Functional languages can be seen as 'executable mathematics'; the notation was designed to be as close as possible to the mathematical way of writing.

● **referential transparency** means that one can freely replace variables by their values and vice versa because expressions can be evaluated at any time. This property, characteristic of mathematical expressions, allows program manipulation or transformation by equational reasoning (substituting equals by equals). Functional programs are thus more tractable mathematically than their imperative counterparts.

● **high-order functions** that can take functions as arguments and return new functions as results. As we have shown in Section 1.2.2, it is possible to abstract computations and reuse them more easily.

● **polymorphism** makes it possible to write a single algorithm that works on many kinds of inputs provided the algorithm does not depend on specific properties of the input.

Unfortunately, these languages also have some disadvantages, mainly:

● **loss of performance** because no state and no update of variables is allowed; while this is a very good mathematical property to have, it can be problematic especially in the case of large data structures which have to be duplicated even though only a small part of their data has changed. States are also important for modelling input–output in a natural way. Recent functional languages such as Haskell have addressed this problem but efficiency concerns are still present.

● **less experience** from the programmers; as these languages are still experimental much less effort has been directed towards providing programming environments and tools. It is precisely the purpose of this book to make functional solutions for some 'classical' problems better known and appreciated.

(1.3) Bibliographical notes

Most of the mathematical background required for the design and analysis of algorithms is presented in Knuth's first book in the series on *The Art of Computer Programming* [73]. The analysis of algorithms is tackled in most algorithm textbooks such as the one by Smith [113]. Euclid's algorithm is described in the translation of 'Euclid's Elements' by Heath [52]. Among the wealth of textbooks on algorithms, two by Harel [49] and Brassard and Bratley [19] are worth mentioning since they do not rely too heavily on the programming language used to implement the algorithms.

The theory of λ-calculus and combinatory logic originates from the work by Church [26] and Curry [30]. Barendregt [7] and Hankin [48] provide a good introduction to these topics. The history and evolution of functional programming languages is well illustrated in an article by Hudak [60]. Most functional programming textbooks ([14, 27, 56, 93, 115, 116, 131] to cite a few) describe the general concepts of functional programming in their introductory chapters. References relating to the Haskell language are listed in the bibliographical notes at the end of the next chapter.

Chapter 2

Functional programming in Haskell

The previous chapter briefly discussed the characteristics of functional programming languages in general. This chapter is devoted to one particular language, called Haskell, which will be used to implement all the algorithms in this book. The syntax of the language is introduced through several examples. At the same time, the reader is exposed to the main concepts of functional programming. The main data structures (lists, trees, and arrays) are also introduced.

2.1 About the language

Haskell is a functional programming language named after the logician Haskell B. Curry. It has been designed over the last few years by a group of scientists in the functional programming community as a vehicle for functional programming teaching, research, and applications.

Although Haskell contains some novel features, we will try to stick as much as possible to a simple subset which is common to several other functional programming languages. The reason is to simplify the analysis by using fewer constructs and allow algorithms to be adapted to other functional languages much more easily.

Efforts in improving the language are still ongoing. In the book, we will be using the Haskell specification which is described in [100]. Many of the features of Haskell are defined in Haskell itself as a library of standard data types, classes and functions, called the 'Standard Prelude' defined in Appendix A of [100]. It is composed of a main module called `Prelude` and three submodules `PreludeList`, `PreludeText` and `PreludeIO` whose components can be used directly in any Haskell program. There are also many predefined 'library modules' which contain less frequently used functions and types; library modules are described in the 'Standard libraries' document [101] which accompanies the Haskell report. Although these libraries are a required part of any Haskell implementation, they must be explicitly imported by a program that uses them. We will show examples of such imports in this chapter.

Haskell has numerous implementations that are freely available over the Internet so the reader is encouraged to implement most of the algorithms described in the book. Details about these implementations are provided in Appendix A.

2.2 Equations and functions

In Haskell, a program is a set of equations. For example, the following equations define the area of a circle of radius r and the Stirling approximation for the factorial of number n given by $(\frac{n}{e})^n \sqrt{2\pi n}$:

```
area r     = pi * r * r


e          = 2.717281828
stirling n = (n/e)**n * sqrt(2*pi*n)
```

An equation can be qualified by a `where` clause for defining values or functions used only within an expression. It is used here for defining the formula for the cube of a number within the formula for computing the volume of a sphere of radius r given by $\frac{4}{3}\pi r^3$:

```
volume r   = 4.0 / 3.0 * pi * (cube r)
    where
    cube x = x * x * x
```

We can also use the `let` construct which is equivalent in the case of a single expression as is used in an alternate definition for computing the volume of a sphere. In this book, we add an apostrophe (quote) at the end of an identifier when it gives an alternative definition of the same function; this is reminiscent of the 'prime' in mathematical formulas.

```
volume' r = let
                 cube x = x * x * x
             in
                 4.0 / 3.0 * pi * (cube r)
```

2.2.1   Function definitions

Functions can have several cases, with the selected case depending on the value of the argument. There are several ways of defining these multiple-case functions in Haskell. We illustrate a few of the common methods below.

Firstly, the if then else construct can be used inside the function. For example, we could define the factorial function as:

```
fact n = if (n == 0)
            then 1
            else n * fact (n - 1)
```

An alternative way of specifying multiple-case functions is to use *guards*:

```
fact n | n == 0    = 1
       | otherwise = n * fact (n - 1)
```

Guards provide a syntax similar to the way functions are specified mathematically. A guard is a boolean expression which, when it evaluates to True, causes its corresponding equation to be selected.

Here is another example of the use of guards:

```
checkVal x y | x > y   = 1
             | x < y   = -1
             | x == y  = 0
```

In the last case we could have used the keyword otherwise instead of the expression x == y. The third approach we illustrate is very common. This uses *pattern matching*:

```
fact 0 = 1
fact n = n * fact (n - 1)
```

The formal parameters in the function definition are specified as *patterns*. When the function is applied to an argument, one of the function equations is selected depending on which formal argument pattern *matches* the actual argument. In this example, if we apply the fact function to the argument 0, this will cause a match with the 0 formal argument pattern in the first equation, so this equation will be selected. Any argument *other* than 0 will not match with the first equation, but *will* match with the pattern consisting of the single identifier n of the second equation. An identifier appearing in a pattern matches *any* argument.

Pattern matching will be elaborated later when structured data types are introduced but, for now, note that there is a subtlety we must be aware of, namely an argument may match more than one pattern. Passing an argument of 0 to the fact function would match with the n pattern in addition to the 0 pattern, the latter being the one we really want it to match with. To achieve our intended match the approach adopted by the implementation is to make the textual ordering of the different cases significant. Matches are tried in the order in which the equations are specified, and the first pattern that matches causes the corresponding equation to be selected. This is different from a language such as Prolog, where if several patterns match they are all tried in turn in a non-deterministic way.

Bindings

When a pattern is successfully matched with an argument, a *binding* occurs. The body of the function is evaluated with any identifiers specified in the pattern (there may be more than one, as we shall see later) taking on the value of the actual argument they matched with. So evaluating fact 3 results in the evaluation of the expression 3 * fact (3 - 1), the value of the argument, that is, 3 being bound to the identifier n.

2.2.2   Infix and prefix operators

As we have seen, operators used in expressions, such as $+$, $-$, and so on, are *infix* functions, that is, function applications are denoted by placing the function name in between the two arguments. This obviously gives us the convenience of writing them down as they would be written in mathematics. If necessary, the user can write down a *prefix* application of an operator function. In this case the infix operator is surrounded by parentheses. In the following example, f and f' define the same function, but use the (*) and (+) operators differently in the body of the function:

```
f  x y z  = x * y + z

f' x y z  = (+) ((*) x y) z
```

Some arithmetic operators such as mod and div are written in prefix form such as in:

```
g x y = (mod x y) + (div x y)
```

The reason for this is that infix operators in Haskell must consist entirely of 'symbols' (such as &, ^, !, etc.) rather than alphanumeric characters, of which mod is composed. However, we can change prefix function applications of two or more arguments into infix function applications by surrounding the function name with backquotes. Thus:

```
mod x y
```

can be written as:

```
x 'mod' y
```

This notation can be used for any prefix function.

Table 2.1 Some basic types in Haskell.

Type	Name	Example value
Integers (limited range)	`Int`	42
Integers (infinite range)	`Integer`	7376541234
Reals	`Float`	3.1415927
Booleans	`Bool`	False
Characters	`Char`	'a'
Strings	`String`	"hello"

Table 2.2 Some basic operations in Haskell.

Name	Operation
`a == b`	Equality ($a = b$)
`a /= b`	Inequality ($a \neq b$)
`a && b`	Logical and ($a \wedge b$)
`a || b`	Logical or ($a \vee b$)
`logBase b x`	Logarithm ($\log_b x$)
`truncate x`	Select integer part only

2.3 Basic types and constructed types

2.3.1 Basic types

Table 2.1 shows some basic types and their names in Haskell and Table 2.2 shows some operations on these basic types (their precise type will be discussed later). There are some other basic types and operations in Haskell that are used less frequently and need not concern us at present.

2.3.2 Constructed types

Haskell has several more sophisticated types which are derived or constructed from other types (which themselves can be basic or constructed). We will describe these in more detail later, but for now we note that there are:

- list types, for example `[Char]` (list of characters).
- tuple types, for example `(Int, Float)` (ordered pair whose first element is an integer, and whose second element is a real).
- function types, for example `Char -> Bool` (function which takes a character argument and returns a boolean result).

2.3.3 Expressing types

We can express the type of an identifier in the program. If we write:

```
i = 68
```

the type of i can be specified as:

```
i :: Int
```

we can specify the types of functions in the same way. For example:

```
isB :: Char -> Bool
```

A specification of the argument and return types for a function is known as its *type signature*. However, type definitions are rarely necessary. The compiler can infer the types of all identifiers in a program. For simple expressions and functions this process can be performed easily by humans. For example:

```
isB c = (c == 'B') || (c == 'b')
```

From the syntax we know that isB is a function, of (say) type *domain* → *range*. Thus we know c must be of type *domain*, and the expression:

```
(c == 'B') || (c == 'b')
```

must be of type *range*. The outermost component of this expression is the application of the || operator, which returns a Bool result; therefore, the type *range* must be Bool. We now need to discover the type of the argument c. There is an application of the (==) operator to c and 'B'. In order for this expression to be correctly typed, c must be of the same type as 'B', in other words Char. Therefore we can substitute Char for *domain*, and we get the final type of the function as being Char -> Bool.

2.3.4   Tuples

Mathematically, a tuple is the *cartesian product* of two or more sets. For example, if the types of the first and second elements of a pair were *A* and *B* respectively, the type of the pair would be:

$$A \times B$$

In Haskell we use a slightly different notation to represent tuple types. We would write the type of a pair as:

```
(A, B)
```

The following are some examples of tuples and their type representations in Haskell:

```
t1 = (3, True)
t1 :: (Int, Bool)

t2 = (14.8, 'd', 34)
t2 :: (Float, Char, Int)

t3 = ((True, "hello"), False, (112, 16.821))
t3 :: ((Bool, String), Bool, (Int, Float))
```

Tuples are constructed types (that is, derived from other types – those of their elements) which are used to keep data items together, much the same way as records do in imperative programs. For example, we could represent a time in hours, minutes and seconds as a three-element tuple such as (14, 32, 27). A function to determine whether one time is later than another could be written as:

```
later (h1, m1, s1) (h2, m2, s2)
    | h1 < h2    = False
    | h1 > h2    = True
    | m1 < m2    = False
    | m1 > m2    = True
    | otherwise = s1 > s2
```

A coordinate in two-dimensional space can also be stored in a two-element tuple (called a *pair*). The distance between two coordinates can be found using the function:

```
distance (x1, y1) (x2, y2)
    = sqrt (dx * dx + dy * dy)
      where
      dx = x2 - x1
      dy = y2 - y1
```

Tuples can be returned from functions, which is the conventional way in functional languages of computing 'more than one value' in a function. This technique, called *tupling*, is illustrated in the following example which returns a tuple with the two real roots for a polynomial of the form $ax^2 + bx + c$. If the discriminant d is negative, the program stops with an error message (more on returning error messages later).

```
roots (a, b, c) = (r1, r2)
    where
    r1          = (-b + r) / f
    r2          = (-b - r) / f
    f           = 2 * a
    r | d >= 0 = sqrt d
      | d < 0  = error "imaginary roots"
    d           = b * b - 4 * a * c
```

For constructed types we can often define general purpose functions that operate on values of those types. Two predefined operations for pairs are those that extract the first and second elements:

```
fst (x, y) = x
snd (x, y) = y
```

For tuples with three elements, we would have to define three new functions, such as:

```
fst3 (x, y, z) = x
snd3 (x, y, z) = y
thd3 (x, y, z) = z
```

2.4 Lists

This section gives a brief introduction to lists and list processing. We will return to lists in more detail in Chapter 4.

2.4.1 Defining lists

A list is a *linear* data structure because it is a variable length sequence of data items that are all of the same type. Some examples of list values and their types are:

```
il = [-3, 12, -14, 56, 0, 121]
il :: [Int]

bl = [True, True, False]
bl :: [Bool]

fll = [[25.3], [-52.75, 0.03, 3.78], [], [14.0, -284.492]]
fll :: [[Float]]

tl = [('a', False), ('1', True), ('d', True), ('y', False)]
tl :: [(Char, Bool)]

el = []
```

The last list is the *empty list*. We have not given a type for it since it can be used to represent a list of any type (more on this later). The list:

```
[1 .. 10]
```

is the list of integers between 1 and 10, and is shorthand for:

```
[1, 2, 3, 4, 5, 6, 7, 8, 9, 10]
```

If we write:

```
[2, 4 .. 100]
```

this is the list of even numbers between 2 and 100 inclusive (the 2 is the first list element, the step from one element to the next is 4 - 2, and the last list element is 100).

If a list does not indicate the final value such as [1..], it defines an *infinite list*; in this case, this is the list of natural numbers. You may wonder how we can have infinitely long lists in a program and expect the program to terminate. This can be achieved if an appropriate evaluation method is used to avoid evaluating values not needed from the infinite list (infinite data structures will be described in Chapter 3). Similarly, we could say:

```
[8, 42 ..]
```

This would represent the infinite list beginning with 8 and increasing in increments of 34.

2.4.2   List comprehensions

In mathematics, we often find it convenient to specify sets in terms of the conditions a value must satisfy to be a member of that set. For example, consider the following specification:

$$\{x^2 \mid x \in N \wedge prime(x)\}$$

This defines the set of primes squared. Defining sets in this way is called Zermelo Frankel set abstraction, and there is an equivalent construct in Haskell. Firstly, there is a *generating set*, from which we are taking potential values for the set being defined (in the above example the generating set is the set of natural numbers, N). Secondly, there is a *filter*, which is a predicate that determines which of the values from the generating set are going to be used to form the set being defined (the filter in our example is the predicate $prime(x)$). Lastly, once we know which values are going to be needed from the generating set, we might wish to manipulate those values in some way before placing them into the set being defined (in our example we are squaring each of the values).

Sets are not directly available in Haskell, but a *list* is rather similar except that elements from a list can be repeated and are ordered. A form of Zermelo Frankel set abstraction can be used to define lists; it is called a *list comprehension*. Basically, we just replace the sets in the definition by lists, and alter some of the symbols used. In Haskell, the above example would become (the definition of the prime function is omitted):

```
[ x * x | x <- [1..], prime x]
```

In some cases, the filter for a list comprehension is unnecessary: we may want to use all the values from the generating set. For example, the set of square roots of all the natural numbers is specified mathematically as:

$$\{\sqrt{x} \mid x \in N\}$$

In Haskell we would define the list of square roots of natural numbers as:

```
[ sqrt x | x <- [1..]]
```

Also, we are not limited to a single generating set. Suppose we wanted the set of all ordered pairs that can be formed from the two sets $\{1, 2, 3\}$ and $\{8, 9\}$. Mathematically, we could express this as:

$$\{(x, y) \mid x \in \{1, 2, 3\} \wedge y \in \{8, 9\}\}$$

In Haskell:

```
[ (x, y) | x <- [1, 2, 3], y <- [8, 9]]
```

This last example brings to light an important aspect of list comprehensions with more than one generating list: the order in which the tuples will appear in the defined list. In fact, it works so that the rightmost generator varies the fastest, and the leftmost the slowest. This means that the 1 will be taken from the left-hand generator, and tupled with all the elements of the right-hand generator before selecting the next element from the left-hand generator. Thus, the sequence of generated tuples will be:

```
[(1, 8), (1, 9), (2, 8), (2, 9), (3, 8), (3, 9)]
```

2.4.3 The (:) operator

Lists can also be built by adding a new element in front of an existing list. This is done with the (:) operator, called 'cons' for 'constructor', which takes two arguments: the first one represents the *head* of the list and the second one the *tail* of the list. Used as an infix operator, (:) separates the head from the tail. The list $[e_1, e_2, e_3 \cdots e_n]$ is thus an abbreviation for $(e_1 : (e_2 : (e_3 \cdots (e_n : []))))$, and as the operator (:) is right associative, the parentheses can be omitted. For example:

```
3 :   [4,5]                      =   [3,4,5]
True :  []                       =   [True]
[2,3] :  [ [1] , [5,6,7] ]       =   [ [2,3] , [1] , [5,6,7] ]
```

In the last example, a list of integers is added in front of a list of lists of integers.

2.4.4 List functions and pattern matching

There is a very rich set of operations that work on lists, some of which are described in this section. We will also extend our view of pattern matching, and see how this technique can be useful when writing list functions.

Simple head–tail patterns

There is a predefined function length which calculates the size or the number of elements in a list. Such a function can be defined with two equations:

```
length []    = 0
length (x:xs) = 1 + length xs
```

The definition uses case analysis on the list argument, to distinguish the empty list case from the non-empty list case. This is our first example of list pattern matching. The pattern in the first equation is the empty list, and consequently matches only with an empty list argument. The pattern in the second equation contains the (:) constructor. This should not be viewed as an application of the constructor; rather it specifies that if an *actual argument* contains an application of the (:) constructor, then it matches with this pattern, and the formal identifiers x and xs are bound to the appropriate components of the list: x is bound to the first element of the list and xs is bound to the rest of the list.

For example, suppose we pass the argument [1, 54, 17], that is (1: [54,17]) to length. This matches the second pattern, and causes the second equation to be evaluated with x bound to the left-hand argument of the (:) constructor (the element 1 at the head of the list), and xs bound to the right-hand argument of the (:) constructor (the rest of the list, namely [54, 17]). The reduction sequence would be:

```
length (1:[54,17])        ⇒   1 + length [54,17]
1 + (length (54:[17]))    ⇒   1 + (1 + length [17])
1 + (1 + length (17:[])) ⇒   1 + ( 1 + (1 + length []))
                          ⇒   1 + ( 1 + (1 + 0))
                          ⇒   3
```

The symbol ⇒, which should read as 'reduces to', is used to denote a *reduction step* (more on this in Chapter 3). The recursive nature of the function is not coincidental, but follows logically from the recursive property of the data type it processes. We will see that functions which operate on other recursive data types such as *trees* also tend to be recursive. Many functions that operate on lists have the same 'form' as this function, a fact which is taken advantage of by defining *higher-order functions* to factor out the structural similarity of the individual functions, discussed in a later section.

As the value bound to x in the second equation of the definition of the length function is not used in the body, we can use an underscore '_' in place of an identifier, meaning 'don't care'. The second equation would then become:

```
length (_:xs) = 1 + length xs
```

In terms of pattern matching, the underscore acts in a similar way to an identifier, in that it matches anything. A final point to notice is that list argument patterns which use the (:) symbol must be placed in parentheses. This is a consequence of the lower precedence of the (:) operator relative to function application. If we wrote:

```
length _:xs = 1 + length xs        -- bad
```

the compiler would parse this as:

```
(length _):xs =  ...
```

which would lead to a syntax error.

Note that the second equation of length should not be written as

```
length [_:xs] = 1 + length xs        -- bad
```

because in this case, this pattern matches a list comprising only one element which is itself a list. This error unfortunately often gives rise to cryptic error messages from the Haskell interpreter or compiler complaining about an 'infinite type'.

Non-exhaustive patterns

Another example which exhibits a similar recursive shape is the last function, which extracts the last element of a list:

```
last [x]    = x
last (_:xs) = last xs
```

Here we have used different list notations in each equation of the definition. The pattern in the first equation matches a list argument with a *single* element. The second equation matches all *multi-element* lists. If given a multi-element list, the function simply discards the head of the list, and applies itself recursively to the remainder of the list. Eventually the list will have a single element (the last element of the original list), which will cause a match with the first equation, and the element will be returned.

We have a potential problem here, in that `last` is not defined for empty list arguments. A program in which this occurs is invalid, but this will only be discovered at evaluation time. Situations like this can only occur when the formal argument patterns in a set of equations for a function definition are not *exhaustive*. If the argument pattern matching for a function is exhaustive, no matter what argument the function is applied to, there will *always* be at least one equation which has a pattern that matches with the argument. The `last` function as defined above does not have exhaustive pattern matching because neither of the two patterns will match with an empty list argument.

Some functional language compilers warn the user when it finds that a function does not have exhaustive pattern matching. Users normally have the option of ignoring the warning, if they are confident that the function will not be applied to an argument which does not cause a match. If they are wrong, the system will inform them during evaluation. However, it is possible to include in the definition of the function a meaningful error message by calling a special function called `error` which expects the error message as its argument:

```
last [] = error "last function called on an empty list"
```

2.4.5 Other list processing functions

Figure 2.1 shows definitions of a few predefined list functions.[1] These definitions are the basic ones and are similar to `length` in that they traverse the list recursively using essentially the same pattern.

We define two infix operators: (`!!`) which is the list indexing operator, the first element having index number 0, and (`++`) which is the list concatenation operator for appending two lists.

There are three sets of related functions for decomposing lists:

● `head` and `tail` return one of the arguments of the (`:`) operator, they return respectively the first element of the list and the rest of the list without the first one;

● `init` and `last` separate the list at the end and return respectively the whole list without the last element and only the last element;

● `take n xs` and `drop n xs` are a generalization of the previous functions because they separate the list after n elements; `take n xs` returns the first n items of list `xs` and `drop n xs` returns list `xs` without its n first elements.

These functions have the following properties for any non-empty list `xs`.

```
hd xs       ++ tl xs      = xs
init xs     ++ last xs    = xs
take n xs ++ drop n xs = xs
```

---

[1] Their exact definitions are given in the submodule `PreludeList` of the Standard Prelude [100] in Appendix A.1; these 'official definitions' often use higher or functions (described in Section 2.5) and check for error cases.

```
(x:_)  !! 0                  = x
(_:xs) !! n                  = xs !! (n-1)


[] ++ ys                     = ys
(x:xs) ++ ys                 = x:(xs ++ ys)


head (x:_)                   = x
tail (_:xs)                  = xs


init [x]                     = []
init (x:xs)                  = x : init xs


last [x]                     = x
last (_:xs)                  = last xs


take 0 _                     = []
take _ []                    = []
take n (x:xs)                = x:take (n-1) xs


drop 0 xs                    = xs
drop _ []                    = []
drop n (_:xs)                = drop (n-1) xs


elem x []                    = False
elem x (y:ys) | x == y       = True
              | otherwise    = elem x ys


sum []                       = 0
sum (x:xs)                   = x + sum xs


reverse []                   = []
reverse (x:xs)               = (reverse xs) ++ [x]
```

Figure 2.1   Simple list processing functions.

More complex patterns

The functions in all the examples we have seen so far have worked by separating a list into its head and tail components. Reflecting this, the patterns in the definition have appeared as:

(x:xs)

The pattern we specify for a formal argument depends on which components of that argument are needed for computing the result. Sometimes, we may need more from a list than just its head and tail components. Consider a function maximum, which returns the maximum value of a list:

```
maximum [x]                   = x
maximum (x:y:ys) | x > y      = maximum (x:ys)
                 | otherwise  = maximum (y:ys)
```

Obviously, the maximum of a one-element list returns that element, a condition satisfied by the first equation. For the case where a list has at least two elements, we compare the top two elements, discard the lesser value, and find the maximum value of the list formed by placing the greater value at the front of the remainder of the list. Finally, note that the function is undefined for empty lists, as would be expected.

We next examine a function that *flattens* a list of lists into a single list; the pre-defined Haskell function for this operation is concat. The elements of the inner lists are extracted and are placed into the outer list, such that the items appear in the same textual order. Below, we show some examples of the result of the flattening operation.

```
concat [[1,43], [-3,12,89,15], [9]]   ⇒   [1,43,-3,12,89,15,9]
concat [[], [False, False], [True]]   ⇒   [False, False, True]
concat []                             ⇒   []
concat [[]]                           ⇒   []
```

The function concat can be defined as:

```
concat []            = []
concat ([]:ys)       = concat ys
concat ((x:xs):ys)   = x:concat (xs:ys)
```

The first equation is self-explanatory, the second simply removes empty list elements from the outer list. The third does most of the work. It removes the head of the first inner list, and adds this element to the list formed by flattening the remaining data structure.

Another useful function is one that transforms two lists into a list of tuples, with the tuple elements taken from corresponding positions in the two lists. We call this function zip. For example:

```
zip [1, 2, 3] [4, 5, 6]   ⇒   [(1, 4), (2, 5), (3, 6)]
```

The definition of zip follows:

```
zip (x:xs) (y:ys) = (x, y):zip xs ys
zip _      _      = []
```

Note that the second equation will be selected whenever *either* of the two list arguments are empty. This means that if the two lists are of different lengths, the resulting list will be the length of the shorter list argument, the rest of the elements from the longer list will be discarded.

A function which performs the opposite of zip can be written. This function is applied to a list of pairs, and returns two lists (in a tuple), whose elements are taken from the pairs. We can define the function unzip as:

```
unzip []        = ([], [])
unzip ((x, y):ps) = (x:xs, y:ys)
                    where (xs, ys) = unzip ps
```

Repeated variables

A useful function is one that removes consecutive duplicate elements from a list. We may be tempted to define the equations of this function as follows:

```
removeDups []       = []
removeDups [x]      = [x]
removeDups (x:x:xs) = removeDups (x:xs)    -- illegal
```

In the third equation we test for the equality of the first and second elements of the list *within the pattern*. This is not allowed in Haskell; instead, we must use another technique such as guards. A correct way to define removeDups is:

```
removeDups []                     = []
removeDups [x]                    = [x]
removeDups (x:y:ys) | x == y      = removeDups (y:ys)
                    | otherwise   = x:removeDups (y:ys)
```

'As' patterns

Suppose we need a function that removes the third and fourth items from a list if they are equal, otherwise it returns the original list. We can write this as:

```
rem34 (p:q:r:s:xs) | r == s    = p:q:xs
                   | otherwise = p:q:r:s:xs
```

The second equation returns the *entire argument*. It sometimes happens in functional programs that one clause of a function needs *part of* an argument, while another operates on the *whole* argument. It is tedious (and inefficient) to write out the structure of the complete argument again when referring to it. Using the @ operator, pronounced 'as', it is possible to label all or part of an argument. We can now write:

```
rem34 lab@(p:q:r:s:xs) | r == s    = p:q:xs
                       | otherwise = lab
```

We have provided a label, lab, for the whole argument in the pattern, and used lab when we referred to the entire argument in the second equation.

Functions and list comprehensions

A function can return a list in the form of a list comprehension. For example, the following function perms produces a list of permutations of a given list.

```
perms [] = [[]]
perms xs = [x:p | x <- xs, p <- perms (removeFirst x xs)]
    where removeFirst x []                  = []
          removeFirst x (y:ys) | x == y     = ys
                               | otherwise = y : removeFirst x ys
```

The removeFirst x xs removes the first occurrence of x from list xs. Each permutation is constructed by placing each element of the argument list, in turn, at the head of each permutation for the remaining elements. For example, perms [1,2,3] takes 1 from the front of the list [1,2,3], finds the permutations of the list [2,3] (these will be [2,3] and [3,2]), and adds the 1 to the front of these permutations, producing the lists [1,2,3] and [1,3,2]. The same is done with the second element of the original list, 2, producing the lists [2,1,3] and [2,3,1]. Finally, we repeat the process with the remaining element of the original list, 3, producing the lists [3,1,2] and [3,2,1]. The final result returned by the perms function is a list containing all these permutations.

2.4.6   Strings

Now that we have described lists, we are in a position to discuss another commonly used data type: the string. Strings are actually lists of characters and the method of writing them in double quotes is shorthand for writing them using normal list notation. Thus, the following are all equivalent:

```
"Parthenon"
['P', 'a', 'r', 't', 'h', 'e', 'n', 'o', 'n']
'P':'a':'r':'t':'h':'e':'n':'o':'n':[]
'P':'a':'r':'t':"henon"
```

The null string "" is therefore an empty list, of type [Char]. Many operations performed on strings are no different from those that operate on any other list. For example, we may want to determine the length of a string, or append two strings together. A function, called show, converts any argument into a string; this is useful for displaying messages to the screen. For example:

```
"The sum of list "++(show l)++" is "++(show (sum l))++"\n"
```

where the string "\n" is an *escape sequence* that causes the cursor to move on to the next line. Details of other escape sequences can be found in the Haskell language definition manual.

2.5 Higher-order functional programming techniques

This section considers the concept of higher-order programming which corresponds to the idea of functions accepting other functions as arguments or returning them as results. Higher-order functions are used extensively in functional programs, since they allow powerful computations to be expressed simply.

Often in what might appear to be quite unrelated functions on data structures, the pattern of access to and the movement through those data structures is quite similar. This section describes some of the more common computation patterns on a list.

2.5.1 Maps

The first computation pattern we will explore involves the creation of a new list from an old list where each element of the new list has a value determined from its corresponding value in the old list according to some *mapping function*.

For example, suppose we require a function `tupleList` to make all the elements of a list tuples, with a zero as the first tuple element, and the original list element as the second tuple element. An example conversion is shown below:

```
tupleList ['d','x','q']   ⇒   [(0,'d'), (0,'x'), (0,'q')]
```

To start off, we define a function to convert a single value into a tuple:

```
makeTuple x = (0, x)
```

We can now write a function to process a complete list in this manner:

```
tupleList []     = []
tupleList (x:xs) = (makeTuple x):(tupleList xs)
```

The computation pattern here is one of traversing the whole list element by element while applying the `makeTuple` function to each element. Now, suppose we wanted to double every element of a list. In a similar manner, we could write this as:

```
double x            = x + x

doubleList []     = []
doubleList (x:xs) = (double x):(doubleList xs)
```

We have the same movement pattern through the list as in the previous example and when we meet each element we perform the same operation, that is, applying a function to it. The difference is in the function that we are applying.

We can define a higher-order function to perform the list traversal and function application. This function is independent of whatever actual operation the function is performing – we can pass this function in as a parameter to the higher-order function. We conventionally call this higher-order function map, since it maps a function over the whole list. We can define it as:

```
map f []    = []
map f (x:xs) = (f x):(map f xs)
```

We can now define the two previous list operation functions in terms of map:

```
tupleList  xs = map makeTuple xs
doubleList xs = map double xs
```

We can use map to carry out other, less obvious, list processing operations, such as in the following alternative definition of the list length function:

```
one _      = 1

length xs = sum (map one xs)
```

Here, we find the length of a list by changing every list element into a 1, and summing the elements of this new list (see sum definition in Figure 2.1). Traversal of a list applying a function to each element is a common operation in functional programming, and map is normally a predefined function available for use in all functional language systems.

2.5.2   Anonymous functions

There is one minor inconvenience in the previous function definitions. The problem relates to functions such as makeTuple which are applied to each list element. It is highly likely that a function such as makeTuple would only be used within the definition of tupleList and nowhere else. If this is the case it is a minor irritant to have to declare this function. Because it is such a small function, and is only used in one place, we would like to be able to introduce and define the function at the point of use only. Haskell allows us to achieve this by means of *anonymous functions*.

The principle behind anonymous functions stems from the view of functions as values. When we need to specify an integer, we write down the value explicitly – we do not have to declare an identifier to represent that integer and then use that identifier. This may seem obvious, but that is exactly what we have been doing in the case of functions. It would be nice, therefore, to have a way of writing down explicit function values directly, rather than always referring to the function indirectly via an identifier. This may seem to have few applications but it is a very convenient feature to have available, and is often used.

In Haskell, the anonymous function corresponding to makeTuple would be written as:

```
\x -> (0, x)
```

This should be interpreted as 'the function that takes a single argument (the identifier x) and returns a tuple with zero as its first element and the argument as its second element'. This notation is akin to the lambda calculus notation $(\lambda x.(0, x))$ (see Section 1.2.1). We can insert this function directly into the definition of tupleList, as follows:

```
tupleList xs = map (\x -> (0, x)) xs
```

Similarly, we can declare doubleList as:

```
doubleList xs = map (\x -> x + x) xs
```

Another way of defining doubleList is as follows:

```
doubleList xs = map ((*)2) xs
```

where the function ((*)2) (multiplication is in prefix form) corresponds to the lambda abstraction (\x->(*)2 x). It is therefore possible to define higher-order functions using first-order functions supplied with fewer arguments than expected. This technique is known as *currying*.

2.5.3   Folds

The next computation pattern we will explore is that of *folding a list*. In the mapping operation we were creating a new list from an old list by mapping each element to a new value. In contrast, folding a list creates a single value from a list.

Right folding

Consider the functions to find the sum and product of the elements of a list of numbers:

```
sum []          = 0
sum (x:xs)      = x + sum xs

product []      = 1
product (x:xs) = x * product xs
```

As in the case of mapping, we can see that there is a common computation pattern between these two functions. We have a function *f* which, when applied to a list, returns the value of a *binary operator* applied to the first list element and the result of applying *f* to the rest of the list. We call this folding or *reducing* the list, because the application can be thought of as laying out all the values of the list and placing the binary operator between them. We then apply the binary operator element by element, always reducing two values to one value, so the list gets 'folded' up, eventually resulting in a single value.

For example, consider the list [15, 3, 5, 7]. The way sum works, applying it to this list is like evaluating the following expression:

```
15 + (3 + (5 + (7 + 0)))
```

We can then imagine the list being folded up from the right, first reducing '7 + 0' to '7', then '5 + 7' to '12', etc. A similar argument applies to the way product works. There are two differences between sum and product. The first is the particular binary operator (call it ⊕) that is applied; the second is the value to be returned for an empty list (call it b). Given the list $[e_0, e_1, e_2, e_3]$ (or $e_0 : (e_1 : (e_2 : (e_3 : [])))$), the fold right operation works as follows:

$$(e_0 \oplus (e_1 \oplus (e_2 \oplus (e_3 \oplus b))))$$

We can abstract out this computation pattern by supplying $\oplus$ and b as arguments to a higher order function we shall call `foldr` (meaning 'fold from the right'), which is defined as follows:

```
foldr f b []     = b
foldr f b (x:xs) = f x (foldr f b xs)
```

The first argument is the binary operator; the second is the 'base' value that will be returned corresponding to the empty list. This looks slightly different syntactically from the two instances above because we are using the conventional prefix function application rather than the infix form which is used by binary operators. If we wanted to, we could define `foldr` in an infix fashion:

```
foldr f b []     = b
foldr f b (x:xs) = x 'f' (foldr f b xs)
```

The `sum` and `product` functions can now be defined as:

```
sum xs     = foldr (+) 0 xs

product xs = foldr (*) 1 xs
```

Note that, in these definitions, binary operators passed as arguments must be enclosed in parentheses. There are some surprising applications of `foldr`, such as appending a list onto the end of another list:

```
xs ++ ys = foldr (:) ys xs
```

We can now redefine the `concat` function (see Section 2.4.5) using `foldr` and the append operator (`++`):

```
concat xs = foldr (++) [] xs
```

The minimum and the maximum value of a list can be determined with the following functions:

```
minimum (x:xs) = foldr min x xs
maximum (x:xs) = foldr max x xs
```

where `min` and `max` compute the minimum and the maximum of two values respectively:

```
min x y | x < y      = x
        | otherwise  = y

max x y | x >= y     = x
        | otherwise  = y
```

We can even define `map` in terms of `foldr`:

```
map f xs = foldr (\x ys ->(f x):ys) [] xs
```

Left folding

Folding a list from the right is not the only way of folding it. We can also perform the fold from the left. If we represent the binary operator by $\oplus$, folding a list $[e_0, e_1, e_2, e_3]$ from the left is analogous to evaluating the expression:

$$((((b \oplus e_0) \oplus e_1) \oplus e_2) \oplus e_3)$$

We can define the function `foldl` to achieve this computation pattern as follows:

```
foldl f b []     = b
foldl f b (x:xs) = foldl f (f b x) xs
```

Though we can use either `foldr` or `foldl` to sum the elements of a list, the distinction between them does matter in some circumstances. A useful application of `foldl` is in a function `revOnto` that reverses a list onto another list, so that `revOnto xs ys = (reverse ys) ++ xs`. For example:

```
    revOnto [1,2,3] [4,5,6]   ⇒   [6,5,4,1,2,3]
```

We define `revOnto` using another function called `consOnto` that simply flips its arguments and applies the `(:)` operator:

```
consOnto xs y = y:xs
revOnto l1 l2 = foldl consOnto l1 l2
```

Another example of using `foldl` is to sum a list of lists:

```
sumll xss = foldl (foldl (+)) 0 xss
```

A list difference function `listDiff`, which deletes from its first argument list the first occurrence of each element of its second argument list, can be defined using `foldl` as follows:

```
listDiff xs1 xs2             = foldl delete xs1 xs2

delete [] _                  = []
delete (x:xs)  y | x == y    = xs
                 | otherwise = x : (delete xs y)
```

Haskell predefines this function under the name of the operator (`\\`) in the library module `List`.

Folding non-empty lists

There are versions of left and right folding which do not need a base case so they only operate on non-empty lists. Their definitions are:

```
foldr1 f [x]     = x
foldr1 f (x:xs) = x 'f' (foldr1 f xs)

foldl1 f (x:xs) = foldl f x xs
```

Applications of these operators include computing the minimum or the maximum of a list:

```
maximum xs = foldl1 max xs
minimum xs = foldl1 min xs
```

2.5.4   Filters

A common requirement is to traverse a list and discover values which satisfy a certain predicate. *Filtering* is the process of forming a new list by selecting elements of the original list which satisfy a predicate. The predicate is a function which returns either True or False, and is passed as an argument to the filter function.

For example (even is predefined in the Standard Prelude):

```
filter even [45, 17, 32, 3, 8, 9, 76]  ⇒  [32, 8, 76]
```

We define filter as:

```
filter _ []                  = []
filter p (x:xs) | p x        = x : filter p xs
                | otherwise  = filter p xs
```

Alternatively, we may only be interested in whether any value in the list *does* satisfy the predicate:

```
any _ []                  = False
any p (x:xs) | p x        = True
             | otherwise  = any p xs
```

We can use any to redefine the function elem (see Figure 2.1) which checks whether an element is a member of a list:

```
elem n xs = any (\x -> x == n) xs
```

There are two other useful functions: the function takeWhile has the same type as filter and collects all elements of the list but stops at the first element that does not satisfy the predicate; dropWhile works similarly but it drops all the elements until one does not satisfy the predicate:

```
takeWhile _ []                = []
takeWhile p (x:xs)  | p x     = x: (takeWhile p xs)
                    | otherwise = []

dropWhile _ []                = []
dropWhile p xs@(x:xs') | p x  = dropWhile p xs'
                     | otherwise = xs
```

2.5.5 Functions in data structures

Functions can be placed into data structures such as lists and user-defined structures. For example:

```
double x        = x * 2
square x        = x * x
bump   x        = x + 1

applyall [] x   = x
applyall (f:fs) x = f (applyall fs x)

y = applyall [bump, square, double] 3
```

The function `applyall` applies a list of functions (which must all have the same type signature) to an initial value. In the above example, y would become equal to:

```
bump (square (double 3))
```

which equals $37 = (3 \times 2)^2 + 1$.

2.6 Algebraic types and polymorphism

In Section 2.4.1, we discussed the structure of a list in terms of applications of the constructor (`:`). This section describes constructors in general and how their types can be expressed. It also introduces polymorphism as a concept which allows one function to operate on different types.

2.6.1 User-defined types

Haskell allows us to define our own types, using *constructors*. A constructor is just like a function, expecting some arguments and delivering a value of the type it defines.

For example, suppose we want a data type to define values which store coordinates in the cartesian plane. We can give a new name to that type, say `CoordType`. We then define a constructor function, call it `Coord`, with two arguments, the x and y components, that returns a value of `CoordType`.

In Haskell we introduce such a type with the following declaration:

```
data CoordType = Coord Float Float deriving Show
```

`deriving Show` at the end of the definition is necessary for user-defined types to make sure that values of these types can be printed in a standard form, as will be explained in Section 2.8.5.

If we want to refer to an actual coordinate (that is, a value of this type) in a program, we write it as an application of the `Coord` constructor. For example, the coordinate which has the x component as 14.0 and the y component as 2.0 can be written as:

```
Coord 14.0 2.0
```

As in the case of lists, we cannot reduce this application to anything simpler (there are no 'rules' telling us how to reduce this expression), so we have to leave it in this form. Once we have defined a new type we can write general purpose functions which work on values of that type using pattern matching such as functions which return the x and y components of a coordinate:

```
xElt (Coord x _) = x
```

```
yElt (Coord _ y) = y
```

Notice the form of pattern matching used in the function definition which is similar to the one used in the case of lists, except that in the latter case the constructor function was an infix function, so it appeared between the formal argument identifiers.

The following function takes a list of coordinates as its argument and checks whether all of the coordinates are in the top-right quadrant of the coordinate system (that is, whether both x and y components are positive).

```
firstQuad []                  = True
firstQuad ((Coord x y):cs)    = (x >= 0) && (y >= 0) && (firstQuad cs)
```

2.6.2   Alternative constructors

Values of a data type do not have to be created by a single constructor. Consider a data type as holding a 'shape' which can either be a rectangle, triangle, or circle with different component information depending on the 'shape'. For example, a rectangle needs the coordinates of its two corners, a triangle, the coordinates of its three vertices, and a circle, the coordinates of its center with the length of its radius. We can define such a data type with alternatives separated by a vertical bar | as:

```
data Shape = Rectangle CoordType CoordType
           | Circle CoordType Float
           | Triangle CoordType CoordType CoordType
     deriving Show
```

A Shape is thus either a Rectangle, a Circle or a Triangle. Here are examples of values of type Shape:

```
Rectangle (Coord 13.0 27.3) (Coord 4.9 12.1)
Circle (Coord 64.0 37.0) 7.5
Triangle (Coord 0.0 0.0) (Coord 45.3 6.0) (Coord 12.8 17.0)
```

A function which accepts an argument of a data type with alternative constructors should have at least one pattern that matches each of the constructors. For example, a function area that calculates the area of a shape is shown below:

Table 2.3   Possible types for the function `fst`.

Context	Type of `fst`
`w = fst (32, 8)`	`fst :: (Int, Int) -> Int`
`x = fst ('c', True)`	`fst :: (Char, Bool) -> Char`
`y = fst ([3, 5, 6], 145.9)`	`fst :: ([Int], Float) -> [Int]`
`z = fst ((True,"s",0), [False])`	`fst :: ((Bool,String,Int),[Bool])`
	`-> (Bool,String,Int)`

```
area (Rectangle corner1 corner2)
    = abs(xElt corner1 - xElt corner2)*
      abs(yElt corner1 - yElt corner2)
area (Circle _ radius)
    = pi*radius*radius
area (Triangle vert1 vert2 vert3)
    = sqrt (h*(h-a)*(h-b)*(h-c))
      where
      h = (a+b+c)/2.0
      a = dist vert1 vert2
      b = dist vert1 vert3
      c = dist vert2 vert3
      dist (Coord x1 y1) (Coord x2 y2)
          = sqrt((x1-x2)*(x1-x2)+(y1-y2)*(y1-y2))
```

If we had only provided the first two equations, the patterns specified in the function definition would not be exhaustive. Applying the function to an argument created by applying the `Triangle` constructor would not cause a match.

2.6.3 Simple polymorphism

Suppose we want to determine the type of the `fst` function, defined as follows:

```
fst (x, _) = x
```

Table 2.3 shows that the type of this function depends on the context in which the call is made. It would seem that we can only give `fst` a type when it is applied to a value. This is unsatisfactory because we want to give a general type to every function independently of where it is used. In Haskell, the type of `fst` is given as:

```
fst :: (a, b) -> a
```

where a and b are *type variables* which can be replaced by *concrete types* (such as `Int`, `Float`, `Bool`, `[Char]`, and so on) when the function is applied. This type definition tells us that `fst` takes an argument which is a pair. It also tells us that the result type of `fst` is the same type as the first element of the pair (because they use the same type variable, a). A function whose type definition contains type variables is known as a *polymorphic* function. The simplest polymorphic function is the identity function:

```
id x = x
```

This simply returns its argument, which can be of *any type*. The type of id is given by:

```
id :: a -> a
```

Consider these other examples of functions:

```
cond (x, y, z) = if x then y else z
apply (f, x)   = f x
```

Their types can be derived as follows:

```
cond   :: (Bool, a, a) -> a
apply  :: (a -> b, a)  -> b
```

2.6.4 List polymorphism

Consider the *list* data type. If this was not already built into Haskell, it could be defined as a data type by specifying the properties of a list. For example, the following (recursive) data type represents a list of integers:

```
data IntList = Nil
             | Cons Int IntList
    deriving Show
```

We could symbolically represent what we understand as the list [14, 9, 12] by the expression:

```
Cons 14 (Cons 9 (Cons 12 Nil))
```

We could similarly define a function to find the length of such a list:

```
lengthIntList  Nil = 0
lengthIntList (Cons _ xs) = 1 + lengthIntList xs
```

However, the list we have defined is restricted to integers. The property of 'listness' has nothing to do with the type of elements in the list (although they *are* constrained to be all of the same type), yet we have had to specify such an unnecessary property when defining the list.

Using *polymorphic data definitions* we can represent such data structures in the way we would like, without unnecessary constraints. Consider the following definition of a list data structure:

```
data List a = Cons' a (List a)
            | Nil'
    deriving Show
```

We have parameterized the type name List with a type variable a. At least one of the arguments of a constructor for that type must be of the type given by this type variable. In this case we have one type variable, and we have specified that the first argument to the Cons' constructor (that is, the list element) will be of this type. The second argument to the Cons' constructor is of type List a, which means that it is a list which must have been constructed with the same type variable, thus ensuring that all list elements are of the same type.

Using this data type, we can write down lists of any element type, for example:

```
Cons' 5 (Cons' 14 (Cons' -3 Nil'))                    = [5, 14, -3]
Cons' False Nil'                                      = [False]
Cons' Nil'(Cons'(Cons' 4.7(Cons' 2.6 Nil'))Nil') = [[],[4.7,2.6]]
```

The last example is a value of type List (List Float).

The predefined list type has the same property and so most general purpose functions which operate on lists are polymorphic. For example:

```
length []     = 0
length (x:xs) = 1 + length xs
```

We know that the argument accepted by length must be a list, but the function is independent of the type of the list elements. Therefore, the type of length is given by:

```
length :: [a] -> Int
```

We are now in a position to determine the type of the empty list (that is, []): it is denoted by [a]. Not all list functions are polymorphic. For example, the formal argument patterns may dictate that the list elements are of a certain type, as in the following case:

```
anyTrue []         = False
anyTrue (True:_) = True
anyTrue (_:xs)   = anyTrue xs
```

Because of the True constant appearing in the argument pattern, the type of anyTrue is given by:

```
anyTrue :: [Bool] -> Bool
```

2.6.5 Trees

The list data structure is the main data structure considered so far. It is called a linear structure because its items appear in a predetermined sequence, that is each item has at most one immediate successor. A tree is a *non-linear* data structure because an item can have one or more successors. Trees have many applications: for example, to represent expressions containing nested function calls.

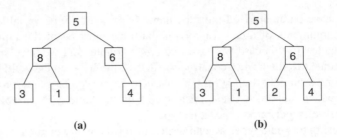

(a)   (b)

Figure 2.2   Examples of binary trees.

Defining trees

Assuming that values are stored in the nodes and that they are all of the same type, a general tree can be declared as:

```
data Tree a = Node a [Tree a]   deriving Show
```

Using this representation, the tree illustrated in Figure 2.2(a) will be expressed as follows provided we do not make any distinction between the successors:

```
Node 5 [Node 8 [Node 3 [], Node 1 []],
        Node 6 [Node 4 []]]
```

A node in a *binary tree* has at most two successors so it can be declared as:

```
data BinTree a  = Empty  | NodeBT a (BinTree a) (BinTree a)
    deriving Show
```

Using this representation, the tree illustrated in Figure 2.2(a) is expressed as:

```
NodeBT 5 (NodeBT 8 (NodeBT 3 Empty Empty) (NodeBT 1 Empty Empty))
         (NodeBT 6 Empty (NodeBT 4 Empty Empty))
```

and the tree in Figure 2.2(b) is represented as:

```
NodeBT 5 (NodeBT 8 (NodeBT 3 Empty Empty) (NodeBT 1 Empty Empty))
         (NodeBT 6 (NodeBT 2 Empty Empty) (NodeBT 4 Empty Empty))
```

If every node of a binary tree is limited to either zero or exactly two successors, some space can be saved by using the following declaration:

```
data BinTree' a = Leaf a | NodeBT' a (BinTree' a) (BinTree' a)
    deriving Show
```

In this case, the tree in Figure 2.2(a) can no longer be represented but the tree in Figure 2.2(b) can be written in a shorter form:

```
NodeBT' 5 (NodeBT' 8 (Leaf 3) (Leaf 1))
          (NodeBT' 6 (Leaf 2) (Leaf 4))
```

Tree operations

Tree operations can be grouped into *single* operations such as insertions or deletions or *global* operations that manipulate the tree as a whole. The most common single operations are adding and removing an item from the tree. An item can be inserted into the tree at different positions, depending on the purpose of the tree and the algorithm. Similarly, deleting an item contained within an interior node can be accomplished in several ways depending on the algorithm used. Examples will be described in Section 5.7.

We now consider global operations that involve traversing the tree as a whole. For example, the depth of a general tree can be computed as follows:

```
depth                  :: Tree a -> Int
depth (Node _ [])    = 1
depth (Node _ succs) = 1 + maximum (map depth succs)
```

because the depth of a node is one more than the maximum depth of its successors. The depth of a binary tree can be determined in the following manner:

```
depth'                  :: BinTree a -> Int
depth' Empty          = 0
depth' (NodeBT _ lf rt) = 1 + max (depth' lf) (depth' rt)
```

Another example is counting the number of empty leaves in a tree:

```
countEmpty                  :: BinTree a -> Int
countEmpty Empty          = 1
countEmpty (NodeBT _ lf rt) = countEmpty lf + countEmpty rt
```

Supposing that nodes contain integers, summing the values in a tree can be achieved as follows depending on the representation we use for the binary trees:

```
tsum                   :: BinTree  Int -> Int
tsum Empty           = 0
tsum (NodeBT a lf rt)  = a + (tsum lf) + (tsum rt)
```

and

```
tsum'                  :: BinTree'  Int -> Int
tsum' (Leaf v)       = v
tsum' (NodeBT' v lf rt) = v + (tsum' lf) + (tsum' rt)
```

Consider now the problem of converting a tree into a list. This can be done in three ways, depending on when the node is visited:

- **Preorder**   the node is visited before its left and right subtrees are visited.
- **Inorder**   the node is visited after the left subtree has been visited and before the right subtree is visited.
- **Postorder**   the node is visited after its left and right subtrees have been visited.

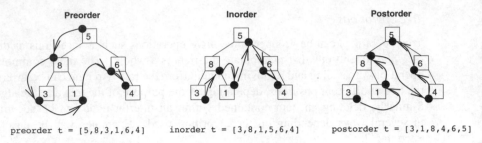

Figure 2.3   Tree traversal strategies.

These strategies are illustrated in Figure 2.3. The corresponding functions for converting a tree into a list are:

```
preorder                     :: BinTree a -> [a]
preorder Empty               = []
preorder (NodeBT a lf rt)    = [a] ++ preorder lf ++ preorder rt

inorder                      :: BinTree a -> [a]
inorder Empty                = []
inorder (NodeBT a lf rt)     = inorder lf ++ [a] ++ inorder rt

postorder                    :: BinTree a -> [a]
postorder Empty              = []
postorder (NodeBT a lf rt)   = postorder lf ++ postorder rt ++ [a]
```

2.7 Arrays

An array is used to store and retrieve a set of elements, each element having a unique *index*. In this section, we describe how arrays are created and manipulated in Haskell. In Haskell, arrays are not part of the Standard Prelude but are provided as the Array library module, so before using any array-related function described in this section, this library should be 'imported' using the following directive:

```
import Array
```

The implementation of arrays will be discussed later in Section 4.3.

2.7.1 Creation of arrays

Arrays are created by three predefined functions called array, listArray and accumArray. The first function:

array *bounds list_of_associations*

is the fundamental array creation mechanism. The first parameter, *bounds*, gives the lowest and highest indices in the array. For example, a zero-origin vector of five elements has bounds (0,4) and a one-origin 10 by 10 matrix has bounds ((1,1),(10,10)). The values of the bounds can be arbitrary expressions. The second parameter is a list of associations where an *association*, of the form (i,x), means that the value of the array element i is x. The list of associations is often defined using a list comprehension (see Section 2.4.2). Here are some examples of building arrays:

```
a'  = array (1,4) [(3 ,'c'),(2 ,'a'), (1 ,'f'), (4 ,'e')]
f n = array (0,n) [(i , i*i) | i <- [0..n]]
m   = array ((1,1),(2,3)) [((i,j) , (i*j)) | i<-[1..2],j<-[1..3]]
```

The type of an array is denoted as `Array a b` where a represents the type of the index and b represents the type of the value. Here are the (possible) type definitions of the previous expressions:

```
a' :: Array Int Char
f  :: Int -> Array Int Int
m  :: Array (Int,Int) Int
```

An array is undefined if any specified index is out of bounds; if two associations in the list have the same index, the value at that index is undefined. As a consequence, `array` is *strict* in the bounds and in the indices but *non-strict* (or *lazy*) in the values. This means that an array can contain 'undefined' elements (we will discuss lazy data structures in Section 3.1.3).

We can thus use recurrences such as:

```
fibs n = a
    where
      a = array (1,n) ([(1, 1), (2, 1)] ++
                       [(i, a!(i-1) + a!(i-2)) | i <- [3..n]])
```

as we will see later in this section, the operator (!) denotes indexing. The second function:

listArray *bounds list_of_values*

is predefined for the frequently occurring case where an array is constructed from a list of values in index order. The following defines a'' to be equivalent to a' above:

```
a''= listArray (1,4) "face"
```

The last function:

accumArray *f init bounds list_of_associations*

removes the restriction that a given index may appear at most once in the association list but instead combines these 'conflicting indices' via an accumulating function *f*. The elements of the array are initialized with *init*. For example, given a list of values vs, `histogram` produces an array giving for each index value within bounds the number of occurrences of the corresponding value in vs.

```
histogram bounds vs = accumArray (+) 0 bounds [(i , 1) | i <- vs]
```

2.7.2   Using arrays

Array subscripting is done using the (!) binary operator. Functions have also been defined for getting the bounds (bounds), the indices (indices), the elements (elems) and associations (assocs) of an array.

For example, consider the two-dimensional array m defined previously:

```
m = array ((1,1),(2,3)) [((i,j) , (i*j)) | i<-[1..2],j<-[1..3]]
```

The use of these array operators is illustrated below:

```
m!(1,2)     ⇒  2
bounds m    ⇒  ((1,1),(2,3))
indices m   ⇒  [(1,1), (1,2), (1,3), (2,1), (2,2), (2,3)]
elems m     ⇒  [1, 2, 3, 2, 4, 6]
assocs m    ⇒  [((1,1) , 1), ((1,2) , 2), ((1,3) , 3),
                ((2,1) , 2), ((2,2) , 4), ((2,3) , 6)]
```

It is also possible to update an array in a functional style, that is return a new array whose values are identical to the old one except for a given index. The operator (//) takes an array and a list of associations and returns a new array identical to the left argument except for every element specified by the right argument list. For example:

```
a'//[(3 , 'r')]
```

redefines the third element of a'. Another example where many updates (on different indices) take place is:

```
m // [((1,1), 4), ((2,2),8)]
```

which redefines $m_{1,1}$ and $m_{2,2}$. For example, the function that constructs a histogram can be redefined as follows:

```
histogram (lower, upper) xs
    = updHist (array (lower,upper) [(i,0) | i <- [lower..upper]])
            xs


updHist a []      = a
updHist a (x:xs) = updHist (a // [(x, (a!x + 1))]) xs
```

For example:

```
histogram (0,9) [3,1,4,1,5,9,2]
    ⇒
            array (0,9) [(0,0),(1,2),(2,1),(3,1),(4,1),
                         (5,1),(6,0),(7,0),(8,0),(9,1)]
```

Instead of replacing the old value, values with the same index could be combined using the predefined:

accum *function array list-of-associations*

For example:

```
accum (+) m [((1,1), 4), ((2,2),8)]
  ⇒   array ((1,1),(2,3))
              [((1,1),5),((1,2),2),((1,3),3),
               ((2,1),2),((2,2),12),((2,3),6)]
```

The result is a new matrix identical to m except for the elements (1,1) and (2,2) to which 4 and 8 have been added respectively.

2.8 Type classes and class methods

This section describes a fundamental issue in the Haskell language that sets Haskell apart from most other functional languages: the concept of *type classes* and *class methods* which are used for structuring predefined and user-defined types. Although Haskell type terminology has some commonality with object-oriented programming, there are many differences between the two views [62, p. 26]; an important difference is the fact that classes and instances are used only for checking types at compilation time in Haskell, but instances of classes are created at execution time in object-oriented languages.

2.8.1 Overloading

Most functional languages use function *overloading* in the sense that the same function name can be used to designate operations of the same nature on values of different types. For example, the addition operator (+) can be used on integers as well as reals. But at the machine level, two different functions (we can call them intAdd and floatAdd) are used depending on the type of the arguments.

It is important to realize that overloading is different from polymorphism. If we had considered the addition operator as a polymorphic function, its type would have been defined as:

```
(+) :: a -> a -> a
```

This would be valid for some types like Int or Float but not for other types like Bool or Char. Any application with arguments of these last two types would result in an error, so the type of the function cannot be expressed as shown above.

Haskell addresses this problem through the concept of a *type class*. Every class consists of several types called *instance types*. An overloaded operation is defined for all types in a given class; such an operation is called a *class method*. When an overloaded operator is called, the implementation chooses the appropriate method according to the type of the arguments.

For example, the class Num represents all numbers including integers or reals. The addition operator (+) is predefined for all numbers so it is a Num class method. Its type definition is similar to the polymorphic definition except that there is a *type restriction* on the type variable a, written on the left of the symbol '=>' which precedes the type definition:

```
(+) :: (Num a) => a -> a -> a
```

To allow the compiler to select the appropriate method, we could assume that the following declarations are predefined:

```
instance Num Int
  where
    x + y   =  x 'intAdd' y

instance Num Float
  where
    x + y   =  x 'floatAdd' y
```

The first line should be read as 'the type Int is an instance of the class Num and every call to the class method + of the form x + y should be interpreted as a call x 'intAdd' y when x and y are of type Int'. The second line should be read in a similar way, replacing Int by Float and intAdd by floatAdd.

Now that we have motivated the importance of type classes, we can show how a type class is defined. A class in Haskell is used to specify the set of operations that can be applied to a value of the type defined by a class (more precisely a value of a type that is an instance of this class). For example, the Num class in Haskell could be defined as

```
class Num a where
  (+),(-),(*)::a -> a -> a
  negate,abs,signum:: a -> a
```

We see that the class defines most of the usual operations that can be applied to any numeric value. As we did for (+), we can define appropriate functions both for Int and Float in instance definitions. The type inference mechanism of Haskell allows the appropriate function to be determined at compilation time even in the context of automatically inferred types.

2.8.2 Overloading on user-defined types

This mechanism is also useful for defining overloaded operations on user-defined data types. For example, consider the following data type which defines records containing a key of type Int and some other information of any type a:

```
data UsDefType1 a = UsConst1 (Int , a)
```

If we want to search for records, we would need to define an overloaded (==) operator that could work on this data type. All the types for which the equality operator is defined are grouped in the Eq class. Therefore, such a definition takes the form:

```
instance Eq (UsDefType1 a)
  where
    UsConst1 (x,_) == UsConst1 (y,_) =  (x == y)
```

This should read as 'when two records are compared, with their first component being respectively x and y, the result of the comparison is the same as (x == y)'.

In fact, the key does not need to be an integer. It could be any type which belongs to the class Eq (such as characters). Therefore, the data type definition can be altered to take into account the new context:

```
data (Eq a) => UsDefType2 a b = UsConst2 (a , b)
```

So the overloaded operator (==) needs to be defined with a context added to it as well:

```
instance (Eq a) => Eq (UsDefType2 a b)
  where
    UsConst2 (x,_) == UsConst2 (y,_) =  (x == y)
```

2.8.3 Type classes and inheritance

So far, we have only discussed the type classes Num and Eq. There are many other Haskell type classes defined in the Standard Prelude and in Standard libraries among which there are:

Ord types for which the comparison operators (i.e. >,<,>=,<=) are defined.

Enum types that can be used to generate lists. For example [1..5] or ['a'..'z'].

Show types that can be converted into strings using the function show.

Ix types are mainly used for indices of arrays.

Real types regrouping all numbers but complex ones.

Integral types regrouping Int for fixed precision integers usually the ones defined by the computer running Haskell, and Integer for arbitrary precision integers.

But some operations are shared among many types; for example, we should be able to test the equality and compare Int, Float, Char and Bool values. It is desirable to define the properties of the equality tests and the comparison functions only once. The properties are defined in type classes which form hierarchies where a parent–child link corresponds to a relationship between a class and a subclass; this relationship is defined by means of a context as was done in the last section. Figure 2.4 shows a more complete view of these hierarchies. For example, any type that belongs to the subclasses Num or Ord also belongs to the Eq class. Therefore, a context like (Eq a , Ord a)=> can safely be replaced by (Ord a)=>. Overloaded functions that belong to a class are *inherited* by its subclasses.

To determine the operations that are available for a value of a type, one must first find the type class that instantiates this type in Table 2.4, then from Figure 2.4 find its operations as well as those inherited either directly or indirectly by the class. For this, one can follow the arrows in reverse order starting from the desired class in Figure 2.4. For example, Table 2.4 (second column) shows that Int is an instance of the class Integral and Figure 2.4 shows its operations as well as operations of the Enum, Real, Ord, Num, and Eq classes that can be applied to it through inheritance.

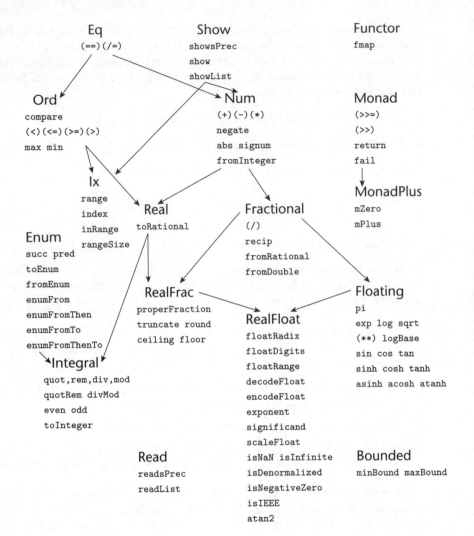

Figure 2.4 Predefined operations in class hierarchies: a class, named in this Type is given with its operators and functions; arrows indicate inheritance relationships between classes. This figure shows, for completeness, all predefined classes of the Standard Prelude and Libraries; they are not all necessarily used in this book.

Moreover, as is shown in the second column of Table 2.4, a type can be an instance of more than one class. For example, Int is also an instance of the following classes: Bounded, Ix, and Read (as well as Show which includes all types in the table). This means that in addition to the Integral operations described above, the set of operations available comprise all operations given and inherited by these classes as well.

Although this type system may seem overwhelming, it provides a principled way of organizing the operations on a type while allowing for the overloading of functions even when types are automatically inferred by the system. This important property sets Haskell apart in the computer language scene.

Table 2.4 Types of the Standard Prelude and of the library modules that are instances of standard Haskell classes and the classes that are automatically derived. All these classes are instances of Show. To save space, not all inherited classes are shown. Not all types in this table are used in this book.

Type	Instance of	Derivation
()	Read	Eq Ord Enum Bounded
[a]	Read Functor Monad	Eq Ord
(a,b)	Read	Eq Ord Bounded
(->)		
Array	Functor Eq Ord Read	
Bool		Eq Ord Enum Read Bounded
Char	Eq Ord Enum Read	
Complex	Floating Read	
Double	RealFloat Read	
Either		Eq Ord Read
Float	RealFloat Read	
Int	Integral Bounded Ix Read	
Integer	Integral Ix Read	
IO	Functor Monad	
IOError	Eq	
Maybe	Functor Monad	Eq Ord Read
Ordering		Eq Ord Enum Read Bounded
Ratio	RealFrac Read	

Combining the information from Figure 2.4 and Table 2.4, it is possible to determine the operations available for any predefined type. For example, here is the type definition of the histogram function (see Section 2.7.2):

```
histogram :: (Num b, Enum i, Ix i) => (i,i) -> [i] -> Array i b
```

The type i of the index belongs to both classes Ix and Enum so that indices can be compared and enumerated within its range. We can use a map function on an array because Array is an instance of Functor (see Figure 2.4). Arrays can be compared because they are instances of Ord and be output because they are instances of Show. Elements of the array can be used in arithmetic operations because they are instances of type Num.

2.8.4   Constraints on instances

Sometimes, there are constraints on defining new instances. For example, we assume the following record declaration:

```
data (Ord a , Ord b) => UsDefType3 a b = UsConst3 (a , b)
```

Suppose that we want to sort records according to the first field, then the second field. Since the comparison operators are defined for the class Ord, we would need to define the data type UsDefType3 as an instance of this class:

```
instance (Ord a, Ord b) => Ord (UsDefType3 a b)
    where
    UsConst3 (x,x') <= UsConst3 (y,y') = if (x==y)
                                            then x'<= y'
                                            else x <= y
```

Unfortunately, this would lead to an error unless the data type UsDefType3 is also defined as an instance of the Eq class which has to be declared as follows:

```
instance (Ord a, Ord b) => Eq (UsDefType3 a b)
    where
    UsConst3 (x, x') == UsConst3 (y,y') = (x==y)&&(x'==y')
```

2.8.5 Derived instances

Haskell provides a mechanism for making it easier to define instances. For example, if we want to sort records without going through the same process as in the previous subsection, an easier way is to use a derived instance clause in the data type declaration:

```
data (Ord a,Ord b) => UsDefType3 a b = UsConst3 (a,b)
    deriving (Eq,Ord)
```

By default, records will be compared according to the first field, then according to the second field. If we also want to be able to display records on the screen, all that is needed is to add the class Show to the list of classes in the data type declaration. This explains the deriving Show that we added to the declaration of user-defined types in Section 2.6.1. The only classes in the Standard Prelude for which derived instances are allowed are Eq, Ord, Enum, Bounded, Show and Read.

The last column of Table 2.4 shows the derived instances of the predefined Haskell types. For example, equality and ordering are automatically derived for list types (noted [a] in the table). The derivation mechanism is described in detail in the Haskell report but in most cases it is quite intuitive. For example, equality and comparisons of composite types are defined in terms of equality and comparisons on their elements. For lists, it means that two lists are equal if their elements are equal and comparison is determined by the first different element. For Read and Show, it means that values can be read and written using the same syntax as they would be written inside a Haskell script.

Exercises

2.1 Using a Haskell interpreter, evaluate the following expressions (try to predict the result):

```
(1 + 2)
if (2>9) then "Hello" else "Bye"
let x= (sqrt 16) in (x+1)
```

2.2 Define and load the following function:

```
fact 1 = 1
fact n = n * fact (n-1)
```

(a) Using the interpreter, evaluate the expression fact 5.

(b) What happens when you try to evaluate fact 0? Alter the above definition to solve this problem.

(c) Modify your definition such that the value −1 is returned when an attempt is made to compute the factorial of a negative value.

2.3 What is wrong with the following expressions? Can you change them to make them valid?

```
1:2:3
[ [2,3]++[] , [2,3]:[] ]
"hello":"world"
```

2.4 Given the following function:

```
f l = reverse (f' l [])
   where f' [] r = r
         f' (x:xs) r = (2*x) : (f' xs r)
```

What is the value of (f [1,2,3,4])? Check your answer with the Haskell interpreter.

2.5 Try to predict the values of the following expressions:

```
[1,2,3] ++ [4]
1:(2:(3:[4]))
head [1,2,3]
tail [1,2,3]
drop 4 [1,2,3,4,5]
[1,2,3,4] !! 2
```

2.6 Write Haskell functions for:

(a) computing the average value of a list of numbers;

(b) selecting the middle element in a list (assuming an odd-length list).

2.7 (a) Try to predict the value of each of the following expressions:

```
[ (x,y) | x <- [1..2] , y <- [2..5], (x+y) /= 4 ]
[ x | x <-[1..10] , (x 'mod' 2)==0 ]
```

(b) Define each of the following lists using a list comprehension:

```
[1, 2, 3, 4, 5, 6, 7, 8, 10, 11, 12, 13, 14, 15]
[2, -3, 4, -5, 6, -7, 8, -9, 10, -11]
```

2.8 (a) Using a list comprehension, define a function `neg` that counts the number of negative values in a list. For example:

$$neg[1, -9, -5, 4, -6, 0] \Rightarrow 3$$

(b) Using a list comprehension, define the function `rep` that takes an argument n and returns a list in which 1 occurs one time, 2 occurs 2 times, and so on until n occurs n times. For example:

$$rep4 \Rightarrow [1, 2, 2, 3, 3, 3, 4, 4, 4, 4]$$

2.9 Define a function `string2int` that converts a string of digits into the corresponding integer. For example:

```
string2int"3454"  ⇒  3454
string2int"76"    ⇒  76
```

Hint: `isDigit` can be used for testing if a character corresponds to a digit or not; the decimal equivalent of a digit character d is given by `digitToInt` d.

2.10 Try to predict the values of the following expressions:

```
map fst [(1,2),(3,8),(0,6),(3,1)]

(foldr f 0 l , foldl f 0 l)
      where l    = [6,9,8,3,10]
            f x y = (x+y) 'div' 2

foldr (++) [] [ [1,2,3],[4,5,6],[], [7]]
```

2.11 What is the type of the following function?

```
compose f g x = f (g x)
```

2.12 Create a one-dimensional array which contains the values:

(a) 11 20 36 47

(b) 1 2 3 4 5 6 7 8 10 11 12 13 14 15

(c) 2 -3 4 -5 6 -7 8 -9 10 -11

2.13 Given the matrix:

$$\begin{vmatrix} 2 & 3 & 4 \\ 5 & 6 & 7 \\ 8 & 9 & 10 \end{vmatrix}$$

(a) Define this matrix by enumerating all values.

(b) Define this matrix using an array comprehension.

(c) Define a function that transposes a square matrix of size 3. If applied to the previous matrix, the result should be:

$$\begin{vmatrix} 2 & 5 & 8 \\ 3 & 6 & 9 \\ 4 & 7 & 10 \end{vmatrix}$$

(d) Extend this definition for a matrix of *any* size.

2.14 Determine the type definitions (with the context) of the following functions:

```
cube x = x * x * x

maxi x y | x >= y    = x
         | otherwise = y

sumAtoB a b = sum [a..b]
```

2.15 Determine the type definitions of the array operators (!), bounds, indices, and elems (see Section 2.7.2).

2.9 Bibliographical notes

A very good starting point to learn Haskell is the 'Gentle Introduction to Haskell' written by Hudak, Peterson and Fasel [62]. Books on functional programming using Haskell include textbooks by Thompson [116] and Bird [14] as well as an introduction to functional programming systems by Davie [32]. The development of Haskell is still an ongoing process [100].

Chapter 3

The efficiency of functional programs

The design of a program is guided by two considerations: first, it should give the correct result, and second, it should run with a reasonable speed. These priorities are reflected throughout the rest of the book: an algorithm is first expressed using a trivial program, then a more efficient version is determined whenever possible.

To improve the efficiency of a program, we must be aware of some of the issues affecting its execution. While avoiding a full description of how functional languages are actually implemented, we examine the costs of running programs as well as a range of transformation techniques aimed at improving the efficiency of programs.

3.1 Reduction order

Functional programs are evaluated by reducing expressions to values. A *reduction strategy* consists of choosing the next expression to reduce, subject to the constraint that an expression must only be evaluated after all the subexpressions on which it depends have already been evaluated. Fortunately, an important property of functional programs states that any reduction strategy, providing that it terminates, produces the same result called the *normal form*.

3.1.1   Examples

In our first example, consider the following function definitions:

```
add x y  = x + y
double x = add x x
```

The expression `double (5*4)` can be evaluated in one of these two orders among others:

```
double (5*4)  ⇒   double 20      double (5*4)  ⇒   add (5*4)(5*4)
              ⇒   add 20 20                    ⇒   (5*4)+(5*4)
              ⇒   20 + 20                      ⇒   20+(5*4)
              ⇒   40                           ⇒   20+20
                                               ⇒   40
```

We can see that the value computed is the same but the number of reduction steps can be different. In some cases, a reduction strategy does not terminate while another one does. In our next example, consider the following definitions:

```
cancel x y = x
f x        = f (x+1)
```

The expression `cancel 2 (f 3)` can be evaluated in at least two ways:

```
cancel 2 (f 3)  ⇒   cancel 2 (f 3)      cancel 2 (f 3)  ⇒   2
                ⇒   cancel 2 (f 4)
                ⇒   ...
```

In the left part, reducing the expression `f 3` leads to a non-terminating evaluation sequence. In contrast, if `cancel` is first reduced as shown in the right part, the evaluation terminates quickly. Fortunately, there is a mechanical way of choosing an evaluation order which always terminates when it is possible to do so. It has been proven that this can be achieved by choosing the *outermost* function application first. Implementations usually take the *leftmost outermost* one, like we did in the right part of our previous examples.

This choice of the outermost reducible expression is sometimes referred to as *call by name*, a terminology introduced by Algol-60 where a parameter is passed unevaluated to a function but is evaluated only when its value is needed in the function. But as such a parameter is re-evaluated each time it is needed, this can lead to more reduction steps especially in the case of loops in imperative languages. But in a functional language, since referential transparency means that the evaluation of an expression always gives the same value, it is possible to replace all occurrences of a parameter by its value once it is evaluated. This would lead to the following reduction steps in our first example:

```
double (5 * 4)  ⇒   add (5*4) (5*4)
                ⇒   (5*4)+(5*4)
                ⇒   20+20
                ⇒   40
```

The second occurrence of 5*4, which corresponds to the second x in the definition of add, is replaced as soon as the value of the first x is determined. This mode of evaluation is called *lazy evaluation* and is often implemented using a *graph reduction* mechanism: when a function application is reduced, a copy of its body is made with the formal parameters replaced by pointers to the graphs of the respective arguments; when an argument is evaluated, its graph is replaced by its value and thus all other occurrences of the same parameter share the result of the evaluation. This is the basis of most implementations of modern functional languages such as Haskell.

Another mode of reduction is *strict evaluation*, where an argument is always evaluated prior to a function call. This is the evaluation mode used in the left part of our previous examples (reducing the expressions double (5*4) and cancel 2 (f 3)). This mode is used in imperative languages and in other functional languages such as Lisp, Scheme or ML because it is more efficient to evaluate the parameter in the context of the caller and pass only the value to the function. Unfortunately, as we have seen, there are cases where this strategy does not give an answer while lazy evaluation does. The possibility of handling infinite data structures is another advantage of lazy evaluation as we will see in Section 3.1.3.

3.1.2 Controlling evaluation order in Haskell

The default evaluation strategy in Haskell is lazy evaluation. However, it is possible to evaluate a given expression strictly using the predefined operator $! which expects two arguments f and x. This operator forces the evaluation of x before applying the function f to it. In our example, strict evaluation can be achieved as follows:

```
double $! (5*4)
```

Some compilers use an optimization called *strictness analysis*; this analyzes the program to determine the situations in which it is safe to evaluate an expression strictly because its value is needed in every execution. In the previous examples, a strictness analyzer would determine that the functions add and double are strict on all their arguments, but that the function cancel is not strict on its second argument. The strictness analyzer cannot always determine if a function is strict on an argument; wherever there is any 'doubt', lazy evaluation will be employed.

3.1.3 Lazy data structures

In a lazy language, algebraic type constructors are also lazy. For example, consider the following declaration of a list:

```
data List a = Cons a (List a) | Nil
```

An application of the form (Cons a b) will not evaluate the expressions a and b until they are needed. For example, consider the following definitions (adapted from well-known list processing functions):

```
map f Nil          = Nil
map f (Cons x xs) = Cons (f x) (map f xs)

head (Cons x xs)  = x
```

The following sequence shows an example of evaluating an application of the head function in a lazy manner:

```
head (map double (Cons 1 (Cons 2 (Cons 3 Nil))))
  ⇒   head (Cons (double 1) (map double (Cons 2 (Cons 3 Nil))))
  ⇒   double 1
  ⇒   add 1 1
  ⇒   1+1
  ⇒   2
```

However, it is also possible to define a strict constructor by preceding the relevant component with the symbol '!'. For example, to define a list where all heads must be evaluated, the following definition is used:

```
data List a = Cons !a (List a) | Nil
```

Applied to the previous example, the evaluation sequence is:

```
head (map double (Cons 1 (Cons 2 (Cons 3 Nil))))
  ⇒   head (Cons (double 1) (map double (Cons 2 (Cons 3 Nil))))
  ⇒   head (Cons (add 1 1) (map double (Cons 2 (Cons 3 Nil))))
  ⇒   head (Cons (1+1) (map double (Cons 2 (Cons 3 Nil))))
  ⇒   head (Cons 2 (map double (Cons 2 (Cons 3 Nil))))
  ⇒   2
```

We can see that the head of the list is evaluated before it is needed. It is also possible to define a list structure which forces the tail of the list to be evaluated:

```
data List a = Cons a !(List a) | Nil
```

In this case, the entire structure of the list is evaluated, although it is not needed in our example:

```
head (map double (Cons 1 (Cons 2 (Cons 3 Nil))))
  ⇒   head (Cons (double 1) (map double (Cons 2 (Cons 3 Nil))))
  ⇒   ...
  ⇒   head (Cons (double 1) (Cons (double 2)
                                      (Cons (double 3) Nil)))
  ⇒   double 1
  ⇒   add 1 1
  ⇒   1+1
  ⇒   2
```

In all these sequences, the result obtained is the same. Here, the lazy structure produces it in fewer steps but there are other cases where strict constructors can improve program efficiency.

3.2 Analyzing the efficiency of programs

3.2.1   Graph reduction

We briefly mentioned graph reduction as a technique in which unevaluated expressions can be shared through pointers. In this section, we examine this technique in more detail. Graph reduction is based on a special data structure called the *heap*, which contains all the objects manipulated by the program. These objects can be constants such as integers and lists, or unevaluated *closures* which represent a function applied to some arguments. An object is referenced through a *pointer*, which is representative of its location in the heap. For example, the heap containing the expression `double (5*4)` is shown at the top of Figure 3.1. The heap contains two closures which correspond to applications of the functions `double` and `(*)`.

Each closure has pointers to the function name and its arguments, which can be constants or other closures. A primitive function application (such as * or +) is displayed in prefix form since we adopt the convention that the leftmost component in a closure is always the name of the function. Evaluation proceeds through a series of *reduction steps*. A reduction step consists of selecting an unevaluated closure and replacing it with the corresponding result. The selection depends on the evaluation strategy adopted (lazy or strict). Figure 3.1 shows the lazy reduction sequence for the previous example. It is similar to the textual representation except that sharing has been made explicit.

Figure 3.2 shows another example which illustrates how algebraic types such as lists are implemented. We can see that a constructor application is just like any other function application. As the evaluation proceeds, some objects (displayed in dotted line) are no longer referenced but still occupy space. Occasionally, the heap is cleared of all unused objects and this process is called *garbage collection*.

3.2.2   Time efficiency analysis

We now discuss time efficiency analysis according to this basic implementation model. The first problem is finding a quantitative measure that will be representative of the 'time'. Most approaches simply define it as *the number of function applications* (or steps) required to compute a given expression. Often, the cost of some primitive operators (such as +, *) will be ignored, while the cost of others will not. For example, the cost of applying primitive list processing functions such as `length` is not constant as it is dependent on the length of the list concerned. The other assumption is that there is always sufficient heap space, so the analysis does not take into account space management overheads (such as garbage collection time). Often, we are only interested in a worst-case analysis of the algorithm or, under some assumption, in an average-case analysis (see Section 1.1.3).

Another problem is that time analysis may give different results depending on whether strict or lazy evaluation is employed. Analyzing strict programs is relatively easy, and will be carried out in most cases. Analyzing programs under lazy evaluation requires more sophisticated techniques which are beyond the scope of this book. In many cases, lazy and strict evaluation result in the same number of function calls to be performed. Considering the example in Section 3.1.1, four reduction steps are required to compute the expression `double (5*4)` under both strategies.

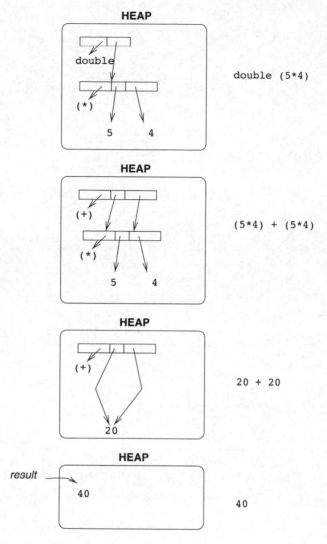

Figure 3.1   Example of reducing an expression.

If we assume that some expressions are never evaluated (such as in the example in Section 3.1.3), lazy evaluation can only result in the same number or less steps being performed. Whenever there is a clear difference between lazy and strict evaluation, we will attempt to analyze the lazy behavior of the program in an ad hoc manner.

3.2.3   Step-counting analysis

This section describes a simple framework for determining the time efficiency of functional programs under strict evaluation. We will use the number of function applications (or steps) as a measure. The analysis proceeds in three successive phases:

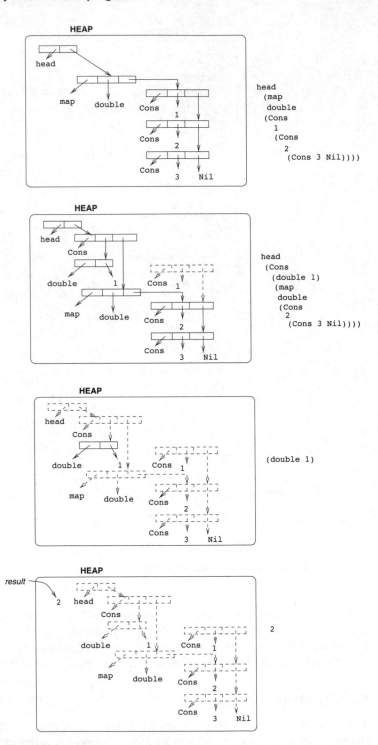

Figure 3.2 Another example of reducing an expression.

1. In the first phase, for each function f we derive a *step-counting* version T_f. By definition, the number of calls required to compute f applied to some arguments under a strict regime is equal to T_f applied to the *same* arguments.

2. The second phase consists of finding for recursive functions the structural property that the complexity depends upon. This is called the *size*.

3. In the last phase, a closed expression expressed in terms of the size of the inputs is derived from the corresponding step-counting version. This often involves solving a system of recurrence equations (Appendix B.4). The closed expression must be a composite of well-known functions such as arithmetic operators, logarithm, exponential, etc.

Transformation rules

Each expression e in the program has a cost denoted $T(e)$ and each function f has a step-counting version denoted T_f. Step-counting versions are directly derived from function definitions as follows:

$$\{f\ a_1\ a_2\ \ldots a_n = e\} \Rightarrow \{T_f\ a_1\ a_2\ \ldots\ a_n = 1 + T(e)\}$$

This is consistent with our definition which states that whenever a function is called, the number of steps performed is the number of steps required to evaluate the body of the function plus one unit of time.

The cost of computing a constant c, or a variable v, is assumed to be 0. The cost of evaluating a conditional expression is the cost of evaluating the predicate plus the cost of evaluating either the 'then' or 'else' clause depending on the value of the predicate. The cost of a primitive function call $p\ a_1\ a_2 \ldots a_n$ is equal to the sum of the costs of evaluating its arguments. Thus:

$$
\begin{aligned}
T(c) &\Rightarrow 0 \\
T(v) &\Rightarrow 0 \\
T(\text{if } a \text{ then } b \text{ else } c) &\Rightarrow T(a) + (\text{if } a \text{ then } T(b) \text{ else } T(c)) \\
T(p\ a_1\ a_2\ \ldots\ a_n) &\Rightarrow T(a_1) + T(a_2) + \ldots + T(a_n)
\end{aligned}
$$

The cost of a function call $(f\ a_1\ a_2\ \ldots\ a_n)$ consists of the costs of evaluating the arguments plus the cost of performing the call to f which is equal to $T_f\ a_1\ a_2\ \ldots\ a_n$.

$$T(f\ a_1\ a_2\ \ldots\ a_n) \Rightarrow T(a_1) + T(a_2) + \ldots + T(a_n) + (T_f\ a_1\ a_2\ \ldots\ a_n)$$

Examples

As a first example, we suppose that the average value of a list of numbers is to be determined using a function `average`, defined using the functions `sum` and `length`:

```
sum []        = 0
sum (x:xs)    = x + (sum xs)
```

```
length []     = 0
length (x:xs) = 1 + (length xs)

average xs    = (sum xs) / fromInt (length xs)
```

Note that fromInt is necessary to convert the Int value returned by length to the corresponding Float expected by the division (/) operator. Haskell uses no implicit conversion. Note also that the type conversion is defined in terms of the source type here Int rather than the target type (such as Float) that would be usually used in other languages. The rationale for this choice is explained in the Haskell report.

The step-counting versions can now be determined as follows:

$$T_{sum} \, [] \qquad\qquad = \quad 1$$
$$T_{sum} \, (x : xs) \qquad = \quad 1 + (T_{sum} \, xs)$$

$$T_{length} \, [] \qquad\qquad = \quad 1$$
$$T_{length} \, (x : xs) \qquad = \quad 1 + (T_{length} \, xs)$$

$$T_{average} \, xs \qquad\quad = \quad 1 + (T_{sum} \, xs) + (T_{length} \, xs)$$

In this case (as for the majority of list processing functions), the 'size' of the problem is the length of the argument list. We can also express these functions using a closed form expression by solving the corresponding set of recurrence equations expressed in function of the size. Both sum and length operate in $(n + 1)$ steps so average performs $2n + 3$ steps for a list of length n. Therefore, its efficiency is in $O(n)$ with a constant of proportionality equal to 2. Another version of this function that operates in just one pass will be described in Section 4.1.6.

Our next example is the reverse function, defined as:

```
reverse []     = []
reverse (x:xs) = reverse xs ++ [x]
```

First, let us start by deriving the complexity of the ++ function denoted T_{++}. Its definition (see Figure 2.1) shows that it requires $(m + 1)$ steps where m is the length of the first argument list. Considering the cost of reversing a list of length n, we can see from the definition that it is equal to the cost of reversing a list of length $(n - 1)$ plus the cost of appending (reverse xs) with [x]. The only potential difficulty is to determine the length of the list (reverse xs) but we know that it is the same as the length of xs. After solving the corresponding set of recurrence equations, the number of steps required to reverse a list of length n is $\frac{n^2}{2} + \frac{3}{2}n + 1$. Compared to the function square which has an $O(1)$ behavior and the function average whose time complexity is in $O(n)$, the function reverse has the worst asymptotic complexity as it is quadratic (that is, in $O(n^2)$).

As a last example, which illustrates the difference between strict and lazy evaluation, consider the function foo defined as follows:

```
foo l = head (map double l)
```

The step-counting analysis of this function yields an $O(n)$ complexity despite the fact that it runs in $O(1)$ under lazy evaluation.

Restrictions

The analysis rules contain a great deal of simplifications. For example, they do not deal with higher-order functions. Another restriction is that we have only considered a very small subset of Haskell. Most of the other constructs can be regarded as 'syntactic sugar' aimed at improving the readability of programs. As an example, consider the following function definition that uses guards:

```
f x | p x       = a
    | otherwise = b
```

This program should be analyzed as:

```
f x = if p x
      then a
      else b
```

The other example of syntactic sugar which may carry high costs is the list comprehension construct (see Section 2.4.2). Consider the two following expressions:

```
[ f x | x <- xs , p x ]

[ f x y | x <- xs , y <- xs , p x y ]
```

If the length of the list xs is n, the cost of evaluating the first expression is in $O(n)$ whereas the cost of evaluating the second expression is in $O(n^2)$. Pattern-matching is also another example of syntactic sugar which can be translated into simpler constructs involving tests and selections. Whenever possible, we will restrict our analysis to programs which consist of primitive constructs only.

3.2.4   Space efficiency analysis

Functional programs can be very greedy for space. We have seen that in graph reduction, a heap is needed to hold constants (such as numbers and lists) and closures. In addition, most implementations use a stack (or stacks) to load the arguments of a function in the correct order, managing function calls and returns, remembering updates, etc. During evaluation, heap nodes that are dereferenced become garbage and we have already mentioned in Section 3.2.1 that the process of freeing the space that they occupy is called garbage collection.

Unlike with time efficiency analysis, which states that lazy evaluation results in at most as many steps as in strict evaluation, lazy evaluation can have a dramatic effect on the space efficiency of a program. More space is needed to pass around unevaluated expressions that may only get evaluated at a very late stage in the computation. This might even cause the computation to abort due to a lack of space. In other situations, lazy evaluation allows several functions to operate on a large data structure without this data structure residing entirely in the memory (for example, infinite data structures). In these cases, a strict evaluation order might fail due to insufficient space!

Incidentally, an increase in space usage results in an increase in execution time due to space management overheads and an increase in the frequency of garbage collection. Therefore, the tradeoff between time and space is always very difficult to determine and a good rule of thumb suggests that we should always go for space first.

Accumulated and largest space efficiency

As with time efficiency analysis, space efficiency analysis involves selecting a measure, then expressing the complexity in terms of this measure. We define two types of space analysis:

● **Accumulated space analysis** where the complexity is expressed in terms of the total of the units selected as a measure; this is the space that would be required if no garbage collection was carried out.

● **Largest space analysis** where the complexity is equal to the largest number of units in use during the reduction sequence; this analysis only takes into account the 'live' space used during the computation so the garbage collector can be invoked as many times as necessary.

The second analysis is more appropriate but is more difficult to carry out. It is relatively easier to do an accumulated space analysis for strict programs as it is very similar to 'step-counting' analysis (see Section 3.2.3). In general, the measure used is a data constructor such as Cons (or (:)), Leaf, Node, etc. Care has to be taken when considering predefined functions with 'hidden' calls to the (:) operator such as the append operator (++).

We cannot provide general rules for determining the largest space used as this can only be carried out on a case-by-case basis by observing how a typical execution proceeds. An example is presented next.

Example

As an example of space efficiency analysis, consider the function reverse as defined in Section 3.2.3. The definition is slightly altered to expose the call to the (:) constructor 'hidden' behind the term [x] used in the second equation. The definition of the append operator (++) is also given:

```
reverse []    = []
reverse (x:xs) = (reverse xs) ++ (x:[])

[]      ++ ys  = ys
(x:xs) ++ ys  = x:(xs ++ ys)
```

To compute the accumulated cost in terms of new list cells, we can first see that the append operation (in general) creates as many list cells as the length of the first argument list. To compute the cost of reversing a list of length n, we add the following costs:

● the cost of reversing a list of length $(n - 1)$;

- the cost of appending (reverse xs) to (x:[]) which is $(n-1)$, since reversing a list of length $(n-1)$ produces a list of length $(n-1)$;
- the cost of building (x:[]) which is 1.

Solving the corresponding system of recurrence relations gives the total cost of reversing a list of length n as $\frac{n^2}{2} + \frac{n}{2}$. This is hardly a surprise since the step-counting analysis also yields an $O(n^2)$ complexity. Note that this function will run in exactly the same sequence under lazy evaluation. Therefore the issue of lazy or strict evaluation does not matter in this case.

As an example, evaluating a call to the function reverse on a list of length 3 using graph reduction would proceed as shown in Figure 3.3. For simplicity, list cells are represented without the calls to the (:) constructor and the empty list is denoted Nil. In this case, the accumulated number of list cells used (in addition to the original list) is $\frac{3^2}{2} + \frac{3}{2} = 6$, so it is consistent with the results of the analysis.

To determine the largest amount of space used during the reduction sequence, the following observations can be made:

- Each call to the reverse function creates a new list cell. However, the list cell containing the head of its argument list is no longer referenced and can be garbage collected immediately.
- Each call to the (++) function creates a new list cell but also consumes the list cell containing the head of its argument list which can also be garbage collected.

When applied to a list of length n, the recursive calls to the reverse function create n list cells but the space used by the original list can be reclaimed. When the function (++) takes over, it does not affect the total number of 'active' list cells in the heap so the largest amount of space used during the computation is n, therefore it is in $O(n)$.

For example, we can see from Figure 3.3 that no more than three list cells are used during the reduction sequence. This is consistent with the observations made for the largest space analysis.

3.2.5   Space leaks

Laziness can produce very strange behavior. In some instances, expressions may be held unevaluated even if their result may occupy less space. In other cases, it may be cheaper to recompute an expression than sharing it. These types of abnormal behavior, called *space leaks*, occur when:

- the memory space leaks away invisibly;
- memory is used when this could have been avoided;
- memory remains referenced although it could be garbage collected.

Such problems are very difficult to detect when examining the program. Recently, the situation has improved with the availability of *heap profiling tools* which allow inspection of heap nodes consumption after execution. More details are provided in the references (see bibliographical notes).

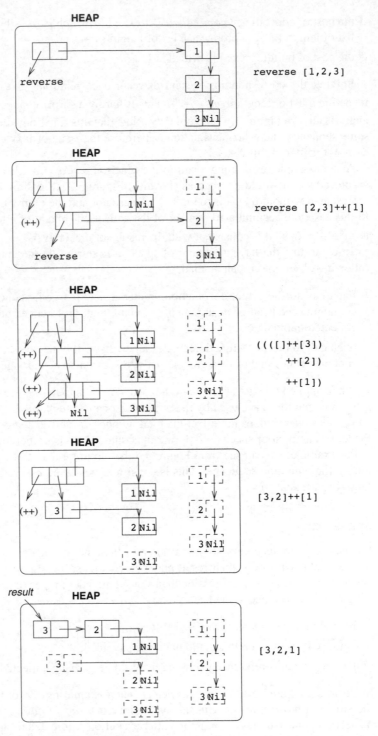

Figure 3.3   Example of heap space usage.

3.3 Program transformation

Transforming a functional program into an equivalent one is possible and can be done for a variety of purposes. In this section, we are mainly interested in transformations that are aimed at increasing efficiency.

3.3.1 The Burstall–Darlington transformation system

Burstall and Darlington [22] proposed a transformation system which is useful for transforming recursive functional programs. The basis of the idea is to treat a program as a set of equations and then perform a series of 'equal-to-equal' substitutions in order to get an equivalent program. For example, consider the following program expressed as two equations:

```
double x = 2 * x
quad   x = double (double x)
```

By replacing calls to double in the definition of quad by their right-hand side definition, we obtain the following definition of quad:

```
quad x   = 2 * (2 * x)
```

This is one type of primitive transformation called *unfolding*. Another transformation would be simply to use the laws of multiplication to replace the expression 2 * (2 * x) by 4 * x. Other primitive transformations include:

- **Definition** introduces a new equation based on known equations.
- **Instantiation** creates a specialization of a given equation, by giving values to some variables.
- **Folding,** the opposite of unfolding, replaces an occurrence of a right-hand side by the appropriate left-hand side definition.
- **Abstraction** introduces local definitions.

In addition, laws for known operators such as arithmetic operations can be used. Rules do not need to be applied in a particular order and can be repeated many times.

Without going too deeply into the details of this system, we will use the rules to transform inefficient functions into more efficient ones. For example, consider the function that computes Fibonacci numbers, expressed as:

$$f\ 0=1 \qquad\qquad\qquad (f.1)$$

$$f\ 1=1 \qquad\qquad\qquad (f.2)$$

$$f\ n=f\ (n-1)+f\ (n-2) \qquad\qquad\qquad (f.3)$$

Suppose that we introduce the following definition of g, based on f, which returns a tuple:

$$g\ n\ =\ (f\ (n+1)\,,\ f\ n) \qquad\qquad\qquad (g.1)$$

If we manage to find a more efficient version of g, then we can easily define another function f' that uses g and is equivalent to f:

$$\text{f' n}\ =\ x + y \text{ where } (x, y) = g\,(n - 2) \tag{$f'.1$}$$

To find an efficient version of g, we need to eliminate references to f in the right hand side of equation ($g.1$). This can be achieved in two stages. The first stage is to instantiate this equation with the particular case n=0:

```
g 0  =  (f 1 , f 0)
```

Now, we can unfold (f 1) and (f 0) using ($f.1$) and ($f.2$) to obtain our first equation for g:

$$\text{g 0}\ =\ (1 , 1) \tag{$g.2$}$$

The second stage is to determine the general case g n. Back to equation ($g.1$), we unfold the term f (n+1) using ($f.3$):

```
g n  =  (f n + f  (n-1)  ,  f n)
```

Next, the expressions (f n) and (f (n-1)) are respectively named x and y using an abstraction rule:

```
g n  =  (x + y , x)  where (x, y) = (f n , f (n − 1))
```

Next, a fold transformation using equation ($g.1$) can be used to replace the expression (f n , f (n-1)) by g (n-1). By combining this definition with ($g.2$), the new definition of g is:

```
g 0  =  (1, 1)
g n  =  (x + y , x)  where (x, y) = g (n − 1)
```

It is easy to prove that f' in ($f'.1$), defined using g as above, produces the required Fibonacci number in fewer steps than f.

Except for introducing the definition of g, all other transformations can be carried out in a mechanical way. There are techniques, mostly based on intuition, for making such introductions, depending on the function being transformed. The next chapter shows some applications of this style of transformation to improve the efficiency of programs.

3.3.2 Tail recursivity optimization

We now move on to a different kind of transformation which only increases space efficiency if the compiler implements one particular optimization. First, consider the following example which illustrates the costs associated with some recursive functions:

```
fact 0 = 1
fact n = n * fact (n-1)
```

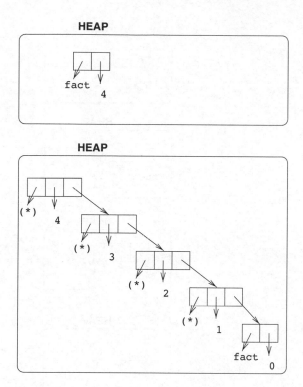

Figure 3.4 Example of reducing a non-tail-recursive function.

This function requires $O(n)$ space to remember the arguments of the operator $(*)$ through the successive recursive calls. Figure 3.4 shows the space used under a graph reduction implementation. We can see that the multiplication cannot start until the recursion has completely unrolled. In addition, since recursive function calls and returns are usually implemented by a stack, the stack growth is also in $O(n)$.

Now suppose that the function `fact` is rewritten as follows:

```
fact n         = fact' n 1

fact' 0 result = result
fact' n result = fact' (n-1) (result*n)
```

Expressed this way, the function is said to be *tail-recursive*. During evaluation, only one instance of the call to the function `fact'` is needed at any time (see Figure 3.5). For this reason, the space occupied by the old function call can be reused by the new function call. Another advantage is that the stack does not need to grow at all. This optimization, carried out by most implementations of functional languages, is called the *tail recursivity optimization*.

Note that in a lazy language, this optimization only works if the parameters of the recursive call are strictly evaluated. If not, the space occupied by the old function call cannot be reused since it contains references to unevaluated arguments. In

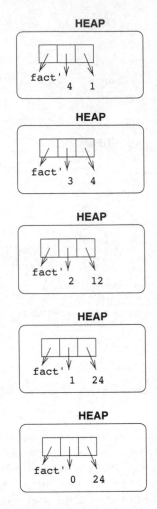

Figure 3.5   Example of reducing a tail-recursive function.

Haskell, to force strict evaluation of both arguments of the recursive call `fact'` `(n-1)` `(result*n)`, the operator `$!` needs to be used (see Section 3.1.2). Therefore, the conditions for tail recursivity optimization are (1) the relevant function must be tail-recursive, (2) the parameters of the recursive call must be evaluated strictly.

Let us now consider the `average` function from Section 3.2.3 which was defined using `sum` and `length`:

```
sum []       = 0
sum (x:xs)   = x + (sum xs)

length []    = 0
length (x:xs) = 1 + (length xs)
```

```
average xs    = (sum xs) / fromInt (length xs)
```

To allow the compiler to carry out the tail recursivity optimization, the `length` and sum functions must be written as:

```
length' xs                  = lengthTR xs 0
    where lengthTR [] r      = r
          lengthTR (x:xs) r  = (lengthTR xs) $! (r+1)

sum' xs                     = sumTR xs 0
    where sumTR [] r         = r
          sumTR (x:xs) r     = (sumTR xs) $! (r+x)

average' xs                 = sum' xs / fromInt(length' xs)
```

Both tail-recursive programs were obtained by using an *accumulating parameter* for the result. The stack space usage in this case is in $O(1)$ since the parameters of the tail-recursive functions are evaluated strictly. Note that the efficient version has been obtained at the expense of simplicity.

3.4 Conclusion

There is a wide gap between the abstract evaluation model of functional languages and traditional architectures. This provides scope for a range of transformations and optimizations aimed at reducing this gap. For this reason, it is very difficult to reason about the efficiency of functional programs since there are few 'standard' optimizations.

Even if the time or space efficiency cannot be determined exactly, in some cases it should be possible to decide which of two programs is the most time/space efficient based on some of the techniques presented in this chapter. However, this is not always possible even for the experienced programmer and the last resort should be to carry out the analysis with the help of a time and/or space profiling tool.

Exercises

3.1 Considering the function call f a b, how would you force the strict evaluation of a only, b only, and both a and b?

3.2 Computing the power k of a number x can be achieved using the following function:

```
power x k = if (k==0)
            then 1
            else if (k 'mod' 2) == 0
                 then power (x*x) (k 'div' 2)
                 else x * (power (x*x) (k 'div' 2))
```

Perform a simple time and space efficiency analysis of this function.

3.3 Assume a list of length n in which every item requires $O(m)$ steps to be computed. Suppose that the functions `length`, `head` and `sum` need to be applied to this list. How many steps would they take (in asymptotic terms) in each of the following cases:

(a) a lazy list,

(b) a list in which all tails are strictly evaluated,

(c) a list in which all heads and all tails are strictly evaluated.

3.4 Consider the following program:

```
prodsum x = prod x + sum x

prod 0 = 1
prod n = n * prod (n - 1)

sum 0 = 0
sum n = n + sum (n - 1)
```

(a) Change the definitions of `sum` and `prod` into tail-recursive ones.

(b) Using the Burstall–Darlington transformation system, write a new definition of `prodsum` (using tuples) such that the result is computed in one pass.

(c) Change this definition into one that avoids using tuples and which is tail-recursive.

3.5 Bibliographical notes

Peyton Jones [94] describes the graph reduction model in detail, as well as some of the optimizations briefly mentioned in this chapter such as strictness analysis. Plasmeijer and van Eekelen describe another model suitable for implementing functional languages called *graph rewriting* [102]. Examples of abstract machines for functional languages include Landin's SECD machine [77], the G-machine [4, 66], TIM [36], and the STG-machine [96]. A good overview of these machines as well as the associated compilation schemes can be found in Lester and Peyton Jones's textbook [97]. Another relevant book on the implementation of functional languages is the one by Field and Harrison [37].

The efficiency of functional programs is addressed in Chapter 7 of Bird's book [14]. However, analyzing the time efficiency of functional programs is still an active research area. The term 'step-counting' technique is due to Rosendahl [106] who provides a framework to analyze a strict first-order language. Other work in this area, notably dealing with higher-order functions and lazy evaluation, include papers by Wadler [124] and Sands [109]. Space efficiency is trickier and the only notable work that has been done is the one by Runciman and Wakeling [107] on heap profiling. Space leaks are discussed by Hughes [63] and Runciman and Rojemo [108].

Chapter 4

Concrete data types

Having discussed the efficiency of functional programs in general, this chapter focuses on the main concrete data types used in functional languages, namely lists, trees, and arrays. It presents some techniques for analyzing and possibly increasing the efficiency of programs that use these data types.

4.1 Lists

The list data structure and its main operations have already been discussed in Chapter 2. This section discusses some efficiency considerations and shows that in some cases it is possible to improve the efficiency of list processing through a change in the programming style. The techniques presented are by no means exhaustive as there are other methods based on experience and/or a specific compiler used. Some techniques reduce the time at the expense of space or vice versa. In other cases, a reduction in cost in one part of the program may result in an increase in the cost of a different part, as we will see later in this section.

4.1.1   Composing list operations

List processing functions are often glued together using function composition. The composition operator (.) is defined as:

$$(f \: . \: g) \: x \;\; = \;\; f \: (g \: x) \hspace{4cm} \text{(composition rule)}$$

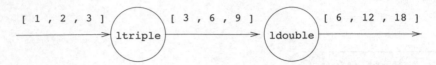

Figure 4.1 Example of a pipeline.

As an example, consider the following definitions:

```
ldouble        :: (Num a) => [a] -> [a]
ldouble []     = []
ldouble (x:xs) = (2*x) : (ldouble xs)


ltriple        :: (Num a) => [a] -> [a]
ltriple []     = []
ltriple (x:xs) = (3*x) : (ltriple xs)
```

The evaluation of the expression (ldouble . ltriple) [1,2,3] is visually illustrated in Figure 4.1. In general, the composition of n list processing functions $f_1, f_2, \ldots, f_n$ forms a *pipeline* where the input of f_i is the output of f_{i+1}.

Under strict evaluation, the computation requires as much space as the largest function in the pipeline. However, under lazy evaluation, it is possible for a part of the result of one function to be passed to the next function 'on demand'. For example, consider the reduction sequence that corresponds to the previous example:

```
(ldouble.ltriple) [1,2,3]  ⟹  ldouble (ltriple [1,2,3])
                           ⟹  ldouble (3:(ltriple [2,3]))
                           ⟹  6:(ldouble (ltriple [2,3]))
                           ⟹  6:12:(ldouble (ltriple [3]))
                           ⟹  [6,12,18]
```

We can see that partial results produced by ltriple are immediately consumed by ldouble, making the intermediate list immediately garbage collectable. Providing that all the functions in the pipeline produce partial results, their composition operates in constant space that is in $O(1)$. We will return to such intermediate lists (called *transient lists*) in Section 4.1.4.

4.1.2 The copying problem

A known disadvantage of functional programs is that space can be considerably replicated. For example, consider the insert function that inserts an item into an ordered list:

```
insert :: (Ord a)            => a -> [a] -> [a]
insert x []                  = [x]
insert x (y:ys) | (x>y)      = y:(insert x ys)
                | otherwise  = x:y:ys
```

If the item is inserted at the end of the list, this list will have to be replicated because other pointers to the old list may exist. In most cases, this problem is unavoidable.

In some cases, some copying can be avoided by a judicious use of sharing. For example, we can introduce a label in the second equation of the above definition as follows:

```
insert x l@(y:ys) | (x>y)      = y:(insert x ys)
                  | otherwise = x:l
```

In this case, only one list cell is saved but such savings can be significant in a context such as:

```
map (insert x) [l1,l2,...ln]
```

4.1.3   Tail strictness and tail recursivity

We have seen in Section 4.1.1 that function composition may lead to the creation of intermediate lists (transient lists). A function that does not produce partial results (that is, it traverses the entire list before producing its result) is called a *tail-strict* function.

As an example, consider the function `filter` that filters a list according to some predicate. A trivial definition is:

```
filter             :: (a -> Bool) -> [a] -> [a]
filter p []      = []
filter p (x:xs) = if (p x)
                    then x:(filter p xs)
                    else filter p xs
```

We could attempt to write a tail-recursive version of `filter` using an accumulating parameter which collects the elements in reverse order (the list must be reversed at the end). The new definition would be:

```
filter'             :: (a -> Bool) -> [a] -> [a]
filter' p xs        = filter'' p xs []

filter''              :: (a -> Bool) -> [a] -> [a] -> [a]
filter'' p [] r     = reverse r
filter'' p (x:xs) r = if (p x)
                        then filter'' p xs (x:r)
                        else filter'' p xs r
```

This version is tail-recursive and tail-strict because the entire list must be traversed before delivering a result. The main advantage is a reduction in stack space usage if the compiler implements tail recursivity optimization (see Section 3.3.2). However, using a tail-strict function may cause an increase of the space used during the computation from $O(1)$ to $O(n)$ if used in a pipeline. This is why care must be taken when changing the definition of a function into its tail-recursive version.

Incidentally, the filter function can also be expressed using the folding operator `foldr` as follows:

```
filter              :: (a -> Bool) -> [a] -> [a]
filter p xs         = foldr f [] xs
  where f x result = if (p x)
                       then (x:result)
                       else result
```

Although this is not obvious, this definition is not tail-strict as the head of the list is produced without unfolding all the calls to the operator foldr.

4.1.4   Deforestation with lists

We have seen that function composition of list functions can lead to the creation of intermediate lists. Despite the fact that these intermediate lists are garbage collectable, it may be desirable to avoid creating them at all. This saves the expense of allocating list cells, testing them, then de-allocating them. In some cases, this can be achieved by program transformation using the Burstall–Darlington transformation system (see Section 3.3.1). For example, consider the program given in Section 4.1.1, expressed as a set of equations:

$$ldouble [] \quad =[] \qquad\qquad\qquad (d.1)$$
$$ldouble (x : xs)=(2 * x) : (ldouble\ xs) \qquad\qquad (d.2)$$

$$ltriple [] \quad =[] \qquad\qquad\qquad (t.1)$$
$$ltriple (x : xs)=(3 * x) : (ltriple\ xs) \qquad\qquad (t.2)$$

Suppose that we introduce a function called ldt that invokes the composition of these two functions:

$$ldt\ xs \quad = \quad (ldouble\ .\ ltriple)\ xs \qquad\qquad (dt.1)$$

An application of this function requires an intermediate list to be passed between the functions ldouble and ltriple. To eliminate this list, another version of ldt is generated by instantiating equation ($dt.1$) with the two cases [] and (x:xs). For the first case, the transformation proceeds as follows:

```
ldt [] =  (ldouble . ltriple) []          (by dt.1)
       =  ldouble (ltriple [])            (by composition rule)
       =  []                              (by t.1, d.1)
```

For the second case (x:xs), the transformation proceeds as follows:

```
ldt (x : xs)
     =  (ldouble . ltriple) (x:xs)         (by dt.1)
     =  ldouble (ltriple (x:xs))           (by composition rule)
     =  ldouble ((3*x):(ltriple xs))       (by t.2)
     =  (2*(3*x)):(ldouble (ltriple xs))   (by d.2)
     =  (6*x):(ldt xs)                     (by dt.1, arithmetic)
```

Putting the two cases together, we have managed to derive an equivalent expression which does not use an intermediate list:

$$\begin{aligned} \text{ldt } [] &= [] \\ \text{ldt } (x:xs) &= (6*x):(\text{ldt } xs) \end{aligned}$$

This procedure to remove intermediate lists forms the basis of Wadler's *deforestation algorithm* and could be automatically implemented by a compiler but is most often done 'by hand'.

4.1.5 Removing appends

In this section, we consider another example of using the Burstall–Darlington transformation approach to remove calls to the append operator (++). The description presented here is based on a technique described by Wadler [123] and inspired by his work on deforestation. First, here are three laws to which (++) obeys:

$$\begin{aligned} [] \mathbin{+\!\!+} x &= x && (a.1) \\ (x:y) \mathbin{+\!\!+} z &= x : (y \mathbin{+\!\!+} z) && (a.2) \\ (x \mathbin{+\!\!+} y) \mathbin{+\!\!+} z &= x \mathbin{+\!\!+} (y \mathbin{+\!\!+} z) && (a.3) \end{aligned}$$

The aim of the transformation is to eliminate the append function from expressions of the form $(f\ x_1 \ldots x_n) \mathbin{+\!\!+} y$ by defining a function f' such that:

$$f'\ x_1 \ldots x_n\ y = (f\ x_1 \ldots x_n) \mathbin{+\!\!+} y \qquad (a.4)$$

Expressions of the form $(f\ x_1 \ldots x_n)$ will be replaced by $(f'\ x_1 \ldots x_n\ [])$. To derive the function f', each definition of the form $\{f\ x_1 \ldots x_n = e\}$ is replaced by $\{f'\ x_1 \ldots x_n\ y = e \mathbin{+\!\!+} y\}$. This technique is known as *generalization* because f' is a generalization of f.

For example, consider the equations of the reverse function as defined in Section 3.2.3:

$$\begin{aligned} \text{reverse } [] &= [] && (r.1) \\ \text{reverse } (x:xs) &= (\text{reverse } xs) \mathbin{+\!\!+} (x:[]) && (r.2) \end{aligned}$$

We need to define a function reverse' according to the rules outlined earlier. We use the following equation derived from $(a.4)$:

$$\text{reverse'}\ xs\ y = (\text{reverse } xs) \mathbin{+\!\!+} y \qquad (a.5)$$

First, consider the case of an empty list:

$$\begin{aligned} \text{reverse'}\ []\ y &= \text{reverse } [] \mathbin{+\!\!+} y && (\text{by } a.5) \\ \text{reverse'}\ []\ y &= [] \mathbin{+\!\!+} y && (\text{by } r.1) \\ &= y && (\text{by } a.1) \end{aligned}$$

Next is the case of a non-empty list:

$$\begin{aligned} \text{reverse'}\ (x:xs)\ y \\ &= ((\text{reverse } xs) \mathbin{+\!\!+} (x:[])) \mathbin{+\!\!+} y && (\text{by } a.5) \\ &= (\text{reverse } xs) \mathbin{+\!\!+} ((x:[]) \mathbin{+\!\!+} y) && (\text{by } a.3) \\ &= (\text{reverse } xs) \mathbin{+\!\!+} (x:([] \mathbin{+\!\!+} y)) && (\text{by } a.2) \\ &= (\text{reverse } xs) \mathbin{+\!\!+} (x:y) && (\text{by } a.1) \\ &= (\text{reverse'}\ xs\ (x:y)) && (\text{by } a.5) \end{aligned}$$

Putting the two cases together, the definition of `reverse'` is:

```
reverse' [] y      =  y
reverse' (x : xs) y  =  reverse' xs (x : y)
```

Replacing calls of the form `reverse xs` by (`reverse' xs []`) leads to a dramatic improvement from $O(n^2)$ to $O(n)$ in both time and space! This technique cannot always guarantee an improvement for every function and requires some skill to carry it out successfully.

4.1.6 Reducing the number of passes

Some functions need to traverse a list several times before delivering a result. Often, it is desirable to reduce the number of passes, particularly if the list involved is large. For example, consider the average function once more:

```
average xs = sum xs / fromInt (length xs)
```

Two list traversals are needed, one for the function `sum` and the other for the function `length`. In addition, the entire list must reside in memory at once because it is shared by both functions `sum` and `length`.

'Tupling' can be used to redefine the above function into a version that operates in just one list traversal:

```
average' xs            = s / fromInt n
    where
        (s,n)          = av xs
        av []          = (0,0)
        av (x:xs)      = (x+s,n+1)
            where
                  (s,n) = av xs
```

However, there are two problems with using tuples to return multiple results: the first one is the extra space needed, and the second one (pointed out by Hughes [63]) is that it is likely to incur a *space leak*, which means that computing the average will not run in constant largest space as the tail-recursive versions of `sum` and `length` will do.

A solution is to include both results *as parameters to the function*. Suppose that we introduce a function `av'` specified as:

```
av' xs s n = (sum xs + s) / fromInt (length xs + n)
```

A more efficient version of `average` can be derived in the usual transformation style, producing the following definition that operates in one pass embedded in a new version of average:

```
average'' xs                = av' xs 0 0
    where av' []      s n = s / fromInt n
          av' (x:xs) s n = av' xs (x+s) (n+1)
```

The advantage of this version is that there is no need for the entire list to reside in memory so the space leak is avoided. Providing that the expressions (x+s) and (n+1) are evaluated strictly, the compiler can implement tail recursivity optimization so the overall space costs are reduced.

4.2 Trees

Trees are useful in many algorithms such as searching and sorting, most of which will be encountered later in the book. Having described the basic definition of the tree data structure in Section 2.6.5, we now introduce some terminology associated with trees, examine various functions that operate on trees and give some examples of how some tree processing programs can be improved.

4.2.1 Terminology

A tree consists of *nodes*; each node, except one given as *root*, has a predecessor (the *parent*) which can be succeeded by one or more nodes (its *children* or *descendants*). A node with no successor is called a *leaf* or a *tip*. The conventional diagrammatic representation shows trees upside down with the leaves at the bottom.

The *root* is the topmost node and a *path* to a node is the sequence of nodes from the root to that node. The *depth* (or *height*) of a tree is the length of its longest path. For example, the height of the tree shown in Figure 4.2 is 3. The *level* of a node is defined as follows: it is 0 if it is the root node or the level of its parent node plus one.

A *binary* tree is a tree in which each node has at most two successors. For example, the tree shown in Figure 4.2 is a binary tree. If a binary tree has n nodes and a depth d, some interesting properties follow:

1. The minimum depth is $d = \lceil \log(n + 1) \rceil$. If n is of the form $2^k - 1$, the minimum depth is k and the tree is said to be *perfectly balanced* in which case there are $2^{k-1} - 1$ interior nodes and 2^{k-1} leaves.

2. The maximum depth is $d = n$ (a chain of nodes).

Unless mentioned otherwise, all logarithms used in this book are of base 2 (see Appendix B.2). In the rest of this section, we assume the following binary tree declaration given in Section 2.6.5:

```
data BinTree a = Empty | NodeBT a (BinTree a) (BinTree a)
                 deriving Show
```

4.2.2 Composing tree operations

Composing various tree-manipulating functions can be achieved in the same way as for lists (see Section 4.1.1). A function taking a tree as input may need to consume either the whole tree or one path at a time before delivering partial results. In the former case,

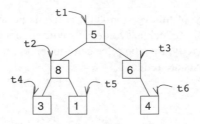

Figure 4.2 An example tree with labeled nodes.

$O(n)$ space is required where n is the total number of nodes in tree and in the latter, $O(d)$ space is required where d is the greatest depth in the tree. For example, consider the following tree-manipulating functions:

```
tcomp                     :: BinTree Int -> Int
tcomp t                   = (tsum . tdouble) t

tdouble                   :: BinTree Int -> BinTree Int
tdouble Empty             = Empty
tdouble (NodeBT v lf rt)  = NodeBT (2 * v)
                                   (tdouble lf)
                                   (tdouble rt)

tsum                      :: BinTree Int -> Int
tsum Empty                = 0
tsum (NodeBT v lf rt)     = v + (tsum lf) + (tsum rt)
```

Applying the function `tcomp` on the tree displayed in Figure 4.2 produces the following reduction sequence:

```
tcomp t1
   ⇒   (tsum . tdouble) t1
   ⇒   tsum (tdouble t1)
   ⇒   tsum (NodeBT 10 (tdouble t2)(tdouble t3))
   ⇒   (10+tsum(tdouble t2))+tsum(tdouble t3)
   ⇒   (10+tsum(NodeBT 16 (tdouble t4)(tdouble t5)))
       +tsum(tdouble t3)
   ⇒   (10+(16+tsum(tdouble t4)+tsum(tdouble t5)))
       +tsum(tdouble t3)
   ⇒   (10+(16+(6+tsum(tdouble t5))))+tsum(tdouble t3)
   ⇒   ...
```

We can see that the largest space used is proportional to the longest path in the tree. We can also see that the intermediate tree built by the function `tdouble` is immediately discarded by the function `tsum`.

As with lists, intermediate trees generated during the composition of tree functions can be eliminated by a series of transformations that can also be carried out by the compiler. The deforestation algorithm mentioned in Section 4.1.4, which involves the usual cycle of instantiation, unfold, and fold transformations, can transform the function tcomp into the following version that docs not use an intermediate tree:

```
tcomp' Empty            = 0
tcomp' (NodeBT v lf rt) = (2*v)+(tcomp' lf)+(tcomp' rt)
```

In addition to lists and trees, the deforestation algorithm can deal with any other algebraic data type.

4.2.3   Reducing the number of passes

As with lists, the Burstall–Darlington transformation style can be used to improve the efficiency of tree processing programs. For example, suppose that we want to compute the number of leaves and the depth of a tree, using the countEmpty and depth functions defined in Section 2.6.5:

```
count_depth t = (countEmpty t, depth t)
```

We can clearly see that the tree needs to be traversed twice. As with lists (see Section 4.1.6), we can derive an equivalent function that uses tupling to deliver the result in one pass:

```
count_depth' Empty = (1,0)
count_depth' (NodeBT v lf rt) = (c1 + c2, 1 + (max d1 d2))
    where (c1,d1) = count_depth' lf
          (c2,d2) = count_depth' rt
```

Sometimes, there might be a dependency between the two traversals, that is, the second traversal needs a value computed by the first traversal. For example, replacing each value in the tree by a percentage value (the original value divided by the total of all the values) can be specified using the following set of equations:

```
comp t                  = perc (tsum t) t

tsum Empty              = 0
tsum (NodeBT v lf rt)   = v + tsum lf + tsum rt

perc x Empty            = Empty
perc x (NodeBT v lf rt) = NodeBT (fromInt v / fromInt x)
                                 (perc x lf)
                                 (perc x rt)
```

We can see that the tree must be traversed twice during evaluation of the function comp. Bird [11] shows a technique to achieve the computation in one traversal. It consists of introducing a function comp'' defined as:

```
comp'' x t = (perc x t, tsum t)
```

Given this function, an alternative function to comp (called comp') can be defined by calling comp'' with one of its arguments being the second component of its result:

```
comp' t = t'
   where (t', x) = comp'' x t
```

So the problem now is to define an efficient version of the comp'' function. To achieve this, the definition of comp'' is instantiated with the two cases corresponding to the constructors Empty and Node. The first case is for the constructor Empty:

```
comp'' x Empty  =  (perc x Empty , tsum Empty)
                =  (Empty, 0)
```

The second case is dealt with as follows:

```
comp'' x (NodeBT v lf rt)
   =  (perc x (NodeBT v lf rt),
       tsum (NodeBT v lf rt))
   =  (NodeBT (fromInt v/fromInt x) (perc x lf) (perc x rt) ,
       v + tsum lf + tsum rt)
   =  (NodeBT (fromInt v/fromInt x) p1 p2 , v + s1 + s2)
       where (p1 , s1)  =  (perc x lf  , tsum lf)
             (p2 , s2)  =  (perc x rt , tsum rt)          (abstraction)
   =  (NodeBT (fromInt v/fromInt x) p1 p2 , v + s1 + s2)
       where (p1 , s1)  =  comp'' x lf
             (p2 , s2)  =  comp'' x rt
```

The two equations of comp'' that correspond to both cases can now be put together:

```
comp'' x Empty           = (Empty,0)
comp'' x (NodeBT v lf rt)= (NodeBT (fromInt v / fromInt x) p1 p2,
                               v + s1 + s2)
   where (p1,s1) = comp'' x lf
         (p2,s2) = comp'' x rt
```

4.2.4   Removing appends revisited

It is often the case that gathering information from a tree into a list produces multiple recursive calls to the (++) operator. For example, consider again the function which converts a tree into list function using the inorder traversal (see Section 2.6.5):

```
inorder Empty             = []
inorder (NodeBT a lf rt) = inorder lf ++ [a] ++ inorder rt
```

In this case, an improvement can be made by removing calls to the append function (see Section 4.1.5). After a series of transformations, the improved version of this function is:

```
inorder' t                  = inorder'' t []
   where inorder'' Empty z = z
         inorder'' (NodeBT a lf rt) z
                            = inorder'' lf (a:(inorder'' rt z))
```

4.2.5 Copying in trees

In some instances, copying can be avoided through the use of labels as we demonstrated with lists (see Section 4.1.2). For example, we assume that binary trees only contain values at the leaves through the following definition (slightly different from the one given in Section 2.6.5) where interior nodes do not contain labels.

```
data BinTree'' a = Leaf'' a
                 | NodeBT'' (BinTree'' a) (BinTree'' a)
```

Now, consider the following function that flips all the left–right branch pairs:

```
flipT                  :: BinTree'' a -> BinTree'' a
flipT (NodeBT'' a b) = NodeBT'' (flipT b) (flipT a)
flipT (Leaf'' a)     = Leaf'' a
```

The evaluation of `flipT` as defined above causes all the leaves in the original tree to be unnecessarily replicated. To avoid this problem, we can rewrite the second pattern in the definition of `flipT` using a label as follows:

```
flipT x@(Leaf'' a) = x
```

In this case, less space is used after evaluation because the new tree shares its leaves with the original tree.

4.2.6 Storing additional information in the tree

In some cases, some additional information can be stored in the nodes to avoid multiple traversals of the tree. For example, consider the problem of inserting a node at the lowest level of the smallest (in size) subtree:

```
tinsert v Empty                  = NodeBT v Empty Empty
tinsert v (NodeBT w lf rt)
    | (size lf) <= (size rt)    = NodeBT w (tinsert v lf) rt
    | otherwise                 = NodeBT w lf (tinsert v rt)
```

We can see that the size of a subtree, defined as the number of elements it contains, is repeatedly calculated. An alternative is to use the following tree declaration where the sizes of the right and the left subtrees are stored together with the value of the root node:

```
data BinTreeSz a = EmptySz
                 | NodeBTSz (Int,Int) a (BinTreeSz a) (BinTreeSz a)
```

In this case, the tree insertion function becomes:

```
tinsertSz        :: a -> BinTreeSz a -> BinTreeSz a
tinsertSz v EmptySz
                 = NodeBTSz (0,0) v EmptySz EmptySz
tinsertSz v (NodeBTSz (s1,s2) w lf rt)
    | s1 <= s2  = NodeBTSz (s1+1, s2) w (tinsertSz v lf) rt
    | otherwise = NodeBTSz (s1,s2+1) w lf (tinsertSz v rt)
```

4.3 Arrays

Arrays and some array operators were introduced in Section 2.7. This section briefly discusses the implementation of arrays and some efficiency considerations.

4.3.1 Functional and imperative arrays

First, we compare functional and imperative arrays and examine how creation, accesses, and updates can be handled.

Arrays in a functional language are somewhat different from arrays in imperative languages. An imperative array has the following advantages:

- A value can be accessed or updated in constant time.
- The update operation does not need extra space.
- There is no need for chaining the array elements with pointers as they can be stored in contiguous memory locations.

A functional array does not have all these features but implementations try to get as close as possible to that of imperative arrays. Since there is no general consensus yet, compilers can greatly vary in the way arrays are implemented. Since all entries in the array are created at once (see Section 2.7.1), it is possible (in principle) for the compiler to allocate a contiguous storage area for the array and allow a direct $O(1)$ access to its elements.

4.3.2 Handling array updates

The main problem is with the update operations. We have seen that the operator $(//)$ can be used to change the value of some entries in an array. The only problem is that the entire array (or part of it) has to be replicated as there may still be pointers to the older version. In many cases, there is no need to replicate the array if only a single version is used at any time, that is there are no pointers to previous versions of the array. In these conditions, the program is said to be *single threaded* and destructive updating can take place. In some circumstances, detecting single threading can be done automatically: either at run-time through the garbage collector or at compile-time by analyzing the program.

However, a recent technique that is becoming increasingly popular is to achieve destructive updating through some designated language constructs that guarantee single threading. For example, operations on one particular array can be chained using some special higher-order functions. As the pointer to the array is not directly accessible, only one version of it exists at any particular time and destructive updating can take place. We will return to this topic in the last chapter (Section 10.2.2) through the concept of *state monad*.

4.3.3 Higher-order array functions†

Higher-order functions can be defined on arrays just as with lists. For the purpose of illustration, we will only discuss mappings. Such a mapping can take place on the elements of an array using map which can be applied either to a list or an array because both are instances of the class Functor (see Figure 2.4). For example, the following expression:

```
map (\x -> x*10) a
```

creates a new array where all elements of a are multiplied by 10.

It is also possible to do mapping on the indices with ixmap, defined in the Array module as:

```
ixmap b f a = array b [(k, a ! f k)| k <- range b]
```

Now consider the following functions that return a row and a column of a matrix:

```
row :: (Ix a, Ix b) => a -> Array (a,b) c -> Array b c
row i m = ixmap (l', u') (\j->(i,j)) m
    where ((l,l'),(u,u'))= bounds m

col :: (Ix a, Ix b) => a -> Array (b,a) c -> Array b c
col j m = ixmap (l, u) (\i->(i,j)) m
    where ((l,l'),(u,u'))= bounds m
```

The function row returns an array comprising the elements of row i of matrix m because the right-hand side of the definition can be reduced as:

```
array (l',u') [(k, m!(i,k))| k <- [l'..u']]
```

which creates a new array comprising the elements of row i of matrix m. Similarly, the function col returns the corresponding column in the matrix.

The following examples illustrate the similarity between mathematical specifications and functional programs (no error checking on the arguments is performed in these definitions):

- the inner product of vectors v and w is $\sum_i v_i w_i$;
- elements c_{ij} of the multiplication of matrices a and b are given by the inner product of row i of a by column j of b.

```
inner :: (Ix a, Num b) => Array a b -> Array a b -> b
inner v w = sum [v!i * w!i | i<-indices v]

matMult :: (Num a,Ix a,Enum a,Num b,Ix b,Num c,Num d,Ix d,Enum d)
           => Array (a,b) c -> Array (b,d) c -> Array (a,d) c
matMult a b = array ((1,1),(m,n))
                [((i,j),inner (row i a)(col j b))
                | i<-[1..m],j<-[1..n]]
    where ((1,1),(m,p)) = bounds a
          ((1,1),(p',n))= bounds b
```

Since there are no updates and assuming that array accesses are in $O(1)$, the efficiency of these two programs is the same as their imperative counterparts, that is $O(n)$ for the inner product and $O(n^3)$ for the matrix multiplication, where n is the dimension of the matrix.

4.1 Compare the efficiencies of these two functions which flatten a list of lists into a single list:

```
concat1 xs = foldr (++) [] xs

concat2 xs = foldl (++) [] xs
```

4.2 Traditional compilation techniques convert list comprehensions into applications of list higher-order functions such as `map` and `filter`. The drawback is that this causes intermediate lists to be created. Consider the following function definition, which uses a list comprehension:

```
comp f g l = [ f x | x <- (map g l) , x > 10 ]
```

Using the deforestation algorithm, derive a more efficient version that does not use intermediate lists.

4.3 Consider the following function which splits a list into two lists depending on its values being less or more than the value of the first argument:

```
split x l = ([ y | y <- l, y <= x] , [ y | y <- l, y > x])
```

(a) Define a version of this function that operates in just one pass.

(b) Derive a tail-recursive function from the previous answer.

4.4 Show how the definition of `average''` in Section 4.1.6 has been derived from the definition of `average`.

4.5 Define a function that determines whether two binary trees have the same structure. Can you provide an idea of the time efficiency of your function?

4.6 Assume the following definition of a function that computes the size of a binary tree:

```
size tr a = length (inorder tr)
```

Derive a more efficient version of `size` by introducing a function `size'` specified as:

```
size' tr a z = (size tr a) + z
```

4.7 The function `flipT` has been presented in Section 4.2.5. Using the transformation rules, define a more efficient version of the following function:

```
ff t = (flipT . flipT) t
```

4.8 Show how the efficient version of the function `inorder`, presented in Section 4.2.4, has been derived according to the rules discussed in Section 4.1.5.

4.4 Bibliographical notes

Several techniques for designing efficient functional data structures are presented by Okasaki [91]. An introduction to the theory of lists and list operations is provided by Bird [13]. Increasing the efficiency of functional programs by program transformation has its roots in the work by Burstall and Darlington [22]. The accumulated parameter technique is described by Bird [12]. The deforestation algorithm is proposed by Wadler [126] and Gill *et al.* [42]. The transformation for removing calls to the append function is based on a paper by Wadler [123]. Most of these transformations are also described in Chapter 7 of Bird's book [14].

All functional programming textbooks [14, 50, 56, 93, 131] include sections on trees and tree algorithms. The elimination of multiple passes in tree processing functions is described by Bird [11]. Functional arrays are discussed by Wadler [122], Hudak [59], and Wise [133]. A sophisticated compiler-based analysis scheme for detecting safe updates is presented by Bloss and Hudak [15]. Another approach, adopted in Clean [102], implements safe destructive updating through the type checking mechanism. References on the monadic approach can be found at the end of the last chapter of this book.

Chapter 5

Abstract data types

This chapter introduces the concept of an abstract data type (ADT) and uses some common data structures such as stacks, queues, and sets as examples of ADTs. These data structures implemented as ADTs will be used in several algorithms described in the rest of the book.

5.1　Introduction

The data types discussed in the previous chapter are called concrete data types because they refer to a particular data structure provided by the language. In contrast, *abstract data types* (ADTs) are not tied to any particular representation. Instead, they are implicitly defined through a set of operations used to manipulate them.

The type definitions of the ADT operations and their specifications form the *interface* to the ADT, but neither the internal structure of an ADT nor the definition of these operations are visible to the user. Given an ADT specification, these operations can have one or several *implementations* depending on the choice of data structure and algorithm for representing and operating on the ADT.

The great benefit of using an ADT is that it enforces the concept of *modularity* in programs. A change in the implementation of a set of operations does not affect other parts of the program as long as the operations have the same type and specifications. Although there is no specific construct to support ADTs in Haskell, an ADT can be easily implemented as a Haskell *module*. We first describe this concept and then give different implementations of some of the more frequently used ADTs, always keeping the same interface for the user of the module.

A module in Haskell defines a collection of functions and data type definitions in a closed environment and can export all or only some of its definitions. A module is defined using the following statement:

module *name* (*export list*) where

In our examples, the name of the module will be the name of the ADT and the *export list* will first export the name of the data type followed by the operations to use the data type.

5.2 Stacks

A Stack is a homogeneous collection of items on which two operations are defined: push x s which pushes the value x on the stack s, returning the new stack with x on top of s; pop s pops an item out of the stack, returning the new stack without the top element of s. The element on top of a stack s is returned by top s. Items are removed according to a Last In First Out (LIFO) strategy, that is the last item pushed is the first one to be popped out of the stack. As the underlying representation is hidden from the user of the ADT, it is necessary to define emptyStack, an operation which creates an empty stack. The function stackEmpty is used to check if a stack has any element in it or not.

In Haskell, a stack implemented as an ADT module can be defined as follows:

module Stack(Stack,push,pop,top,emptyStack,stackEmpty) where

```
push       :: a-> Stack a -> Stack a
pop        :: Stack a -> Stack a
top        :: Stack a -> a
emptyStack :: Stack a
stackEmpty :: Stack a -> Bool
```

The type definitions are not strictly necessary because Haskell deduces them from the implementation but it is quite useful to write them as documentation for the user of the ADT; Haskell will also check if the implementation conforms to the intention described by the type definitions.

A first implementation can be done using a user-defined type:

```
data Stack a          = EmptyStk
                      | Stk a (Stack a)

push x s              = Stk x s

pop EmptyStk          = error "pop from an empty stack"
pop (Stk _ s)         = s

top EmptyStk          = error "top from an empty stack"
top (Stk x _)         = x

emptyStack            = EmptyStk

stackEmpty EmptyStk = True
stackEmpty _        = False
```

As pop and top are not meaningful on an empty stack, we merely stop the program by issuing an error message.

Another possible implementation can be obtained using the predefined list data structure because push and pop are similar to the (:) and tail operations. But to make sure that the only available operations on a Stack are the ones defined in the ADT and not the whole gamut of predefined list functions (it would not be meaningful to index within a Stack or to reverse it), we create a new type using the newtype keyword of Haskell with a constructor (here Stk) to differentiate between predefined lists and lists used within the ADT for implementing a Stack. The presence of newtype can make Haskell aware that the constructor is only used for type checking. This constructor thus incurs no overhead at execution time. Within the module though, it is possible to access the list representation and use the predefined list operations for manipulating it.

```
newtype Stack a       = Stk [a]

push x (Stk xs)       = Stk (x:xs)

pop (Stk [])          = error "pop from an empty stack"
pop (Stk (_:xs))      = Stk  xs

top (Stk [])          = error "top from an empty stack"
top (Stk (x:_))       = x

emptyStack            = Stk []

stackEmpty (Stk []) = True
stackEmpty (Stk _ ) = False
```

All these operations on Stacks are efficient because they operate in $O(1)$ steps.

5.2.1   Displaying an abstract data type

Because the constructors EmptyStk and Stk are not exported from the module, they are not mentioned in the export list. The user of the module cannot use or create a Stack by any other way than the operations exported by the module. The user (or the interpreter) cannot even display a value of type Stack for debugging, for example. Of course, the user could always pop the entire stack to access the values on the stack but this would be cumbersome.

In Haskell, there are two ways of making 'showable' values from an abstract data type. The first way is simple and uses a deriving Show clause as we did in Section 2.6.1; this has the drawback, however, of revealing the implementation of the ADT to the user although the representation cannot be accessed in any way outside the module definition of the ADT. If we use this clause in both our Stack ADT implementations, then printing a Stack value will result in two different outputs.

For example, consider the first implementation where a stack is defined as:

```
data Stack a = EmptyStk
             | Stk a (Stack a)
   deriving Show
```

then evaluating an expression creating a stack would give an output showing its implementation like the following

```
push 3 (push 2 (push 1 emptyStack)
   ⇒   Stk 3 (Stk 2 (Stk 1 EmptyStk))
```

But if we consider the second implementation where a stack is defined as:

```
newtype Stack a = Stk [a] deriving Show
```

then evaluating the same expression would give

```
push 3 (push 2 (push 1 emptyStack)   ⇒   Stk [3, 2, 1]
```

Although this way of making a user-defined data type is simple for the programmer, it is not really abstract.

Fortunately, there is a better way of hiding the internal representation of an ADT by making the representation of the type an instance of the class Show and defining the showsPrec p v function which is the fundamental operation called by all other functions used for displaying values; p is a precedence value not relevant here. Our implementation of showsPrec uses the functions shows, showChar and showString defined in the 'Standard Prelude'.[1] If we want Stack values to be output always in the same way, we merely define the showsPrec function for each representation. For example, we will always display a stack value by listing each value in the stack separated by a vertical bar and ending with a dash such as the following:

```
push 3 (push 2 (push 1 emptyStack)   ⇒   3|2|1|-
```

---

[1] In the Haskell report [100], these functions are defined in their curried form but here we make the input string explicit.

In our first implementation using the `EmptyStk` and `Stk` constructors, we can make the `Stack` type an instance of `Show` and then define the `showsPrec` function as follows:

```
instance (Show a) => Show (Stack a) where
    showsPrec _  EmptyStk str = showChar '-' str
    showsPrec _  (Stk x s) str
        = shows x (showChar '|' (shows s str))
```

For the second implementation, we define another instance declaration that uses the `Stk` declaration and the list properties.

```
instance (Show a) => Show (Stack a) where
    showsPrec p (Stk [])     str = showChar '-' str
    showsPrec p (Stk (x:xs)) str
        = shows x (showChar '|' (shows (Stk xs) str))
```

We can see that `Stack` values are displayed in the same way in both user-defined type and list implementations. As the derivation and the `showsPrec` function is defined within the module, it can access the internal representation of the abstract data type.

5.3 Queues

A Queue is a data structure similar to a stack but in which items are removed in a First In First Out (FIFO) order, that is the first one inserted in the queue is the first one to be removed. The type of each operation is similar to its counterpart in the stack ADT:

```
module Queue(Queue,emptyQueue,queueEmpty,
             enqueue,dequeue,front) where

emptyQueue :: Queue a
queueEmpty :: Queue a -> Bool
enqueue    :: a -> Queue a -> Queue a
dequeue    :: Queue a -> Queue a
front      :: Queue a -> a
```

As with stacks, a straightforward implementation of a queue is to hold the items in a list:

```
newtype Queue a    = Q [a]
    deriving Show

emptyQueue         = Q []

queueEmpty (Q []) = True
queueEmpty (Q _ ) = False

enqueue x (Q q)    = Q (q ++ [x])
```

```
dequeue (Q (_:xs)) = Q xs
dequeue (Q [])     = error "dequeue: empty queue"

front (Q (x:_))    = x
front (Q [])       = error "front: empty queue"
```

In this implementation, the enqueuing operation takes $O(n)$ steps because an item is inserted at the end of a list (of length n). Of course, we could insert items at the front of the list and remove them from the tail of the list but the dequeuing function would take $O(n)$ steps in this case.

Another implementation, proposed by Burton [24], is to use a pair of lists: one representing the front of the queue and the other representing the rear of the queue in reverse order. When a dequeue operation depletes the front of the queue, it is replaced by the rear of the queue in reverse order and the rear of the queue becomes empty. So, now dequeuing takes $O(1)$ steps as do most of the dequeuing operations except when the first list is empty. The corresponding implementation is:

```
newtype Queue a        = Q ([a],[a])

queueEmpty (Q ([],[])) = True
queueEmpty _           = False

emptyQueue             = Q ([],[])

enqueue x (Q ([],[]))  = Q ([x],[])
enqueue y (Q (xs,ys))  = Q (xs,y:ys)

dequeue (Q ([],[]))    = error "dequeue:empty queue"
dequeue (Q ([],ys))    = Q (tail(reverse ys) , [])
dequeue (Q (x:xs,ys))  = Q (xs,ys)

front (Q ([],[]))      = error "front:empty queue"
front (Q ([],ys))      = last ys
front (Q (x:xs,ys))    = x

instance (Show a) => Show (Queue a) where
   showsPrec p (Q (front, rear)) str
        = showString "Q " (showList (front ++ reverse rear) str)
```

We define the showsPrec function so that the tuple implementation of queues is displayed in the same way as the derived display of the list implementation. We assume that the reverse operation is the one defined in Section 4.1.5 which takes $O(n)$ steps to reverse a list of length n. In this case, the average access time over a sequence of queue operations is in $O(1)$ steps but in the worst case it can be in $O(n)$ steps. Okasaki [90, 91] describes a method in which a list is reversed progressively during dequeue operations so that the worst case for any dequeue operation is in $O(\log n)$.

5.4 Priority queues

A priority queue is a queue in which each item has a priority associated with it. The dequeue operation always removes the item with the highest (or lowest) priority. The interface presented here is the same as with queues except that there must now be a class restriction on the type of items held in the queue, that is, their type must belong to the Ord class (see Section 2.8):

```
module PQueue(PQueue,emptyPQ,pqEmpty,enPQ,dePQ,frontPQ) where

emptyPQ :: PQueue a
pqEmpty :: PQueue a -> Bool
enPQ    :: (Ord a) => a -> PQueue a -> PQueue a
dePQ    :: (Ord a) => PQueue a -> PQueue a
frontPQ :: (Ord a) => PQueue a -> a
```

In the rest of this section, we assume that ordering is based on the (<=) operator and that the dequeue operation always selects the 'smallest' item according to this operator.

5.4.1 List implementation

In this implementation, items are held in a sorted list. In this case, the priority queue ADT operations are defined as follows:

```
newtype PQueue a   = PQ [a]
    deriving Show

emptyPQ            = PQ []

pqEmpty (PQ [])    = True
pqEmpty _          = False

enPQ x (PQ q)      = PQ (insert x q)
    where insert x []                      = [x]
          insert x r@(e:r') | x <= e    = x:r
                            | otherwise = e:insert x r'

dePQ (PQ [])       = error "dePQ:empty priority queue"
dePQ (PQ (x:xs))   = PQ xs

frontPQ (PQ [])    = error "frontPQ:empty priority queue"
frontPQ (PQ(x:xs)) = x
```

In this case, the dequeue operation takes $O(1)$ steps but the enqueue operation can take up to $O(n)$ steps in the worst case. If an unordered list is used, it takes $O(1)$ steps to enqueue an item and $O(n)$ steps to dequeue an item because it corresponds to a list minimum operation.

5.4.2   Heap implementation

The implementation of an ADT can be based on another ADT. For example, a priority queue ADT can be implemented using a *heap* ADT, the details of which will be described in Section 5.8.1.

5.5   Sets

A set is a collection of distinct items in which an item can be tested for membership, inserted into or deleted from this collection. The number of distinct items in the set is called the *size* of the set. Among many possible operations, the set ADT operations presented here are:

```
module Set (Set,emptySet,setEmpty,inSet,addSet,delSet) where

emptySet  :: Set a
setEmpty  :: Set a -> Bool
inSet     :: (Eq a) => a -> Set a -> Bool
addSet    :: (Eq a) => a -> Set a -> Set a
delSet    :: (Eq a) => a -> Set a -> Set a
```

Since we need to test items for equality, the type of items must belong to the class Eq. Other operations such as union, intersection, and difference of sets can be expressed using these simple operations. Some implementations may require other class restrictions on the type of items.

There are several ways of implementing sets. Some operations are more efficient in one representation and less efficient in another. In general, the best representation is selected depending on which operations are used most frequently.

5.5.1   List implementations

This section describes several list-based implementations of sets.

Unordered lists with duplicates

The first way to implement a set is using a list where elements may be duplicated. The corresponding operations are presented below:

```
newtype Set a      = St [a]

emptySet           = St []

setEmpty (St [])   = True
setEmpty _         = False

inSet x (St xs)    = elem x xs
```

```
addSet x (St a)   = St (x:a)

delSet x (St xs)  = St (filter (/= x) xs)

instance (Show a) => Show (Set a) where
    showsPrec _ (St s) str = showSet s str

showSet []     str = showString "{}" str
showSet (x:xs) str = showChar '{' ( shows x ( showl xs str))
   where showl []     str = showChar '}' str
         showl (x:xs) str = showChar ',' (shows x (showl xs str))
```

As duplicates are allowed, addSet is very simple because it merely adds a new element in front of the list. inSet checks if a value is element of the list, an operation which can imply looking at all elements of the list, especially if the element is not in the set. delSet must remove all occurrences of x in xs, an operation again requiring going through the whole list which can be longer than the size of the set.

Unordered lists without duplicates

To avoid these problems, sets can be represented as lists without duplicates. The corresponding inSet, addSet and delSet operations are:

```
addSet x s@(St xs) | inSet x s  = s
                   | otherwise  = St (x:xs)

delSet x (St s) = St (delete x s)
```

assuming a function delete x s which removes an item x from a list s.

In this case, the size of a list holding a set equals the size of the set. delSet is more efficient as it does not have to traverse the entire list every time. However, addSet is now taking $O(n)$ steps (where n is the size of the set) because every element to be inserted has to be tested for membership first.

Ordered lists without duplicates

Testing for membership can be done faster if the items are ordered in the list according to some relational operator, which means that their type must belong to the Ord class instead of the Eq class. If items are ordered in ascending order, the corresponding operations, with the revised type declarations, are:

```
inSet  :: (Ord a) => a -> Set a -> Bool
inSet x (St s) = elem x (takeWhile (<= x) s)

addSet :: (Ord a) => a -> Set a -> Set a
addSet x (St s) = St (add x s)
```

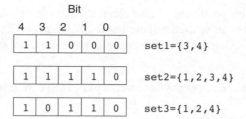

Figure 5.1 Example of three sets represented as binary numbers.

```
    where add x []                    = [x]
          add x s@(y:ys)| (x>y)       = y : (add x ys)
                        | (x<y)       = x : s
                        | otherwise   = s

delSet :: (Ord a) => a -> Set a -> Set a
delSet x (St s) = St (del x s)
    where del x []                    = []
          del x s@(y:ys)| (x>y)       = y : (del x ys)
                        | (x<y)       = s
                        | otherwise   = ys
```

If the element is not in the set, the test for membership and the deletion operation can be terminated earlier than in the second implementation. In the worst case, these operations take a linear number of steps. Therefore, keeping the set as an ordered list can be achieved quite easily but does not significantly improve the efficiency of its operations.

5.5.2   Tree representations

A tree representation of a set is also possible. Items can be stored in a binary search tree (see Section 5.7) or an AVL tree (see Section 5.9) such that an inorder traversal produces a sorted list. If the tree is kept balanced, testing for membership, insertion, and deletion all take logarithmic time.

5.5.3   Bit vector representation

If we wish to define a set that only contains numbers (of type Int) between 0 and $(n-1)$, this set can be represented as a binary number with n bits where bit i $(0 \le i < n)$ is 1 if and only if number i is in the set. For example, Figure 5.1 shows three sets and their associated binary numbers.

The efficiency of this representation depends largely on the compiler and the architecture used. Our representation rests upon the assumption that division and module operation for powers of 2 and parity tests are implemented efficiently using shifts and binary masks on the binary representation of the integer. This representation induces supplementary constraints on the elements that can be added in this Set; only a small range of Ints can be used and our implementation checks that elements are within this range. The definition of the module stays the same but the types of the functions are different.

```
module Set (Set,emptySet,setEmpty,inSet,addSet,delSet) where

emptySet  :: Set
setEmpty  :: Set -> Bool
inSet     :: Int -> Set -> Bool
addSet    :: Int -> Set -> Set
delSet    :: Int -> Set -> Set
```

These set ADT operations can be implemented as follows:

```
newtype Set    = St Int

maxSet = truncate (logBase 2 (fromInt (maxBound::Int))) - 1

emptySet       = St 0

setEmpty (St n) = n==0

inSet i (St s)
  | (i>=0) && (i<=maxSet) = odd (s `div` (2^i))
  | otherwise             = error ("inSet:illegal element ="
                                        ++ show i)

addSet i (St s)
  | (i>=0) && (i<=maxSet) = St (d'*e+m)
  | otherwise             = error ("addSet:illegal element ="
                                        ++ show i)
    where (d,m) = divMod s e
          e     = 2^i
          d'    = if odd d then d else d+1

delSet i (St s)
  | (i>=0) && (i<=maxSet) = St (d'*e+m)
  | otherwise             = error ("delSet:illegal element ="
                                        ++ show i)
    where (d,m) = divMod s e
          e     = 2^i
          d'    = if odd d then d-1 else d


instance  Show Set where
    showsPrec _  s str = showSet (set2List s) str
```

```
set2List (St s) = s2l s 0
    where s2l 0 _               = []
          s2l n i | odd n       = i : s2l (n 'div' 2) (i+1)
                  | otherwise = s2l (n 'div' 2) (i+1)
```

The maximum allowed integer in the Set, is given by $\log_2$ maxBound $- 1$. maxBound being overloaded for all instances of the class Bounded, a type constraint is necessary to get its value for Int types. Because of the lazy evaluation regime of Haskell, this expression will be evaluated once because all occurrences of this expression will share the result of the first evaluation. inSet checks if element i is in the set by dividing the integer by 2^i. If the quotient is odd then the element is in the set. Both addSet and delSet separate the integer representation in two parts corresponding to the quotient and remainder of the division by 2^i. If the quotient is odd then the element is present so addSet will not change it and delSet does by subtracting one; the number is then recomposed by multiplying the new quotient by 2^i and adding the remainder. A similar operation is performed if the element is absent from the set.

In an alternative representation of Set, any interval of integers could be specified by supplying bounds. The implementation would have to use an array of the appropriate number of Int; it would also be possible to use an Integer, which is of arbitrary precision and thus can have a large number of bits. We could also make Set more general by accepting as an element any type which can be enumerated (class Enum) such as the Char type; this is left as an exercise for the reader.

5.6 Tables

A table allows values to be stored and retrieved according to an *index*. In other words, a table implements a function of type (b -> a) by means of a data structure instead of an algorithm. Assuming a type (Table a b), the type definitions of the table ADT operations are:

```
module Table(Table,newTable,findTable,updTable) where

newTable    :: (Eq b) => [(b,a)] -> Table a b
findTable   :: (Eq b) => Table a b -> b -> a
updTable    :: (Eq b) => (b,a) -> Table a b -> Table a b
```

The operation newTable takes a list of (index,value) pairs and returns the corresponding table. The functions findTable and updTable are used to retrieve and update values in the table.

5.6.1 Implementing a table as a function

Since functional languages have the capacity to manipulate functions like any other data objects, it is possible to implement a table simply as a function. When a new item x with an index i is inserted, a new function is created. This function returns x for the index i and applies the old function for all other indices.

In this case, the table operations are defined as follows:

```
newtype Table a b          = Tbl (b -> a)

newTable assocs            =
              foldr updTable
                   (Tbl (\_ -> error "updTable:item not found"))
                   assocs

findTable (Tbl f) i        = f i

updTable (i,x) (Tbl f)     = Tbl g
     where g j | j==i      = x
               | otherwise = f j

instance Show (Table a b) where
     showsPrec _ _ str = showString "<<A Table>>" str
```

The cost of the findTable operation depends on when the update operation for the corresponding element was last performed. The later the update was performed the faster the selection of a particular element can be made. In the worst case, the select operation is linear. Because there is no meaningful way to show a function, the showing of a table is also minimal.

5.6.2 List implementation

Another implementation of a table is to use a list of index-value pairs called an *association list*. The corresponding definitions of its operations are:

```
newtype Table a b     = Tbl [(b,a)]
     deriving Show

newTable   t          = Tbl t

findTable (Tbl []) i  = error "findTable: item not found in table"
findTable (Tbl ((j,v):r)) i
     | (i==j)         = v
     | otherwise      = findTable (Tbl r) i

updTable e (Tbl [])   = Tbl [e]
updTable e'@(i,_) (Tbl (e@(j,_):r))
     | (i==j)         = Tbl (e':r)
     | otherwise      = Tbl (e:r')
     where Tbl r'     = updTable e' (Tbl r)
```

This representation is very inefficient because an update or select operation takes $O(n)$ steps in the worst case where n is the number of entries in the table. In addition, each update requires $O(n)$ new list cells in the worst case. As we did with sets, access time can be reduced by sorting items in increasing index values but it will still remain linear in the worst case.

5.6.3 Array implementation

If the type of the index is restricted to the class `Ix`, tables can be implemented as arrays. Another restriction is that it is not possible to insert a new value or update a value outside the boundaries of the first table. The corresponding definitions, with the revised type declarations for the interface, are:

```
newTable    :: (Ix b) => [(b,a)] -> Table a b
findTable   :: (Ix b) => Table a b -> b -> a
updTable    :: (Ix b) => (b,a) -> Table a b -> Table a b

newtype Table a b       = Tbl (Array b a)
    deriving Show

newTable l              = Tbl (array (lo,hi) l)
    where indices       = map fst l
            lo          = minimum indices
            hi          = maximum indices

findTable (Tbl a) i     = a ! i

updTable p@(i,x) (Tbl a) = Tbl (a // [p])
```

The function `newTable` determines the boundaries of the new table by computing the maximum and the minimum key in the association list. Note that in the function `findTable`, access to an invalid key now returns a system error instead of a user error.

The efficiency of this implementation depends on how arrays are implemented (see our discussion in Section 4.3.2). At best, access is achieved in constant $O(1)$ time but the array cannot be updated in place.

5.6.4 Tree representations

Another representation is to use a binary search tree (see next section) or a heap (see Section 5.8) where selecting and updating can be done in $O(\log n)$ steps. Each node in the tree or heap will contain one index-value pair that represents one entry in the table.

5.7 Binary search trees

A binary search tree contains a number of items such that every item contained in a node must be larger than all the items contained in its left subtree and smaller than all the items contained in its right subtree. An example of storing the values [2,3,4,5,6,8,9]

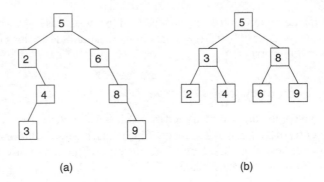

Figure 5.2 Example of two binary search trees.

using two binary search trees is illustrated in Figure 5.2. The main purpose of using the binary search tree is to reduce the time to access an item. The type definitions of some of the operations that manipulate such trees are:

```
module BinTree (BinTree,emptyTree,inTree,addTree,delTree,
                     buildTree,inorder) where

inTree     :: (Ord a,Show a) => a -> BinTree a -> Bool
addTree    :: (Ord a,Show a) => a -> BinTree a -> BinTree a
delTree    :: (Ord a,Show a) => a -> BinTree a -> BinTree a
buildTree  :: (Ord a,Show a) => [a] -> BinTree a
inorder    :: (Ord a,Show a) => BinTree a -> [a]
```

The operation `inTree` checks if a value appears in the tree, `addTree` inserts a new value in the tree and `delTree` removes a value from the tree. `buildTree` builds a search tree from a list of items. `inorder` returns the values of the tree following an inorder traversal of the tree. In the rest of this section, we describe one particular implementation of these operations. Since the items must be ordered, we assume the following binary tree declaration taken from Section 2.6.5:

```
data (Ord a) => BinTree a = EmptyBT
                          | NodeBT a (BinTree a) (BinTree a)
     deriving Show

emptyTree = EmptyBT
```

5.7.1 Testing for membership

Testing for membership is achieved through the following function:

```
inTree v' EmptyBT                     = False
inTree v' (NodeBT v lf rt) | v==v'  = True
                           | v'<v   = inTree v' lf
                           | v'>v   = inTree v' rt
```

The time needed to search for a value depends on the position of that value in the tree. The worst case is when the value is at the bottom of the tree, so the number of steps is proportional to the depth of the tree. The depth of a binary search tree with n nodes can vary from n to $\lceil \log(n + 1) \rceil$ (see Section 4.2.1). Consequently, the efficiency is in $O(n)$ in the worst case and $O(\log n)$ in the best case, which implies that the better the tree is balanced, the less steps it takes to retrieve an item.

5.7.2 Adding an item

Adding an item to the search tree can be done using this function which adds the item as a leaf, provided that the item is not already in the tree, in which case it is not added:

```
addTree v' EmptyBT          = NodeBT v' EmptyBT EmptyBT
addTree v' (NodeBT v lf rt)
              | v'==v      = NodeBT v lf rt
              | v' < v     = NodeBT v (addTree v' lf) rt
              | otherwise = NodeBT v lf (addTree v' rt)
```

As with the membership test, inserting an item takes $O(n)$ steps in the worst case and $O(\log n)$ in the best case.

5.7.3 Building a search tree

Building a search tree from a list of items could be done by folding the list using the insertion function defined previously, that is:

```
buildTree lf = foldr addTree EmptyBT lf
```

However, there is the likelihood of building unbalanced trees. For example, the call `buildTree [1,2,3,4,5,6,7]` will produce a chain of seven nodes. If the list of values is always presented in a sorted order, it is possible to build a tree with a minimum depth as follows:

```
buildTree' []      = EmptyBT
buildTree' lf      = NodeBT x (buildTree' l1) (buildTree' l2)
    where l1       = take n lf
          (x:l2)   = drop n lf
          n        = (length lf) 'div' 2
```

To transform a tree into a list of values in increasing order is only a matter of traversing the tree according to an 'in order' strategy such as the following (taken from Section 2.6.5):

```
inorder EmptyBT           = []
inorder (NodeBT v lf rt) = inorder lf ++ [v] ++ inorder rt
```

Recall that a more efficient version (without appends) has been described in Section 4.2.4. In general, it is not guaranteed that the tree will be balanced. A different type of search tree which carries such a guarantee will be described in the next section.

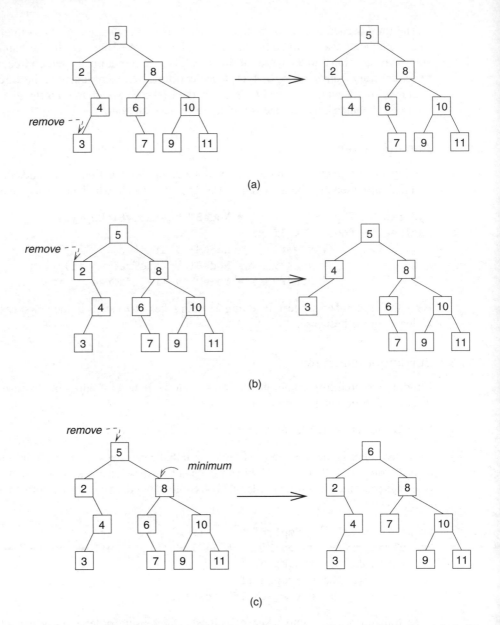

Figure 5.3 Examples of removing a node from a binary search tree. (a) Removing a leaf; (b) removing a node with one descendant; (c) removing a node with two descendants.

5.7.4   Removing an item

We now consider the operation of removing an item from a binary search tree. If the value is at the bottom of the tree, or if it has only one descendant, the removal is a simple operation as the examples in Figures 5.3(a) and 5.3(b) show.

The difficult case is when the node has two descendants. A simple solution is to replace the value to be deleted with the minimum value in the right subtree and delete that value from the tree. Since this value, found by following all left descendants, has at most one descendant, the second deletion operation is simpler. This is illustrated in Figure 5.3(c). Similarly, we could have selected the maximum value from the left subtree instead. The function that implements this procedure is:

```
-- value not found
delTree v' EmptyBT = EmptyBT
-- one descendant
delTree v' (NodeBT v lf EmptyBT)
           | v'==v = lf
delTree v' (NodeBT v EmptyBT rt)
           | v'==v = rt
-- two descendants
delTree v' (NodeBT v lf rt)
     | v'<v        = NodeBT v (delTree v' lf) rt
     | v'>v        = NodeBT v lf (delTree v' rt)
     | v'==v       = let k = minTree rt
                     in NodeBT k lf (delTree k rt)

minTree (NodeBT v EmptyBT _)
                  = v
minTree (NodeBT _ lf _)
                  = minTree lf
```

Deleting items from the tree can also lead to tree imbalances in the same way as the insertion of items does. If the value to be deleted does not appear in the tree, the tree is left unchanged.

5.7.5   Concluding remarks

A binary search tree would be appropriate for implementing a set if the most frequently used operations are membership test, insertion and deletion. However, the efficiency drops if the tree becomes unbalanced. Although it is possible to build a balanced tree initially, some tree operations (such as insertion and deletion) may introduce imbalances in the tree. Besides implementing sets, binary search trees are useful in other applications such as sorting, hash tables and priority queues.

5.8   Heaps

Since we mentioned that priority queues and tables can be implemented using heaps, this section examines the heap, as an ADT, in more detail. Applications using a heap also include the heapsort algorithm described in the next chapter (Section 6.4.1).

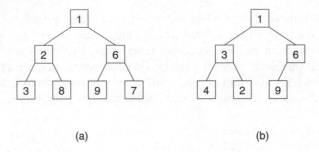

(a)   (b)

Figure 5.4   (a) is a heap but (b) is not.

A heap is a binary tree whose leaves respect the *heap order property* which states that a key stored in a node must be smaller than the keys contained in its left and right child nodes (if any). Consequently the value contained in the root of the heap is always the minimum value. For example, the *heap order property* is preserved in Figure 5.4(a) but not in Figure 5.4(b) because there is a node containing the value 3 which is greater than the value 2 of its right child node.

The interface for the heap ADT operations is:

```
module Heap(Heap,emptyHeap,heapEmpty,findHeap,insHeap,delHeap)
   where
```

```
emptyHeap:: (Ord a) => Heap a
heapEmpty:: (Ord a) => Heap a -> Bool
findHeap :: (Ord a) => Heap a -> a
insHeap  :: (Ord a) => a -> Heap a -> Heap a
delHeap  :: (Ord a) => Heap a -> Heap a
```

The first two operations represent the empty heap and the test for an empty heap. `findHeap` returns the minimum value in the heap. `insHeap` inserts a new value in the heap and returns the modified heap. `delHeap` returns the modified heap once its minimum value is removed and the rest of the heap is modified so that it still respects the *heap order property*.

The rest of this section describes an implementation of the heap ADT operations based on the *leftist* tree representation described by Okasaki [91]: a heap is represented by a binary tree where each node has a value and a 'rank', an integer giving the least number of nodes to go to an empty node. A tree is *leftist* if the rank of the left child of each node is greater or equal to the rank of its right child. Figure 5.5 shows three examples of leftist trees; each node contains a value (in the left part) and the rank (in the right part). This property makes the tree 'lean' heavily on the left, hence its name. This also means that the shortest path to a leaf may always be obtained by moving to the right. A heap implementation by a leftist tree can be defined as follows:

```
data (Ord a) => Heap a = EmptyHP
                       | HP a Int (Heap a) (Heap a)
      deriving Show
```

The first three ADT operations are very simple given the fact that the minimum value is at the top of the tree:

```
emptyHeap            = EmptyHP

heapEmpty EmptyHP    = True
heapEmpty _          = False

findHeap EmptyHP       = error "findHeap:empty heap"
findHeap (HP x _ a b) = x
```

Insertion of a new value and deletion of the minimum value are built on a single basic operation on leftist trees: the merging of two leftist trees to build a new leftist tree.

Because of the *heap order property*, each value in a node is smaller than or equal to those in its children, so by going down a tree we get a list in ascending order. Because the trees lean so much on the left, always going to the right will give a list of nodes in ascending order of the shortest length which is at most $\log(n + 1)$ for a tree of n nodes. Indeed, a rank of value r in node p implies the existence of at least 2^r leaf nodes below p, otherwise there would be a shorter path from p to a leaf.

Merging sorted lists is done by going through these lists and producing a new one by always choosing the smallest value of the two. This can be done in linear time and will be used for sorting in the next chapter (see Figure 6.5). Merging the right spines of two leftist trees uses the same mechanism but it possibly swaps the children of a node to restore the leftist property; this also runs in $O(\log n)$.

The following merge function first deals with the case of merging with an empty heap which only returns the other heap. The last case is more interesting: it first compares the values at the root of the heaps and creates a new heap containing as a value the smallest value at the root of the original heaps; the new left heap will be the left heap of the value put in the root node; the new right heap is the result of merging the right heap of the value put in the root node and the other original heap. The creation of the new heap is done by makeHP which adjusts the rank of the new node and possibly swaps the children to ensure that the rank of the left child is greater or equal to the rank of the right child.

```
rank :: (Ord a) => Heap a -> Int
rank EmptyHP      = 0
rank (HP _ r _ _) = r

makeHP :: (Ord a) => a -> Heap a -> Heap a -> Heap a
makeHP x a b | rank a >= rank b = HP x (rank b + 1) a b
             | otherwise        = HP x (rank a + 1) b a

merge ::(Ord a) =>  Heap a -> Heap a -> Heap a
merge h EmptyHP = h
merge EmptyHP h = h
merge h1@(HP x _ a1 b1) h2@(HP y _ a2 b2)
        | x <= y    = makeHP x a1 (merge b1 h2)
        | otherwise = makeHP y a2 (merge h1 b2)
```

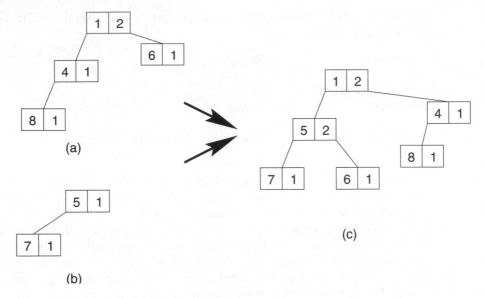

Figure 5.5 Merging two leftist trees into one.

Figure 5.5 shows two leftist trees (a) and (b) and the resulting merged leftist tree (c). This process merges node 6 (nodes are identified here with their value), which is the heap to the right of node 1, with heap (b). This gives a rank of 2 for node 5. As this rank is greater than the left heap starting with node 4, makeHP interchanges the two children of node 1 to restore the rank of the left child to being greater or equal to the rank of the right child.

This process may seem a bit devious and often results in non-intuitive transformations because of the embedded recursive calls to merge and makeHP which both can swap the children of the resulting tree. But as we must in any event create new cells for merging the right spines to insure the property, implementation remains efficient. There are at most $O(\log n)$ new cells to merge two heaps into one. In Figure 5.5, only new cells for nodes 1 and 5 have been created by merging trees (a) and (b).

Once merging is implemented, insertion is then only a matter of merging the original heap with a heap consisting of only the element to insert.

```
insHeap x h = merge (HP x 1 EmptyHP EmptyHP) h
```

Deletion is also easily done by merging the children of the first node.

```
delHeap EmptyHP      = error "delHeap:empty heap"
delHeap (HP x _ a b) = merge a b
```

5.8.1   Implementation of the priority queue ADT

A priority queue (described in Section 5.4) can be implemented as a heap by merely renaming the functions. The main advantage is an efficient access to the minimum value since it is always placed at the root of the heap. In the following implementation, a priority queue is merely an access to a heap with the interface of Section 5.4.

```
newtype PQueue a = PQ (Heap a)
                     deriving Show

emptyPQ          = PQ emptyHeap

pqEmpty (PQ h)   = heapEmpty h

enPQ v (PQ h)    = PQ (insHeap v h)

frontPQ (PQ h)   = findHeap h

dePQ (PQ h)      = PQ (delHeap h)
```

Compared to the list implementation of a priority queue, the efficiencies of the operations enPQ and dePQ are at most logarithmic instead of linear.

5.9 AVL trees†

In the previous section, we saw that it is desirable to keep the maximum depth of search tree at around $O(\log n)$ despite eventual modifications. The AVL tree, named after Adelson-Velskii and Landis [2], is a binary search tree with a *balance* condition. The condition stipulates that for every node, the difference between the height of the left subtree and the height of the right subtree should not be greater than 1. For example, the trees in Figure 5.6(a) and 5.6(b) are AVL trees whereas the tree displayed in 5.6(c) is not.

```
module AVLTree(AVLTree,emptyAVL,addAVL) where

data (Ord a,Show a) => AVLTree a = EmptyAVL
                                 | NodeAVL a (AVLTree a)
                                             (AVLTree a)
     deriving Show

emptyAVL = EmptyAVL
```

Therefore, the search operation on an AVL tree always takes $O(\log n)$ steps. Assuming a tree in AVL form, we only need to make sure that modifications (such as insertions and deletions) do not alter the balance condition.

5.9.1 Rotations

This section examines some transformations on binary search trees which modify the shape without affecting the ordering property. If an insert operation violates the AVL

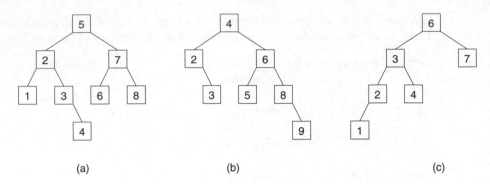

(a)   (b)   (c)

Figure 5.6   Only (a) and (b) are AVL trees.

balance condition, it is always possible to apply one of these transformations to get back to an AVL tree.

Single rotation

Given a tree whose value at the root node is v with two descendants: the left subtree's root has a value `lv` and descendants `lflf` and `lfrt` and the right subtree is denoted `rt` as illustrated on the left of Figure 5.7(a). It is possible to replace this node with a node containing `lv` with a left subtree equal to `lflf` and a right subtree comprising v as the root value and `lfrt` and `rt` as its descendants. This is called *left rotation* and is illustrated in Figure 5.7(a). A symmetric rotation, called *right rotation*, is illustrated in Figure 5.7(b).

The functions that implement these two rotations are defined using pattern-matching as follows:

```
rotateLeft,rotateRight :: (Ord a,Show a)=> AVLTree a -> AVLTree a
rotateLeft EmptyAVL    = EmptyAVL
rotateLeft (NodeAVL v (NodeAVL lv lflf lfrt)
                      rt)
                  = NodeAVL lv lflf
                          (NodeAVL v lfrt rt)


rotateRight EmptyAVL   = EmptyAVL
rotateRight (NodeAVL v lf
                  (NodeAVL rv rtlf rtrt))
                = NodeAVL rv (NodeAVL v lf rtlf)
                          rtrt
```

Rotations are used to rebalance a tree after a modification has taken place. For example, consider the tree in Figure 5.6(c) and suppose that the insertion of item 1 has violated the AVL property. Figure 5.8 shows how a left rotation puts the tree back into AVL shape.

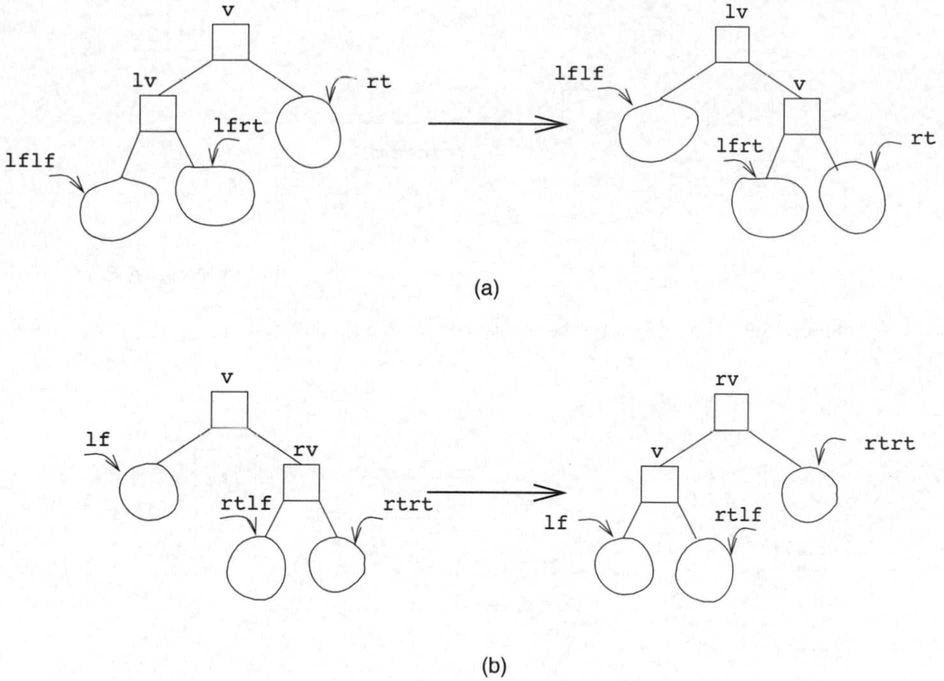

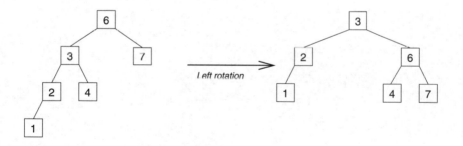

Figure 5.7 Single rotations. (a) Left rotation; (b) right rotation.

Figure 5.8 Example of applying a single rotation.

5.9.2 Double rotation

There are situations in which neither a left nor right rotation can rebalance the tree. For example, consider the tree on the left of Figure 5.9, where the imbalance is caused by the insertion of item 5. The same figure shows that a left rotation still does not solve the problem.

A more complex transformation, called *double rotation*, is needed. It can take two forms: right–left double rotation and left–right double rotation. Both are illustrated in Figure 5.10.

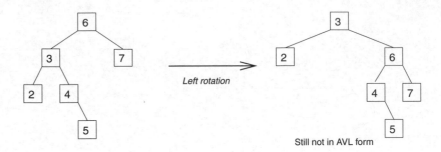

Figure 5.9   The tree cannot be rebalanced using a single rotation.

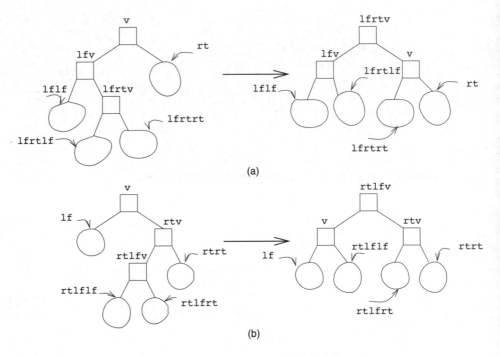

Figure 5.10   Double rotations. (a) Left–right rotation; (b) right–left rotation.

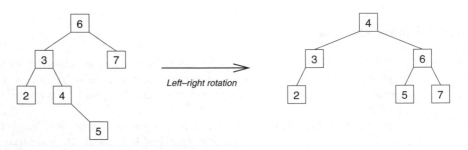

Figure 5.11   Example of a double rotation.

The corresponding functions are:

```
dRotLeftRight , dRotRightLeft
    :: (Ord a,Show a) => AVLTree a -> AVLTree a
dRotRightLeft (NodeAVL v lf
                        (NodeAVL rv (NodeAVL rtlv rtlflf rtlfrt)
                                    rtrt))
    = NodeAVL rtlv (NodeAVL v lf rtlflf)
                (NodeAVL rv rtlfrt rtrt)

dRotLeftRight (NodeAVL v (NodeAVL lv lflf
                                    (NodeAVL lfrv lfrtlf
                                                    lfrtrt))
                        rt)
    = NodeAVL lfrv (NodeAVL lv lflf lfrtlf)
                (NodeAVL v lfrtrt rt)
```

We can see now from Figure 5.11 that a non-AVL tree (from our previous example) can be made into AVL form using a left–right double rotation. Note that double rotations can also be expressed as a combination of two single rotations.

5.9.3 Inserting an item

We now show how to insert an item i into an AVL tree. Given a node with a value v, the insert operation proceeds in a similar way as in a binary search tree (see Section 5.7.2) but with the following differences:

1. If an insertion on the left subtree has taken place, and if the height of the left subtree differs by 2 from the height of the right subtree:

— if *i* is smaller than the value of the root of the left subtree, a single left rotation takes place,

— otherwise, a left–right double rotation occurs.

2. Similarly, if an insertion on the right subtree has taken place, and if the height of the right subtree differs by 2 from the height of the left subtree:

— if *i* is greater than the value of the root of the right subtree, a single right rotation takes place,

— otherwise, a right–left double rotation occurs.

```
height EmptyAVL          = 0
height (NodeAVL _ lf rt) = 1 + max (height lf) (height rt)
```

```
addAVL i EmptyAVL= NodeAVL i EmptyAVL EmptyAVL
addAVL i (NodeAVL v lf rt)
    | i < v     = let
                    newlf@(NodeAVL newlfv _ _)  = addAVL i lf
                  in
                  if ((height newlf - height rt) == 2)
                  then if i < newlfv
                          then rotateLeft (NodeAVL v newlf rt)
                          else dRotLeftRight (NodeAVL v newlf rt)
                  else (NodeAVL v newlf rt)
    | otherwise = let
                    newrt@(NodeAVL newrtv _ _)  = addAVL i rt
                  in
                  if ((height newrt - height lf) == 2)
                  then if i > newrtv
                          then rotateRight (NodeAVL v lf newrt)
                          else dRotRightLeft (NodeAVL v lf newrt)
                  else (NodeAVL v lf newrt)
```

We can see that height information must be available at all times. An improved version could store height information at the nodes. A similar technique was suggested in Section 4.2.6 where the size of subtrees was stored at the nodes to avoid a repeated calculation of these values.

Exercises

5.1 Given a set of points represented by their coordinates (x, y) in a 2-D space, the distance of a point of coordinates (x, y) from the origin is defined as:

$$\sqrt{x^2 + y^2}$$

Define an appropriate type in Haskell and the corresponding overloading operation (<=) to handle these points in a priority queue. We always want the point closer to the origin to be at the front of the queue.

5.2 Change the interface and the list implementation of the priority queue such that ordering does not depend on the overloading of the operator (<=) but on a comparison function supplied as a parameter.

5.3 Considering the basic list representation of a set, define the following set operations using list comprehensions:

inSet s x : returns True if x is an element of s and False otherwise.

included s1 s2 : returns True if all the elements of s1 are inside s2.

inter s1 s2 : returns the intersection between the sets s1 and s2.

union s1 s2 : computes the union between the sets s1 and s2.

5.4 Considering the ordered lists representation of a set, define an efficient version of the operations `inter` and `union`.

5.5 Define the interface and an efficient implementation of multisets (or bags). Multisets are similar to sets except that items can be duplicated.

5.6 Define the interface and an implementation of a two-dimensional table. Define matrix multiplication using these ADT operations.

5.7 The following function `listToHeap` produces a leftist heap from an unordered list of elements by inserting each element one by one into an initial empty heap:

```
list2heap xs = foldr insHeap EmptyHP xs
```

Implement a new version of `listToHeap` by recursively merging heaps formed by separating `xs` in two lists of (almost) equal length.

5.8 Rewrite the definition of the function `insHeap` (see Section 5.8) so that it inserts the value directly rather than going through a call to `merge`.

5.9 Rewrite the insert procedure for the AVL tree storing height information in the nodes to avoid calculating them repeatedly.

5.10 Write the function `delAVL` for removing an item from an AVL tree.

(5.10) Bibliographical notes

A significant contribution to the work on abstract data types was made by Guttag [46, 47]. Azmoodeh's book [5] discusses the use of ADTs in algorithms. Implementations of ADTs using the ML functional language are covered extensively in Harrison's textbook [50]. Other functional programming textbooks (such as [14, 56, 93, 131]) also mention ADTs to a lesser extent.

Representing queues as a pair of lists was proposed by Burton [24]. Okasaki [90] reviews some other similar schemes and proposes a technique using lazy lists. Binary search trees are described by Knuth [74] and in most textbooks on algorithms and data structures. Weiss's textbook [130] contains a comprehensive description of several types of search trees and AVL trees originally described in [2]. The description of heaps is taken from Okasaki [91] which also presents another implementation by means of binomial heaps. Paulson's textbook [93] presents another approach to heaps based on functional arrays.

Chapter 6

Sorting

The sorting of values is frequently used in real life to organize records in a database; in fact, it is often a prerequisite for other operations like searching records, consolidating values, comparing lists, etc. This chapter describes some sorting algorithms and their implementation in a functional language.

6.1 Introduction

Sorting often operates on records having a special field, called a *key*, that identifies the record and serves as comparison criteria between two records. But here, as we are mainly interested in explaining the operations involved by the different sorting algorithms, our algorithms only deal with keys. We also assume that the records (keys in our case) can be kept in main memory and do not have to be stored on disk; otherwise, we would have to change our algorithms because accessing a random key might have a much greater cost than accessing the next element in sequence.

So for the sake of this chapter the sorting problem consists of arranging a list of keys according to some relational operator. The aim is to produce a sequence of keys in increasing value, the first key being the minimum value and the last one being the

114

maximum value. There are two main approaches to sorting values: the first is based
on the successive comparison of two values and the exchange of their relative position
and is called 'comparison-based sorting'. The second approach is based on properties
of the internal representations of the keys to separate the elements of the sequence into
many subsequences that are then put together; this approach is known as 'radix-based
sorting'. In this chapter, we first present different methods of comparison-based sorting
with some of their improvements; the last section then briefly presents an example of
radix sorting to show the difference between the two approaches but does not elaborate,
as this method is usually quite dependent on the representation chosen for the keys.

6.2 Comparison-based sorting

In Haskell, non-numeric keys can be compared as long as their type belongs to the Ord
class. Therefore, the type declaration of a comparison-based algorithm is:

```
sort :: (Ord a) => [a] -> [a]
```

These algorithms rely on the following principle: split the original list L into two lists
$L1$ and $L2$, sort these lists recursively, then join the results together (see Figure 6.1).
Depending on exactly how these operations are defined and whether each operation is
'hard' or 'easy', we get different sorting algorithms with distinct properties.

Following Azmoodeh [5], comparison-based algorithms can be characterized by the
following properties:

- **Hard/easy split**   refers to the complexity of the split operation, for example it is
  easier to split a list after the first element than to find the minimum value and then
  split the list around it.
- **Singleton/equal size lists**   refers to the length of $L1$ compared to the length of $L2$
- **Hard/easy join**   which refers to the complexity of the join operation, for example
  it is easier to join by concatenating two sublists than to merge them which involves
  running through each of them in parallel and always taking the smallest of each one.

Ideally we would like to have a sorting method that combines easy split and easy
join but unfortunately the law of 'entropy' says that to do a 'hard job' like sorting, one
must combine either an easy split and a hard join or a hard join and an easy split.

Table 6.1 classifies each of the comparison-based sorting algorithms. Each slot
identifies two types of algorithms: a simple and intuitive one and another one (given in
italics) that can be seen as an optimization of the same scheme. The number following
each algorithm identifies the section where this algorithm is described in detail and
analyzed.

Before giving the details and the analysis of each algorithm, we first present in
Figures 6.2 to 6.5 the principles behind the four types of algorithms and provide a
simple implementation. The main transformation steps are illustrated using a small
sequence of values. In each case, the selected element (elements) is (are) emphasized
in italics.

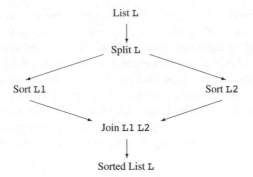

Figure 6.1   Abstract description of a comparison-based sorting algorithm.

Table 6.1   Classifying sorting algorithms.

	Singleton	Equal Size
hard split/easy join	Selection sort (6.3.1)	Quicksort (6.3.3)
	Heapsort(6.4.1)	
easy split/hard join	Insertion sort (6.3.2)	Mergesort (6.3.4)
	Tree sort (6.4.2)	

Example

```
ssort  [3,1,4,1,5,9,2]     ⇒    1:(ssort  [3,4,1,5,9,2])|
ssort  [3,4,1,5,9,2]       ⇒    1:(ssort  [3,4,5,9,2])
ssort  [3,4,5,9,2]         ⇒    2:(ssort  [3,4,5,9])
ssort  [3,4,5,9]           ⇒    3:(ssort  [4,5,9])
ssort  [4,5,9]             ⇒    4:(ssort  [5,9])
ssort  [5,9]               ⇒    5:(ssort  [9])
ssort  [9]                 ⇒    9:(ssort  [])
ssort  []                  ⇒    []
```

Naive implementation

```
ssort [] = []
ssort xs = m : ssort (delete m xs)
          where m = minimum xs
```

Figure 6.2   Selection sort: hard split/easy join with singleton.

● **Selection sort** (Figure 6.2)   extracts the key with the minimum value from the original list of keys and puts it into a result list. This is repeated until the original list is empty.

● **Quicksort** (Figure 6.3)   selects the first element as a pivot and splits the rest into two sublists: one containing all the keys that at most equal the pivot and the other containing the keys greater than the pivot. These sublists are recursively sorted, then joined together with the pivot in the middle.

Example

```
qsort [3,1,4,1,5,9,2]   ⇒   (qsort [1,1,2])++[3]++(qsort [4,5,9])
qsort [1,1,2]           ⇒   (qsort [1])++[1]++(qsort [2])
qsort [1]               ⇒   (qsort [])++[1]++(qsort [])
qsort [2]               ⇒   (qsort [])++[2]++(qsort [])
qsort []                ⇒   []

qsort [4,5,9]           ⇒   (qsort [])++[4]++(qsort [5,9])
qsort [5,9]             ⇒   (qsort [])++[5]++(qsort [9])
qsort [9]               ⇒   (qsort [])++[9]++(qsort [])
```

Naive implementation

```
qsort []           = []
qsort (pivot:rest) = qsort [ x | x <- rest, x <= pivot] ++
                     [pivot] ++
                     qsort [ x | x <- rest, x > pivot]
```

Figure 6.3   Quicksort: hard split/easy join with equal size lists.

Example

```
isort [3,1,4,1,5,9,2]   ⇒   insert 3 (isort [1,4,1,5,9,2])
isort [1,4,1,5,9,2]     ⇒   insert 1 (isort [4,1,5,9,2])
....
isort [2]               ⇒   insert 2 (isort [])
isort []                ⇒   []
insert 2 []             ⇒   [2]
....
insert 4 [1,2,5,9]      ⇒   [1,2,4,5,9]
insert 1 [1,2,4,5,9]    ⇒   [1,1,2,4,5,9]
insert 3 [1,1,2,4,5,9]  ⇒   [1,1,2,3,4,5,9]
```

Naive implementation

```
isort []     = []
isort (x:xs) = insert x (isort xs)

insert x xs = takeWhile ((<=)x) xs ++ [x] ++ dropWhile ((<=)x) xs
```

Figure 6.4   Insertion sort: easy split/hard join with singleton.

● **Insertion sort** (Figure 6.4)   takes the first element and inserts it in the right place in the resulting sequence.

● **Mergesort** (Figure 6.5)   splits the original sequence into two equal halves that are recursively sorted and merged to make an ordered list.

After this overview of the different sorting methods, we now present them in more detail. We then present other sorting methods that fall into the same categories but that can be seen as optimizations of the same schemes.

Example

```
msort [3,1,4,1,5,9,2]    ⇒    merge (msort [3,1,4])(msort [1,5,9,2])
msort [3,1,4]            ⇒    merge (msort [3])(msort [1,4])
msort [1,5,9,2]          ⇒    merge (msort [1,5])(msort [9,2])
msort [3]                ⇒    [3]
msort [1,4]              ⇒    merge (msort [1])(msort [4])
                              . . . .
```

Naive implementation

```
msort []   = []
msort [x]  = [x]
msort xs   = merge (msort xs1)(msort xs2)
           where xs1 = take k xs
                 xs2 = drop k xs
                 k   = (length xs) `div` 2
```

Figure 6.5   Mergesort: easy split/hard join with equal size lists.

6.3 Basic sorting algorithms

6.3.1 Selection sort

As mentioned in the previous section, this algorithm works by removing the minimum value of the list and inserting it at the appropriate place in the result list until the original list is empty. A simple example is illustrated in Figure 6.2 and a trivial program that implements it is the following (we repeat the one given in Figure 6.2):

```
ssort :: (Ord a) => [a] -> [a]
ssort [] = []
ssort xs  = m : ssort (delete m xs)
            where m = minimum xs
```

where the `delete` function removes the first occurrence of m from xs.

Based on the observation that once the minimum is removed, the order of remaining keys does not matter, it is possible to apply a transformation which reduces the number of passes, similar to the one described in Section 4.1.6. The final program for the selection sort function is:

```
split :: (Ord a) => [a] -> a -> [a] -> [a]
split [] m r     = m : (ssort' r)
split (x:xs) m r = if x < m
                     then split xs x (m:r)
                     else split xs m (x:r)

ssort' []        = []
ssort' (x:xs)    = split xs x []
```

The `split` function returns the remaining keys in reverse order. As expected, this version is more efficient than but not as clear as the trivial one.

6.3.2   Insertion sort

This algorithm is the most used in everyday life. As an example, sorting a pack of cards consists of picking one card after the other and inserting it at the appropriate place in the hand. The insertion sort algorithm operates on a similar principle, as in the example shown in Figure 6.4. At the heart of the algorithm is the `insert` function which inserts a key into an already sorted list.

```
insert      :: (Ord a) => a -> [a] -> [a]
insert x xs = takeWhile ((<=)x) xs ++ [x] ++ dropWhile ((<=)x) xs
```

The insertion sort function is defined using the following argument: sorting a list consists of removing one key, sorting the rest, and then inserting this key back into the sorted list (taken from Figure 6.4).

```
isort        :: (Ord a) => [a] -> [a]
isort []     = []
isort (x:xs) = insert x (isort xs)
```

Alternatively, insertion sort can be expressed using a folding operator:

```
isort' xs = foldr insert [] xs
```

To improve the program, the two list traversals and the calls to the append function can be eliminated by defining the insert function with an accumulating result. The new insertion sort program is:

```
insert' key []                    = [key]
insert' key l@(x:xs) | key <=x    = key : l
                     | otherwise  = x : (insert key xs)

isort'' xs                        = foldr insert' [] xs
```

6.3.3   Quicksort

Quicksort is one of the most popular sorting algorithms because of its efficiency. It operates by selecting a key as a pivot, then splits the list into two sublists: one containing all the keys less than or equal to the pivot and the other containing the keys greater than the pivot. These sublists are recursively sorted, then joined together with the pivot in the middle.

Quicksort is nicely expressed using list comprehensions, as the following program (slightly modified from Figure 6.3) shows:

```
qsort :: (Ord a) => [a] -> [a]
qsort []             = []
qsort (pivot:rest) = qsort lower ++ [pivot] ++ qsort upper
                       where lower = [ x | x <- rest, x <= pivot]
                             upper = [ x | x <- rest,  x > pivot]
```

An example of using this function was illustrated in Figure 6.3. One way to improve the program is by removing the calls to the append function using the transformation described in Section 4.1.5. The new definition is:

```
qsort' :: (Ord a) => [a] -> [a] -> [a]
qsort' [] s = s
qsort' (pivot:rest) s
            = qsort' lower (pivot : (qsort' upper s))
              where lower = [ x | x <- rest, x <= pivot]
                    upper = [ x | x <- rest,  x > pivot]
```

As the order in which the keys appear in the lower and upper list does not matter, a function called split' that computes the lower and the upper lists in just one pass can be derived from the above definition (see transformation described in Section 4.1.6). We thus get the following more efficient version.

```
qsort'' l           = qs l []
    where qs []  s  = s
          qs [x] s  = (x:s)
          qs (pivot:rest) s
                    = split pivot rest [] [] s

split pivot [] lower upper s
                  = qsort' lower (pivot : (qsort' upper s))
split pivot (x:xs) lower upper s
                  = if x < pivot
                    then split pivot xs (x:lower) upper s
                    else split pivot xs lower (x:upper) s
```

Note that the efficiency of the modified version depends on the tail recursivity optimization.

6.3.4   Mergesort

We have just demonstrated that good performance of the quicksort algorithm depends on how equally balanced are the two lists produced by the split function. The mergesort algorithm is always well balanced because it splits the original list into two equal halves. These lists are recursively sorted then combined in such a way as to make an ordered list. Combining two ordered lists, which is called a *merge* operation, traverses the two lists from head to tail and puts the smallest key from the two lists in the resulting list.

```
merge :: (Ord a)  => [a] -> [a] -> [a]
merge [] b       = b
merge a []       = a
merge a@(x:xs) b@(y:ys)
      | (x<=y)   = x : (merge xs b)
      | otherwise = y : (merge a ys)
```

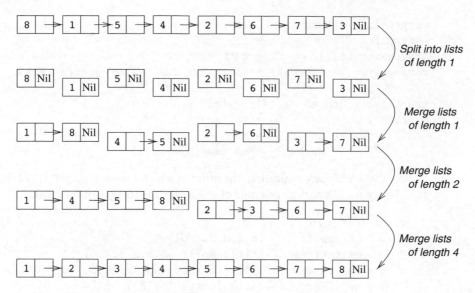

Figure 6.6 An example of bottom-up merging.

Having defined the merge operation, the mergesort algorithm can be expressed as follows (repeated from Figure 6.5):

```
msort :: (Ord a)=> [a] -> [a]
msort []          = []
msort [x]         = [x]
msort xs          = merge (msort xs1)(msort xs2)
    where
            xs1 = take k xs
            xs2 = drop k xs
            k   = (length xs) 'div' 2
```

Bottom-up mergesort

Mergesort divides a list of length n into two lists of length $\frac{n}{2}$, then into four lists of length $\frac{n}{4}$ and so on, until we get about n lists of length 1 before it starts to merge. It is more space efficient to start the algorithm with n lists of length 1, and then successively merge them by pairs. In this case there is no need to use take and drop to split the list. This technique is also referred to as *bottom-up mergesort*. An example is illustrated in Figure 6.6.

The corresponding program is shown below:

```
split :: (Ord a) => [a] -> [[a]]
split []          = []
split (x:xs)      = [x] : split xs
```

```
mergepairs :: (Ord a) => [[a]] -> [[a]]
mergepairs []           = []
mergepairs x@[1]        = x
mergepairs (11:12:rest) = (merge 11 12) : (mergepairs rest)

msort'' :: (Ord a) => [a] -> [a]
msort'' 1                 = ms (split 1)
        where ms [r]    = r
              ms l      = ms (mergepairs l)
```

Note that under lazy evaluation, the order in which lists are merged is not the same as in Figure 6.6. Here is an example of evaluating the mergesort function:

```
msort'' [4,1,5,8,2,3,7,6]
 ⇒   ms (split [4,1,5,8,2,3,7,6])
 ⇒   ms (mergep ([4]:[1]:(split [5,8,2,3,7,6])))
 ⇒   ms ((merge [4] [1]):(mergep (split [5,8,2,3,7,6])))
 ⇒   ms ((merge [4] [1]):(merge [5][8])
          :(mergep (split [2,3,7,6])))
 ⇒   ms (mergep (((merge [4] [1]):(merge [5][8]):
                      (mergep (split [2,3,7,6])))))
 ⇒   ms ((merge (merge [4] [1]) (merge [5][8]))
          :(mergep (mergep (split [2,3,7,6]))))
 ⇒   ...
 ⇒   merge ((merge (merge [4] [1])(merge [5][8]))
                      (((merge (merge [2] [3]) (merge [7][6]))))))
```

We can see that the program builds the entire network of calls to the merge function before starting the first merge operation. This function can be made more efficient by changing the evaluation order. This is further discussed in Section 6.5.4.

6.4 Tree-based sorting

We now consider two sorting algorithms, called heapsort and tree sort, which both use a tree data structure and can be regarded as optimizations of two previous algorithms.

6.4.1 Heapsort

We have seen in Chapter 5 that a priority queue is an ADT which gives access to the smallest item among a collection of items. Assuming such an ADT, the heapsort algorithm simply works by initially placing all the original items in the priority queue, then repeatedly dequeuing the smallest item in the priority queue and placing it in the result list until the queue is empty. Therefore, the heapsort algorithm is an optimization of the selection sort algorithm which uses a special data structure in which the minimum key can be immediately accessed. For greatest efficiency, the priority queue ADT must be implemented using a heap as described in Section 5.8.1.

Given a priority queue ADT and its interface as defined in Section 5.4, this algorithm is implemented by the following function:

```
mkPQ  :: (Ord a) => [a] -> PQueue a
mkPQ xs  = foldr enPQ emptyPQ xs

hsort :: (Ord a) => [a] -> [a]
hsort xs = hsort' (mkPQ xs)
            where hsort' pq
                    | (pqEmpty pq) = []
                    | otherwise    = (frontPQ pq):(hsort' (dePQ pq))
```

6.4.2   Tree sort

The tree sort algorithm builds a binary search tree (see Section 5.7) containing all the elements to be sorted, then performs an inorder traversal of the tree to get these elements in an increasing order.

Therefore, this algorithm is simply expressed as:

```
tsort xs = (inorder . buildTree) xs
```

The function `inorder` flattens the tree according to an inorder traversal (see Section 4.2.4) and the function `buildTree` builds a binary search tree from a list of items (see Section 5.7.3).

Note the similarity between building a search tree and building an ordered list in the insertion sort algorithm (see Section 6.3.2). The difference is that inserting a key in a tree is likely to take less steps than in a list because it is in $O(\log n)$ instead of $O(n)$. For this reason, the tree sort algorithm can be considered as an optimization of the insertion sort algorithm.

6.5   Efficiency of comparison-based algorithms†

6.5.1   Selection sort

Using the analysis rules presented in Section 3.2.3, the selection sort function performs the following number of steps under strict evaluation:

$$T_{\text{ssort}}(n) = \frac{n^2}{2} + \frac{3n}{2} + 1$$

where n is the length of the list concerned. This shows that the time complexity of the selection sort algorithm is in $O(n^2)$. The comparison operator forces the evaluation of each key so there will not be any difference under lazy evaluation.

We now turn to the accumulated space efficiency. The measure employed will be the additional number of list cells used. Under strict evaluation, the accumulated space usage is:

$$S_{\text{ssort}}(n) = \frac{n^2}{2} + \frac{n}{2}$$

This means that the accumulated space complexity of the selection sort algorithm is also in $O(n^2)$. To determine the largest space used, the following observations can be made:

- the `split` function creates a new list cell, but the first list cell in its first argument can be reclaimed by the garbage collector;

- the `ssort` function also creates a new list cell, but the first list cell in its first argument can be reclaimed.

These remarks show that the largest space usage of the selection sort algorithm is in $O(n)$ if the result list is stored. If the result list is immediately consumed (for instance, by the display function) then the space usage is in $O(1)$ (see our discussion on pipelines in Section 4.1.1).

6.5.2 Insertion sort

Analyzing the efficiency of the insert function is not easy since it depends on the future position of the key in the list. For a list of length n, the key is inserted at the end of the list (requiring $(n + 1)$ steps) in the worst case and at the front of the list (requiring 1 step only) in the best case.

If the key is *always* inserted at the end of the list, for example when the original list is in reverse order, a worst-case analysis of the insertion sort function gives the following result:

$$T_{\texttt{isort}_{WC}}(n) = \frac{n^2}{2} + \frac{3n}{2} + 1$$

Therefore, insertion sort in the worst case has the same time efficiency as selection sort, that is in $O(n^2)$.

If the insert function always places the key at the front of the list, for example when the original list is already sorted, a best-case analysis yields:

$$T_{\texttt{isort}_{BC}}(n) = 2n + 1$$

which corresponds to a linear complexity. A good analysis assumes an 'average' of $\frac{i}{2}$ steps to insert a key into a list of length i, leading to the following solution for the average time complexity:

$$T_{\texttt{isort}_{AC}}(n) = \frac{n^2}{4} + \frac{3n}{4} + 1$$

which still corresponds to an order of complexity of $O(n^2)$. In conclusion, the insertion sort algorithm is efficient for lists with only a few keys out of order.

Considering the accumulated space used by the program, we have similar results as with step-counting analysis:

$$
\begin{aligned}
S_{\texttt{isort}_{WC}}(n) &= \frac{n^2}{2} + \frac{n}{2} \\
S_{\texttt{isort}_{BC}}(n) &= n \\
S_{\texttt{isort}_{AC}}(n) &= \frac{n^2}{4} + \frac{n}{4}
\end{aligned}
$$

We can see that the average insertion sort is slightly more list-space efficient than selection sort. When executed lazily, a chain of calls to the insert function is created as follows:

insert x₁ (insert x₂ ... (insert xₙ []) ...)

There will be n calls to this function that will be operating in a pipeline fashion. In this case, the result list is built progressively as the original list is consumed so the largest space used is in $O(n)$ if the result list is saved or $O(1)$ if it is immediately consumed.

6.5.3 Quicksort

An exact analysis of the efficiency of the quicksort function is impossible because the size of the lower and the upper lists cannot be determined in advance. The worst case is when one of the halves of the split list always contains all the keys (minus the pivot), which means that the other half is always empty. Under this assumption, step-counting analysis yields:

$$T_{\text{qsort}_{WC}}(n) = \frac{n^2}{2} + \frac{5n}{2} - 1$$

This is worse than all the sorting algorithms we have seen so far! However, such cases are highly unlikely so a more 'realistic' analysis assumes that the original list is split into two roughly equal halves. Under these assumptions, the average time efficiency analysis leads to the following solution:

$$T_{\text{qsort}_{AC}}(n) \approx n \log n + 2n - 1$$

Therefore, quicksort has an average running time of $O(n \log n)$, which is the first to be asymptotically better than the previous $O(n^2)$ algorithms.

As expected, accumulated space efficiency analysis leads to similar results:

$$
\begin{aligned}
S_{\text{qsort}_{WC}}(n) &= \frac{n^2}{2} + \frac{n}{2} \\
S_{\text{qsort}_{AC}}(n) &\approx n \log n + n
\end{aligned}
$$

This shows that the average space complexity of the quicksort algorithm is also in $O(n \log n)$.

During execution, the function qsort' discards one list cell, then passes control to the split' function which creates as well as discards one list cell at each recursive call. At the end of the recursive call, it hands back the control to the qsort' function with one list cell created. This means that as the list is being split, the old list can be discarded. Therefore, there are $O(n)$ list cells that coexist at any moment.

6.5.4 Mergesort

To simplify the analysis, we assume a list whose length is an integral power of 2. The first difficulty is to estimate the cost of merging two lists of length k and l as it depends on the content of these two lists. An example is illustrated in Figure 6.7. In the worst

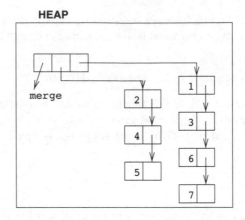

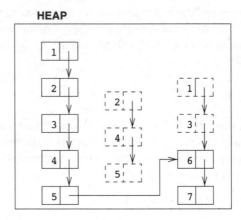

Figure 6.7 Example of merging two lists.

case, all keys from the two lists except one are selected resulting in $(k + l - 1) + 1$ steps being performed. In the best case, only keys from the shortest of the two lists are selected resulting in $min(k, l) + 1$ steps being performed.

Under the worst-case scenario, the time efficiency is:

$$T_{\text{msort}_{WC}}(n) = n \log n + 2n + 2 \log n + 2$$

Asymptotically, this is an improvement over quicksort because the time complexity is in $O(n \log n)$ even in the worst case. Assuming that in the average case, merging two lists takes half as many steps, we have $T_{\text{msort}_{AC}}(n) \in O(\frac{3}{4}n \log n)$. This means that bottom-up mergesort has a slightly better average time efficiency than quicksort but this is highly dependent on the content of the lists.

Considering the accumulated space usage of the bottom-up mergesort algorithm, the analysis proceeds in the same way as with time efficiency analysis. Under the same assumptions, we can determine the following results:

$$\begin{aligned} S_{\text{msort}_{WC}}(n) &= n \log n + 2n + \log n \\ S_{\text{msort}_{AC}}(n) &\approx \tfrac{3}{4}n \log n + 2n \end{aligned}$$

This shows that bottom-up mergesort uses less total space than quicksort on average. However, the stack space usage is in $O(n)$ because the merge operation cannot benefit from tail recursivity optimization.

We now examine how the computation proceeds under lazy evaluation. We have already seen that the program builds the entire network of calls to the merge function before starting the first merge operation. A more efficient version would perform the merge operations in a strict manner while the rest of the program executes lazily as the following example shows:

```
msort'' [4,1,5,8,2,3,7,6]
  ⇒   ms (split [4,1,5,8,2,3,7,6])
  ⇒   ms (mergep ([4]:[1]:(split [5,8,2,3,7,6])))
  ⇒   ms ((merge [4] [1]):(mergep (split [5,8,2,3,7,6])))
  ⇒   ms ([1,4]:(merge [5][8]):(mergep (split [2,3,7,6])))
  ⇒   ms (mergep (([4,1]:[5,8]:(mergep
                              (split [2,3,7,6])))))
  ⇒   ms ((merge [4,1] [5,8]):(mergep (mergep
                              (split [2,3,7,6]))))
  ⇒   ms ([1,4,5,8]:(mergep (mergep (split [2,3,7,6]))))
  ⇒   ...
  ⇒   [1,2,3,4,5,6,7,8]
```

As the merge operation is applied successively from the left, the order of execution is also different from the one illustrated in Figure 6.6. This is more space efficient because not all partitions need to reside in memory at the same time and the largest number of list cells used is in $O(n)$. If we evaluate the same program under strict evaluation, more space would be used as all lists of length 1, then all lists of length 2, etc. are generated instead of successive merges as in the lazy/strict program. To enable the definition of a strict merge function, we need to use a strict list constructor (:) (see Section 3.1.3). This program is the first we have considered in which the most efficient space usage depends on a combination of strict and lazy evaluation. A different program that exhibits the same behavior in a strict functional language is described by Paulson [93].

6.5.5   Heapsort

Since we assumed that the priority queue is implemented using a heap, the average heap access time is in $O(\log n)$. The worst-case situation is when the keys are always inserted at the bottom level during the reorganization of the heap which takes place during a dequeue operation (percolating down operation). Under this scenario, we get the following results:

$$T_{\text{hsort}_{WC}}(n) \in O(3n \log(n))$$
$$S_{\text{hsort}_{WC}}(n) \in O(3n \log(n))$$

As with quicksort and mergesort, the asymptotic time complexity of the heapsort algorithm is in $O(n \log n)$. However, it has a higher constant of proportionality.

The accumulated space efficiency is measured by the number of heap nodes used. Using the heap as a lazy tree structure is inefficient due to the number of insertions and deletions that are carried out. The process of building the heap generates $O(n)$ heap nodes and each delete operation creates $O(\log n)$ additional nodes. Therefore, it is preferable to use a *strict* node constructor (see Section 3.1.3) so that insertions and deletions are immediately propagated. After each iteration in the algorithm, there is one less node in the tree and one additional list cell. Therefore, the largest space used is when the first deletion takes place where $O(n + \log n)$ nodes are used.

6.5.6   Tree sort

We already mentioned that the advantage of tree sort over insertion sort is that inserting a key in a tree is likely to take less steps than in a list ($O(\log n)$ instead of $O(n)$). However, unlike with a heap, there are no guarantees that the search tree will be balanced. In the worst-case scenario, the tree consists of a chain of i nodes resulting in $(i + 1)$ steps performed for each node insertion. In the average case, it is estimated that the tree is roughly balanced, resulting in $\lfloor \log(i + 1) \rfloor + 1$ steps to insert a node. Assuming that $n = 2^k - 1$ with $k \geq 1$, the solutions for both cases are:

$$
\begin{array}{rcl}
T_{\text{tsort}_{WC}}(n) & = & \frac{n^2}{2} + \frac{7n}{2} + \frac{5}{2} \\
T_{\text{tsort}_{AC}}(n) & = & n \log(n + 1) + 2n + \log(n + 1) + 2
\end{array}
$$

As expected, if the tree is always a chain (worst case), tree sort behaves like insertion sort so it has the same asymptotic complexity that is in $O(n^2)$. In the average case, it has an $O(n \log n)$ complexity.

If space efficiency is measured using the total number of tree nodes and list cells used, we also get:

$$
\begin{array}{rcl}
S_{\text{tsort}_{WC}}(n) & = & \frac{n^2}{2} + \frac{3n}{2} \\
S_{\text{tsort}_{AC}}(n) & = & n \log(n + 1) + \log(n + 1)
\end{array}
$$

If the building up of the tree is carried out lazily, there is no need for the whole tree to reside in memory at once as the left tree can be consumed while the right tree can still contain calls to the insert function. Therefore the lazy version operates in $O(\log n)$ space (see our discussion in Section 4.2.2).

If the final list is stored, it does not matter whether a strict or lazy tree is used as the number of insert closures added to the number of tree constructor nodes remains the same as that in $O(n)$. A strict version is obtained by using a strict tree constructor and strict folding.

6.5.7   Summary

The time efficiencies of the sorting algorithms considered so far, using the most significant term, are summarized in Table 6.2.

Theoretical analysis of the time efficiency shows that the best average performance is in $O(n \log n)$. When comparing constants of proportionality, bottom-up mergesort performs best with $O(\frac{3}{4}n \log n)$ followed by the quicksort and tree sort algorithms

Table 6.2   Comparing time efficiency.

Algorithm	Worst case	Average	Algorithm	Worst case	Average
Selection sort	$0.5n^2$	$0.5n^2$	Quicksort	$0.5n^2$	$n \log n$
Heapsort	$3n \log n$	–			
Insertion sort	$0.5n^2$	$0.25n^2$	Mergesort	$n \log n$	$0.75n \log n$
Tree sort	$0.5n^2$	$n \log n$			

Table 6.3   Comparing accumulated space efficiency.

Algorithm	Worst case	Average	Algorithm	Worst case	Average
Selection sort	$0.5n^2$	$0.5n^2$	Quicksort	$0.5n^2$	$n \log n$
Heapsort	$3n \log n$	–			
Insertion sort	$0.5n^2$	$0.25n^2$	Mergesort	$n \log n$	$0.75n \log n$
Tree sort	$0.5n^2$	$n \log n$			

with $O(n \log n)$. Compared to imperative implementations, time analysis leads to the same asymptotic complexity, although functional versions have a higher constant of proportionality.

The space used under strict evaluation is summarized in Table 6.3. Again, bottom-up mergesort is still the most efficient on average, followed by quicksort and insertion sort. As mentioned in our discussion in Chapter 1, these figures must be taken with care since the constants of proportionality do not mean much and may safely be ignored.

6.6 Representation-based sorting

In all the previous algorithms, sorting was performed by comparing key values. There is another category of algorithms that operate using the internal representation of the keys; they are commonly called *bucket sort* algorithms. A bucket sort algorithm divides the keys into several buckets according to some key property. Buckets are then sorted, either recursively using the same technique, or using another sorting algorithm. Finally, the buckets are combined to obtain the sorted list. Dividing and combining keys can be achieved faster because the bucket sort algorithm takes advantage of some key representation property.

6.6.1 The radix sort algorithm

One of these algorithms is called *radix sort* which assumes that a key consists of exactly p positions. The values in each position are between a minimum m to a maximum m' so there is a range r of $m' - m + 1$ possible values for each of the p positions that make up a key. Radix sort works on the principle that if keys are sorted with respect to the $(p - 1)$ least significant positions, they can be sorted completely by sorting them according to the pth position.

```
[[2,3,2],[2,3,1],[4,2,8],[1,1,1],[2,1,3],[8,2,1],[7,9,7],[3,9,8],[5,2,1]]
```

split according to least significant digit

array of buckets

digit=0	[ ]
digit=1	[[2,3,1],[1,1,1],[8,2,1],[5,2,1]]
digit=2	[[2,3,2]]
digit=3	[[2,1,3]]
digit=4	[ ]
digit=5	[ ]
digit=6	[ ]
digit=7	[[7,9,7]]
digit=8	[[4,2,8],[3,9,8]]
digit=9	[ ]

concatenate array

```
[[2,3,1],[1,1,1],[8,2,1],[5,2,1],[2,3,2],[2,1,3],[7,9,7],[4,2,8],[3,9,8]]
```

Figure 6.8 Splitting a list into buckets.

To implement the radix sort algorithm, we choose to represent keys as lists of values. For example, in the case of non-negative integers, the key can be represented as a list of decimal digits, so the list [5,2,8] represents the key 528. We use the !! operator to access the individual components of a key. We also assume that all lists representing keys have the same length.

The following type definitions show that the buckets are represented as an array of lists of keys, that is as an array of lists of lists of values, so that the access to an individual bucket can be done in $O(1)$ and the values can be updated efficiently.

```
type Key val    = [val]
type Bucket  val = [Key val]
type Buckets val = Array val (Bucket val)
```

We first define a function split k bnds xs that splits the list of keys xs returning an array of buckets; each bucket contains keys whose digit k is equal to one particular value (see the example in Figure 6.8). The parameter bnds indicates the minimum and maximum values that can appear at a position. Splitting is achieved by accumulating in a list the keys with equal values at a given position. Figure 6.8 also shows that after splitting, the array is converted into a list with the function concatA. The corresponding functions are presented below:

```
split :: (Ix a) => Int -> (a,a) -> [Key a] -> Buckets a
```

```
[[2,3,2],[2,3,1],[4,2,8],[1,1,1],[2,1,3],[8,2,1],[7,9,7],[3,9,8],[5,2,1]]
```

split and concatenate

```
[[2,3,1],[1,1,1],[8,2,1],[5,2,1],[2,3,2],[2,1,3],[7,9,7],[4,2,8],[3,9,8]]
```

split and concatenate

```
[[1,1,1],[2,1,3],[8,2,1],[5,2,1],[4,2,8],[2,3,1],[2,3,2],[7,9,7],[3,9,8]]
```

split and concatenate

```
[[1,1,1],[2,1,3],[2,3,1],[2,3,2],[3,9,8],[4,2,8],[5,2,1],[7,9,7],[8,2,1]]
```

Figure 6.9 Example of using the radix sort function.

```
split k bnds xs  = accumArray f [] bnds [(x!!k , x) | x <- xs]
                   where f xs key = xs ++ [key]

concatA:: (Ix a)=> Buckets a ->. [Key a]
concatA bckts = concat (elems bckts)
```

This is based on the fact that the Haskell function elems returns a list containing all the elements in an array in increasing index order (see Section 2.7.2). Given these two functions, the radix sort function simply splits and flattens from the least significant digit to the most significant one. It takes p (the length of the key) and bnds (the bounds for the array of buckets) as additional parameters:

```
rsort :: Ix a => Int -> (a,a) -> [Key a] -> [Key a]
rsort 0       bnds l = l
rsort (p+1) bnds l = rsort p bnds (concatA (split p bnds l))
```

An example of executing this program is illustrated in Figure 6.9. It corresponds to the following call:

```
rsort 3 (0,9) [[2,3,2],[2,3,1],[4,2,8],[1,1,1],[2,1,3],
               [8,2,1],[7,9,7],[3,9,8],[5,2,1]]
```

Thanks to the polymorphic nature of these definitions, rsort can also be used to sort other kinds of keys such as Strings:

```
rsort 6 (' ','z') ["jasmin","amiel ","latif ","ervig "]
   ⇒  ["amiel ", "ervig ", "jasmin", "latif "]
```

6.6.2   Improving the program

The improvement consists of eliminating the call to the append operator (++) in the definition of the split function. The idea is to gather the keys in reverse order before putting them back in order during the concatenate operation. The final program is:

```
split' :: (Ix a) => Int -> (a,a) -> [Key a] -> Buckets a
split' k bnds l = accumArray f [] bnds [(x!!k,x) | x <- l]
                    where f l key = key : l
```

```
concatA':: Ix a => Buckets a -> [Key a]
concatA' bckts = concat (map reverse (elems bckts))
```

The program can be further improved by concatenating the lists and reversing at the same time using the following definition of the concatA function:

```
concatA'' :: Ix a => Buckets a -> [Key a]
concatA'' = (foldr rev []) . elems
    where
    rev []      res = res
    rev (x:xs) res = rev xs (x:res)
```

where the rev function is the efficient $O(n)$ list reversing function (reverse') described in Section 4.1.5.

6.6.3   Efficiency of radix sort†

To split a list of length n, $O(n)$ steps are required if we assume that array accesses are performed in constant time. We do not take into account the steps needed to access the value of a given position within a key. The cost of the flatten function is still in $O(n)$ because it is just a matter of combining all the keys into one list. There are p split/flatten steps in this algorithm. Assuming that p is constant with respect to n, this is the first algorithm that performs sorting in $O(pn)$, when ignoring the time to access the value at a given position within a key. The accumulated space usage is also in $O(pn)$ which corresponds to a linear complexity with a high constant of proportionality. The largest space used is in $O(n)$ providing that the arguments of the recursive call to the rsort function are evaluated strictly to take advantage of tail recursivity optimization.

Exercises

    6.1 Sort the list [4,2,5,6,10,3,7] using insertion sort.

    6.2 A person is represented by a tuple containing a name (of type String) and an age (of type Int). Is it possible to sort this list by increasing age using insertion sort without any change to its function definition?

    6.3 (a) Implement the *Bubblesort* algorithm, another sorting technique which according to Knuth [74] 'seems to have nothing to recommend it except a catchy name'. It works by making several passes through the list, comparing pairs of keys in adjacent positions and swapping them if they are out of order. After the first pass, the largest key should be at the end of the list. The second pass will traverse all keys except the last one. The third pass will traverse all keys except the last two which constitute the sorted part of the list. This is repeated until the unsorted part of the list has only got one element.

(b) Modify your solution such that after any pass, if no keys have been swapped, the algorithm terminates. What is the best-case and worst-case efficiency of this new version?

6.4 Perform the time efficiency analysis of the quicksort function assuming n keys in reverse order.

6.5 One of the disadvantages of quicksort is that unnecessary overheads are incurred when the sizes of the argument lists are small. Develop a version of quicksort that reverts to insertion sort once the size of the list to be sorted falls below a threshold given as a parameter.

6.6 The basic quicksort algorithm chooses the first item in the list as a pivot. Develop another version that chooses the median of the first element, the middle element and the last element in the list. The median of a group of n numbers is defined as the $\lceil n/2 \rceil$th largest number. For example, if the list is [93,25,51,95,40,64,31,82,19], the first, middle and last elements are 93, 40 and 19 respectively so the pivot should be 40. Are there any advantages of using this technique?

6.7 Build a worst-case list of length 8 for the mergesort function.

6.8 Considering the basic mergesort algorithm in Section 6.3.4, develop a version that divides the original list into three sublists instead of two sublists. Analyze the asymptotic efficiency of this version (use recurrence relations solutions in Appendix B.4).

6.9 Show the content of the heap when heapsort processes the list [23,63,21,15,64,96,66,52,20,33,90,19].

6.10 Build a list of length 7 that is a best case for tree sort. Determine experimentally the number of steps needed to sort it.

6.11 Show that it is possible to derive the quicksort basic program from the tree sort program using the tree deforestation technique presented in Section 4.1.4.

6.12 Define a version of the radix sort algorithm in which each bucket is sorted using quicksort. Repeat the time analysis accordingly.

6.7 Bibliographical notes

Most textbooks treat sorting algorithms in the context of imperative languages. Knuth's book [74] is a comprehensive reference for sorting. A more recent one is by Gonnet and Baeza-Yates [44]. Quicksort was originally invented by Hoare [55] and heapsort by Williams [132]. The taxonomy of sorting algorithms presented in this chapter is based on the one by Azmoodeh [5].

On the functional programming side, Paulson [93] describes most of the sorting algorithms in the strict functional language ML and discusses their performance based on profiling information. He also describes the bottom-up mergesort which was originally devised by O'Keefe [92]. A derivation of quicksort from tree sort through tree deforestation is described by Bird [14].

Graph algorithms

....

This chapter introduces the concept of a graph and describes some of the algorithms that operate on graphs and their applicability to a variety of problems.

7.1 Definitions and terminology

First, we need to introduce some of the terminology associated with graphs. Formally, a graph denoted $G = \langle V, E \rangle$ consists of a finite set of *nodes* (or *vertices*) V and a set of *edges* E, where an edge ij represents a connection between two nodes, i and j. In other words, a graph can be defined as a set and a relation over that set, where every element in the set corresponds to a node in the graph, and where there is a relation between two elements if there is an edge between the corresponding nodes. If the edge has a direction, it is called an *arc* (that is, the relation is not symmetric). In the rest of the chapter, the number of nodes and the number of edges in the graph are respectively denoted as $|V|$ and $|E|$.

Informally, graphs are represented visually as the examples in Figure 7.1 show. The graph on the left is *undirected* (that is, the edges have no direction) and the graph in the

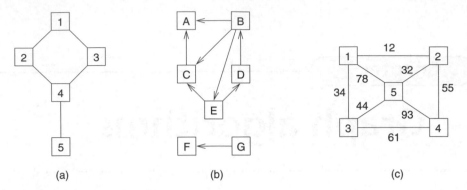

Figure 7.1 Examples of graphs.   (a) Undirected graph; (b) directed graph; (c) weighted (undirected) graph.

middle is *directed* (all the arcs are pointing in one direction). Therefore, just like a tree, a directed graph is also a non-linear data structure since an item can have more than one successor. The difference with trees is that in a graph, a node can have zero or more predecessors whereas each node in a tree (except the root) has only one predecessor.

A *path* from v_1 to v_n is a sequence of nodes $v_1, v_2, \ldots, v_n$ such that every pair $v_{i-1}v_i$ constitutes an edge (or arc). A *simple path* is a path where all the v_i in the path are distinct. A *cycle* is like a simple path except that $v_1 = v_n$, that is, it starts and ends at the same node. A graph is said to be acyclic if it has no cycles. In the example graph in Figure 7.1(b), the sequence $\{D, B, C, A\}$ constitutes a simple path between D and A whereas the sequence $\{B, E, D, B\}$ forms a cycle.

If there is a path between each pair of the nodes, the graph is said to be *connected* as in Figures 7.1(a) and 7.1(c), otherwise, it is disconnected as in Figure 7.1(b). Therefore, a tree can be defined as a connected acyclic graph.

The set of nodes directly connected by an edge to a particular node are said to be *adjacent* to that node. In Figure 7.1(a), the nodes that are adjacent to 4 are $\{2, 3, 5\}$ whereas in Figure 7.1(b), the nodes that are adjacent to B are $\{A, C, E\}$. In a directed graph, the number of nodes adjacent to a given node is called the *out degree* of that node and the number of nodes to which a particular node is adjacent to is called the *in degree*. For example, node C in the graph in Figure 7.1(b) has an in degree of 2 and an out degree of 1. In an undirected graph, the in degree is equal to the out degree and often, it is referred to simply as the degree of the node.

Sometimes, it is useful to associate a *cost* (or *weight*) with every edge in the graph. A weighted graph is illustrated in Figure 7.1(c).

7.2 The graph ADT

We now discuss how to handle graphs in a functional language. Since there are many possible representations, a graph will be manipulated as an ADT (cf. Chapter 5). The description presented here is for a weighted graph but it could equally apply to an unweighted graph by ignoring weight information.

First, we need a suitable definition of a type (Graph n w) where:

● n is the type of the nodes: we assume it can be an index (class Ix). We are only making this assumption in order to use a node as an array index.

● w is the type of the weight: we assume that weights are numbers (class Num).

Given this type, the operations needed to manipulate the graph ADT are:

```
mkGraph ::   (Ix n,Num w) => Bool->(n,n)->[(n,n,w)]->(Graph n w)
```
takes the lower and upper bound of the vertices set, a list of edges (each edge consists of the two end vertices and the weight) and returns a graph; the first boolean parameter indicates whether the graph is directed; if False then the given arcs are added in both directions.

```
adjacent ::   (Ix n,Num w) => (Graph n w) -> n -> [n]
```
returns the nodes adjacent to a particular node.

```
nodes ::   (Ix n,Num w) => (Graph n w) -> [n]
```
returns all the nodes in the graph.

```
edgesD,edgesU ::   (Ix n,Num w) => (Graph n w) -> [(n,n,w)]
```
returns all the edges in a directed and an undirected graph respectively.

```
edgeIn ::   (Ix n,Num w) => (Graph n w) -> (n,n) -> Bool
```
returns True only if the corresponding edge is in the graph.

```
weight ::   (Ix n,Num w) => n -> n -> (Graph n w) -> w
```
returns the weight of the edge connecting two nodes.

The graph of Figure 7.1(c) can then be created with the following expression:

```
mkGraph False (1,5) [(1,2,12),(1,3,34),(1,5,78),(2,4,55),
                     (2,5,32),(3,4,61),(3,5,44),(4,5,93)]
```

The rest of this section describes possible implementations of the graph ADT.

7.2.1   Pointer representation

One way of representing a graph is to declare it just like a general tree using the following declaration:

```
data Graph n w = Vertex n [((Graph n w),w)]
```

In this representation, circular references are possible using local variables to reference nodes. For example, the graph of Figure 7.1(c) is represented as:

```
graphPTR = v1
     where
         v1 = Vertex 1 [(v2,12),(v3,34),(v5,78)]
         v2 = Vertex 2 [(v1,12),(v4,55),(v5,32)]
         v3 = Vertex 3 [(v1,34),(v4,61),(v5,44)]
         v4 = Vertex 4 [(v2,55),(v3,61),(v5,93)]
         v5 = Vertex 5 [(v1,78),(v2,32),(v3,44),(v4,93)]
```

This representation is very space efficient because traversing the graph does not involve the creation of intermediate data structures. One problem is that if the graph is not connected, each component has to be defined separately. Another problem is that since pointers that denote circularly defined values cannot be manipulated directly or compared, constructing or traversing the graph cannot be achieved in a simple manner. Because of these drawbacks, we will not elaborate further on this representation but in some cases this representation might prove useful.

7.2.2 Adjacency list representation

Another representation is the *adjacency list* representation. A linear structure holds every node in the graph together with its adjacent nodes. For example, if we decide to use a list to hold the nodes, a graph is defined as:

```
type Graph n w = [(n,[(n,w)])]
```

In this representation, access to the adjacency list of a node would be in $O(|V|)$. A better representation uses an array to allow a constant access to any adjacency list:

```
type Graph n w = Array n [(n,w)]
```

In this case, the graph of Figure 7.1(c) can be directly defined as:

```
graphAL = array (1,5) [(1,[(2,12),(3,34),(5,78)]),
                       (2,[(1,12),(4,55),(5,32)]),
                       (3,[(1,34),(4,61),(5,44)]),
                       (4,[(2,55),(3,61),(5,93)]),
                       (5,[(1,78),(2,32),(3,44),(4,93)])]
```

or created with the following call:[1]

```
graphAL' = mkGraph False (1,5) [(1,2,12),(1,3,34),(1,5,78),
                                (2,4,55),(2,5,32),(3,4,61),
                                (3,5,44),(4,5,93)]
```

Unlike with a list, modifications to the shape of the array (needed when adding or removing vertices) cannot be easily achieved. However, this is sufficient for our purpose since the algorithms described later consider a graph as a static entity that is not modified.

We now show an adjacency list implementation of the graph ADT. We can see that for undirected graphs, listing the edges without duplicates is achieved by ordering vertices in an edge in increasing value order.

```
mkGraph dir bnds es =
    accumArray (\xs x -> x:xs) [] bnds
             ([(x1,(x2,w)) | (x1,x2,w) <- es] ++
              if dir then []
              else [(x2,(x1,w))|(x1,x2,w)<-es,x1/=x2])
```

---

[1] `graphAL` and `graphAL'` are equivalent graphs but the ordering of the arcs might be different depending on the implementation of `mkGraph`.

```
adjacent g v  = map fst (g!v)

nodes g       = indices g

edgeIn g (x,y)= elem y (adjacent g x)

weight x y g  = head [c | (a,c)<-g!x , (a==y)]

edgesD g      = [(v1,v2,w) | v1<- nodes g ,(v2,w) <-g!v1]

edgesU g      = [(v1,v2,w) | v1<- nodes g ,(v2,w) <-g!v1 ,v1<v2]
```

MkGraph starts from an empty array and then creates for each vertex the list of destination nodes and weights by adding a tuple in front of its list. If the graph is undirected then the reverse arcs are added, except for arcs that would start and end at the same vertex. The main characteristic of this representation is that traversing adjacent nodes as well as computing the weight of an edge takes a time proportional to the length of the adjacency list. In the worst case, the length is equal to $|V| - 1$ when the node is connected to all other nodes.

7.2.3 Adjacency matrix representation

The next representation uses a two-dimensional square array of values of dimension $|V| \times |V|$ where both coordinates i and j are nodes and where the entry (i, j) is equal to the weight of the corresponding edge (or arc) between nodes i and j:

```
type Graph a b = Array (a,a) b
```

The main problem with using this representation is that we need a value that corresponds to non-existent edges. For this, we use the predefined Maybe algebraic type with two constructors, Nothing and Just b. It is then possible to detect whether there is an edge between two nodes by testing for the value Nothing. Given this type, the adjacency matrix implementation of the graph ADT now becomes:

```
type Graph n w = Array (n,n) (Maybe w)

mkGraph dir bnds@(l,u) es
    = emptyArray // ([((x1,x2),Just w) |(x1,x2,w)<-es] ++
                     if dir then []
                     else [((x2,x1),Just w) |(x1,x2,w)<-es,x1/=x2])
        where emptyArray
                = array ((1,1),(u,u)) [((x1,x2),Nothing) |
                                       x1 <- range bnds,
                                       x2 <- range bnds]

adjacent g v1 = [ v2 | v2 <-nodes g,(g!(v1,v2))/= Nothing]
```

```
nodes g        = range (l,u) where ((l,_),(u,_)) = bounds g

edgeIn g (x,y)= (g!(x,y)) /= Nothing

weight x y g   = w where (Just w) = g!(x,y)

edgesD g       = [(v1,v2,unwrap(g!(v1,v2)))
                      | v1 <-nodes g, v2 <- nodes g,
                        edgeIn g (v1,v2)]
       where unwrap (Just w) = w

edgesU g       = [(v1,v2,unwrap(g!(v1,v2)))
                      | v1 <-nodes g, v2 <- range (v1,u),
                        edgeIn g (v1,v2)]
       where (_,(u,_)) = bounds g
             unwrap (Just w) = w
```

mkGraph first creates an array filled with Nothing values which are then replaced by
Just v according to the given list of arcs. Note that the edgesU function works by
scanning half of the adjacency matrix only. It uses the function range which produces
the list of indices that exist between a pair of bounds. The main inefficiency of this
representation is having to build the matrix with Nothing constructors then updating
it with weight values. We could avoid this problem by assuming that the list of edges
supplied to the mkGraph function contains all possible combinations and that a special
value represents a non-existent edge.

As with the previous implementation, using an adjacency matrix is only suitable if
there are no (or few) changes to the structure of the graph. The main advantage over it
is that access to the weight of an edge is constant. However, computing the adjacency
list of any node now takes $O(|V|)$ steps.

7.2.4   Comparison between the representations

The pointer representation is very space efficient but all its operations are complicated
and time inefficient. When comparing between the adjacency list and the adjacency
matrix representations, the efficiencies of their graph-manipulating functions depend
on the parameters $|V|$ and $|E|$ of the graph, or on the *degree of sparsity*. Informally,
when there is a large number of edges, the graph is said to be *dense*, and when there
are few connections, it is *sparse*. In some textbooks, a graph is said to be sparse when
$|E| < |V| \log |V|$. In general, the matrix representation is better with dense graphs and
the adjacency list representation with sparse graphs.

7.3   Depth-first and breadth-first search

We can identify two main strategies for traversing a graph:

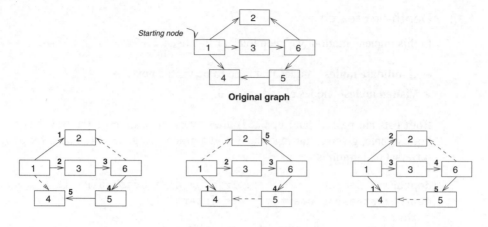

Original graph

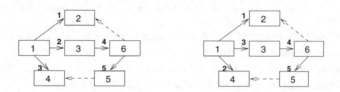

Examples of depth-first traversals

Examples of breadth-first traversals

Figure 7.2   Depth-first and breadth-first traversals of a graph.

- **Depth-first search**   after visiting a node, all its (non-visited) adjacent nodes are recursively visited using a depth-first search. This is a generalization of the preorder traversal of the tree.

- **Breadth-first search**   after visiting a node, all its (non-visited) adjacent nodes are visited. Then, the algorithm is applied to each of these adjacent nodes separately.

For example, Figure 7.2 shows how a graph can be traversed in different ways using a depth-first or a breadth-first strategy. This example shows a directed graph but the strategy is the same for undirected graphs if we consider an edge to be equivalent to two arcs, one in each direction.

These graph traversal strategies constitute a framework which can be used to design other graph algorithms. The *topological sort* algorithm, considered later in this chapter, is an example of graph traversal that uses a depth-first strategy.

The remaining part of this section examines different ways of implementing these graph traversals. In Section 2.6.5, we have described several strategies for traversing the tree data structure. A graph traversal is similar to a tree traversal but in the presence of cycles we need to remember which nodes have been visited so that they will not be visited again.

7.3.1   Depth-first search

In this implementation, we keep track of two lists:

- **Candidate nodes**   nodes that need to be visited next;
- **Visited nodes**   nodes already visited.

Both lists are passed (and updated) after every invocation of the traversal function. For example, given a starting node s and a graph g, a general function for depth-first traversal of a graph is:

```
depthFirstSearch            :: Ix a => a -> Graph a -> [a]
depthFirstSearch start g = dfs [start] []
  where
    dfs [] vis    = vis
    dfs (c:cs) vis
      | elem c vis = dfs cs vis
      | otherwise  = dfs ((adjacent g c)++cs) (vis++[c])
```

The first argument of the dfs function represents the list of candidate nodes and the second argument the list of visited nodes. To avoid calling the (++) operator in the second argument of the recursive call to dfs, visited nodes can be accumulated in reverse order then reversed just before delivering the result:

```
depthFirstSearch'           :: Ix a => a -> Graph a -> [a]
depthFirstSearch' start g = reverse (dfs [start] [])
  where
    dfs [] vis    = vis
    dfs (c:cs) vis
      | elem c vis = dfs cs vis
      | otherwise  = dfs ((adjacent g c)++cs) (c:vis)
```

When applied to the graph in Figure 7.2, the evaluation proceeds as follows:

```
depthFirstSearch' 1 g  ⇒    dfs [1] []
                       ⇒    dfs [2,3,4] [1]
                       ⇒    dfs [3,4] [2,1]
                       ⇒    dfs [6,4] [3,2,1]
                       ⇒    dfs [5,4] [6,3,2,1]
                       ⇒    dfs [4,4] [5,6,3,2,1]
                       ⇒    dfs [4] [4,5,6,3,2,1]
                       ⇒    dfs [] [4,5,6,3,2,1]
                       ⇒    reverse [4,5,6,3,2,1]
                       ⇒    [1,2,3,6,5,4]
```

In this program, adjacent nodes are added and retrieved from the front of the candidate nodes list during the search. Therefore, we can use a stack ADT (see Section 5.2) to hold candidate nodes since they are processed in a last-in-first-out (LIFO) fashion:

```
depthFirstSearch''      :: Ix a => a -> Graph a -> [a]
depthFirstSearch'' start g
                    = reverse (dfs (push start emptyStack) [])
 where
  dfs s vis
    | (stackEmpty s)   = vis
    | elem (top s) vis = dfs (pop s) vis
    | otherwise        = let c = top s
                          in
                            dfs (foldr push (pop s) (adjacent g c))
                                (c:vis)
```

7.3.2 Breadth-first search

The function that implements breadth-first traversal is identical to the depth-first function except that this time, a queue ADT (see Section 5.3) is used to hold the candidate nodes. This function is defined as:

```
breadthFirstSearch :: Ix a => a -> Graph a -> [a]
breadthFirstSearch start g
                    = reverse (bfs (enqueue start emptyQueue) [])
 where
  bfs q vis
    | (queueEmpty q)= vis
    | elem (front q) vis
                    = bfs (dequeue q) vis
    | otherwise     = let c = front q
                       in
                         bfs (foldr enqueue
                                    (dequeue q)
                                    (adjacent g c))
                             (c:vis)
```

In the previous example, it generates the following reduction sequence:

```
breadthFirstSearch 1 g  ⇒  bfs [1] []
                        ⇒  bfs [2,3,4] [1]
                        ⇒  bfs [3,4] [2,1]
                        ⇒  bfs [4,6] [3,2,1]
                        ⇒  bfs [6] [4,3,2,1]
                        ⇒  bfs [5] [6,4,3,2,1]
                        ⇒  bfs [4] [5,6,4,3,2,1]
                        ⇒  bfs [] [5,6,4,3,2,1]
                        ⇒  reverse [5,6,4,3,2,1]
                        ⇒  [1,2,3,4,6,5]
```

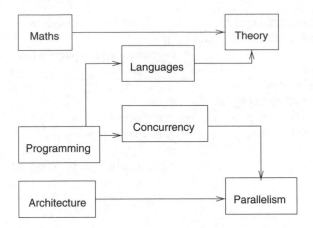

Figure 7.3 Representing a course prerequisite structure as a graph.

If the graph is not connected, the depth-first search and breadth-first search functions presented here only produce the list of all graph nodes reachable from the starting node. Section 7.6 describes depth-first search for non-connected graphs.

7.4 Topological sort

We now consider a graph problem with numerous applications. Given a directed acyclic graph, a *topological sort* is an ordering of vertices such that if there is a path from v_i to v_j, then v_j appears after v_i in the ordering. As the example in Figure 7.3 shows, we may want to represent the modules in a course as a graph, in which an arc from module i to module j indicates that i is a prerequisite module for the module j.

A topological sort of a graph corresponds to an appropriate sequence in the choice of modules that conforms to the prerequisite structure. An example is the sequence *Maths, Programming, Languages, Concurrency, Architecture, Parallelism, Theory*. Note that the sequence is not unique: the modules *Concurrency* and *Architecture* could have been swapped in the sequence.

A simple program for the topological sort will be developed based on the depth-first traversal function depthFirstSearch function presented in Section 7.3.1. First, a closer look at the body of the dfs function reveals how these argument lists are modified from one recursive call to the next:

Candidate nodes:	(c:cs)	$\rightarrow$	(adjacent g c)++cs
Visited nodes:	vis	$\rightarrow$	vis++[c]

In the topological sort program, these lists must be updated as follows:

Candidate nodes:	(c:cs)	$\rightarrow$	cs
Visited nodes:	vis	$\rightarrow$	c:(tsort' (adjacent g c) vis)

This means that when a node is inserted in the solution, it precedes the topological sort (called recursively) of all its adjacent nodes. Also, the initial list of candidate nodes must consist of all nodes with no incoming edges (that is, nodes with an in degree equal to zero). The complete program is:

```
inDegree g n  = length [t | v<-nodes g, t<-adjacent g v, (n==t)]

topologicalSort g = tsort [n | n<-nodes g , (inDegree g n == 0)]
                          []
  where
    tsort [] r   = r
    tsort (c:cs) vis
      | elem c vis = tsort cs vis
      | otherwise  = tsort cs (c:(tsort (adjacent g c) vis))
```

When applied to the example in Figure 7.2 created by the following expression:

```
g = mkGraph True (1,6) [(1,2,0),(1,3,0),(1,4,0),(3,6,0),
                        (5,4,0),(6,2,0), (6,5,0)]
```

it generates the following reduction sequence:

```
topologicalSort g
    ⇒   tsort' [1] []
    ⇒   tsort' [] (1:(tsort' [2,3,4] []))
    ⇒   (1:(tsort' [2,3,4] []))
    ⇒   1:(tsort' [2,3,4] [])
    ⇒   1:(tsort' [3,4] (2:(tsort' [] [])))
    ⇒   1:(tsort' [3,4] [2])
    ⇒   1:(tsort' [4] (3:(tsort' [6] [2])))
    ⇒   1:(tsort' [4] (3:(tsort' [] (6:(tsort' [2,5] [2])))))
    ⇒   1:(tsort' [4] (3:(6:(tsort' [2,5] [2]))))
    ⇒   1:(tsort' [4] (3:(6:(tsort' [5] [2]))))
    ⇒   1:(tsort' [4] (3:(6:(tsort' [] (5:(tsort' [4] [2]))))))
    ⇒   1:(tsort' [4] (3:(6:(5:(tsort' [4] [2])))))
    ⇒   1:(tsort' [4] (3:(6:(5:(tsort' []
                                   (4:(tsort' [] [2])))))))
    ⇒   1:(tsort' [4] (3:(6:(5:(4:(tsort' [] [2]))))))
    ⇒   1:(tsort' [4] [3,6,5,4,2])
    ⇒   1:(tsort' [] [3,6,5,4,2])
    ⇒   [1,3,6,5,4,2]
```

A topological sort sequence corresponds to a depth-first search but not every depth-first search is a topological sort. For example, the depth-first sequence [1,2,3,6,5,4] is not a topological sort because the value 2 appears before 6.

The course graph of Figure 7.3 can be created by the following definitions:

```
data Courses = Maths | Theory | Languages | Programming
             | Concurrency | Architecture | Parallelism
     deriving (Eq,Ord,Enum,Ix,Show)

cg = mkGraph True (Maths,Parallelism)
        [(Maths,Theory,1),(Languages,Theory,1),
         (Programming,Languages,1),(Programming,Concurrency,1),
         (Concurrency,Parallelism,1),(Architecture,Parallelism,1)]
```

A topological sort of this graph then returns the following result:

```
topologicalSort cg
   ⇒   [Architecture, Programming, Concurrency, Parallelism,
        Languages, Maths, Theory]
```

which is also a topological sort different from the one we gave before, but finishing with Maths and Theory is surely a much less pedagogical approach!

7.5 Minimum spanning tree

Given a connected, weighted undirected graph $G = \langle V, E \rangle$, a spanning tree is a subgraph of G, $G' = \langle V, E' \rangle$ such that G' is acyclic and connected. In other words, G' is a tree that 'covers' all the nodes in the graph. For example, the graph in Figure 7.4 has several spanning trees, three of them depicted below the original graph. Note that the number of edges in a spanning tree is always equal to $|V - 1|$.

The cost of a spanning tree is the sum of the weights of the edges that constitute it. In the previous example, the costs of the three spanning trees is 194, 185 and 133 respectively. The minimum spanning tree problem is to find the spanning tree with the minimum cost. This graph problem has several practical applications such as building a computer network with minimal cost or designing a telephone exchange for n locations.

7.5.1 Kruskal's algorithm

The first algorithm described is called Kruskal's algorithm. Starting with an empty tree, it works by successively adding the lowest cost edge to this tree providing that no cycles are created. An example of how the algorithm works is illustrated in Figure 7.5.

However, this algorithm could be extremely expensive to implement if we have to test a graph continuously for cycles. For this reason, it is implemented as follows:

1. Initially, there is a table containing one entry per vertex, each vertex being allocated an arbitrary distinct number (we could give every vertex its own value to start with).

2. All edges are placed in a priority queue, ordered according to the weight of the edge.

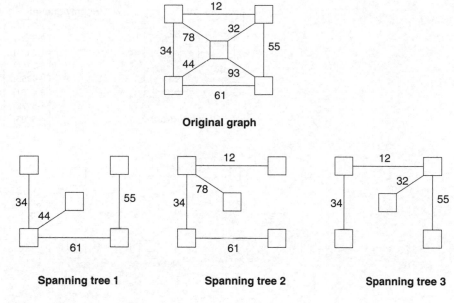

Original graph

Spanning tree 1   **Spanning tree 2**   **Spanning tree 3**

Figure 7.4 Examples of spanning trees.

3. Add the edge at the front of the priority queue (that is, with the lowest cost) until $|V| - 1$ edges have been added using the following algorithm:

(a) if both vertices that constitute this edge have different numbers in the table, this edge is added to the solution and both numbers in the table are replaced by the same number (for example, the minimum of both of them);

(b) otherwise the edge is rejected and the table is left untouched.

Step 3 of this algorithm uses the function `unionFind` which, given a pair of vertices and a table, returns a pair consisting of a boolean and the updated table, the boolean indicates whether the table has been updated according to the rules stated above. This function, which uses the table ADT (see Section 5.6), is defined as:

```
unionFind :: (Eq n, Ord w) => (n,n)->Table w n->(Bool,Table w n)
unionFind (x,y) t
  = let xv = findTable t x
        yv = findTable t y
    in  if (xv == yv)
        then (False,t)
        else (True,updTable (if yv<xv then (x,yv) else (y,xv)) t)
```

Now here is an implementation of Kruskal's algorithm. The function `fillPQ` places edges in the priority queue in the order (`weight,v,w`) so that the tuples are sorted according to weight.

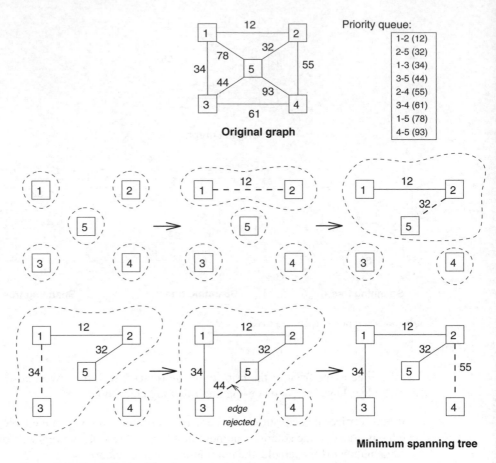

Figure 7.5 Kruskal's algorithm for computing the minimum spanning tree.

```
fillPQ :: (Ord n, Ord w, Ord c) => [(n,w,c)] -> PQueue (c,n,w)
                                          -> PQueue (c,n,w)

fillPQ [] pq           = pq
fillPQ ((x,y,w):es) pq = fillPQ es (enPQ (w,x,y) pq)


kruskal :: (Num w, Ix n, Ord w) => Graph n w -> [(w,n,n)]
kruskal g = kruskal' (fillPQ (edgesU g) emptyPQ)
                     (newTable [(x,x) | x<- nodes g])
                     [] 1
      where n          = length (nodes g)
            kruskal' pq t mst i
                | i==n      = mst
                | otherwise = let e@(_,x,y)    = frontPQ pq
                                  pq'          = dePQ pq
                                  (updated,t') = unionFind (x,y) t
```

```
in if updated
   then kruskal' pq' t'(e:mst) (i+1)
   else kruskal' pq' t   mst      i
```

kruskal' implements Step 3 of the algorithm, mst is the list containing the edges of the minimum spanning tree and the last parameter keeps track of its length to avoid recomputing it at each step. The iteration stops when $n-1$ edges (where n is the number of nodes) have been added to the solution since a minimum spanning tree always consists of $n-1$ edges. Notice that this program uses no less than three ADTs. Therefore, the efficiency of this algorithm depends on how these ADTs are implemented. Potentially every edge is examined resulting in $O(|E|)$ iterations at the outer level in the worst case.

7.5.2   Prim's algorithm

The second algorithm described is called Prim's algorithm. It works by considering all vertices instead of all edges in the graph. The algorithm divides vertices into two sets: those which have been included in the tree (denoted T) and those which have not (denoted R). Initially, one vertex is arbitrarily placed into the set T (for example, the vertex 1). Then at each stage in the algorithm, among all the edges (u, v) where $u \in T$ and $v \in R$, the edge with the minimum weight is selected. An example is illustrated in Figure 7.6.

The advantage of this algorithm over the previous one is that there is no need to sort all edges and repeatedly update a table of vertices. We now show an implementation of Prim's algorithm. In the next chapter, we will show that this is an example of a *greedy* algorithm.

```
prim g           = prim' [n] ns []
  where (n:ns)   = nodes g
    es           = edgesU g
  prim' t [] mst = mst
       prim' t r mst
              = let e@(c,u',v') = minimum[(c,u,v)|(u,v,c)<-es,
                                          elem u t, elem v r]
                in prim' (v':t) (delete v' r) (e:mst)
```

where the function delete removes an item from a list.

⑦.⑥   Depth-first search trees and forests†

The depth-first search traversal program described in Section 7.3.1 essentially indicates the order in which nodes are visited. A *depth-first search tree* shows not only the nodes but also the edges traversed. Figure 7.7 shows the depth-first search trees that correspond to the depth-first search traversals displayed in Figure 7.2.

This section describes how to implement algorithms that generate depth-first search trees.

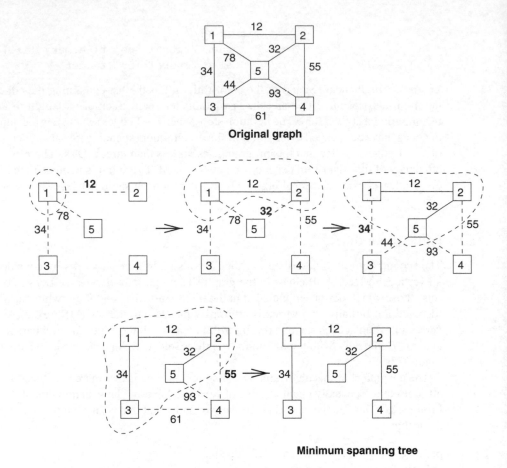

Figure 7.6   Prim's algorithm for computing the minimum spanning tree.

7.6.1   Extending the basic approach

First, we need to define the depth-first search tree as a general tree (see Section 2.6.5):

```
data Tree a = NodeGT a [Tree a]
```

Generating the depth-first search tree can now be accomplished using the following function, derived from the `depthFirstSearch` function in Section 7.3.1. We use a set (see the interface in Section 5.5) to record the nodes that have been visited to avoid having to inspect the tree to check whether a particular node is part of the tree. `foldl` is used to compute the list of trees that depend on a node because they are derived from its adjacent nodes.

```
depthFirstTree :: (Num w,Ix n) => n -> Graph n w -> Tree n
depthFirstTree s g = head (snd (dfst g (emptySet,[]) s))
```

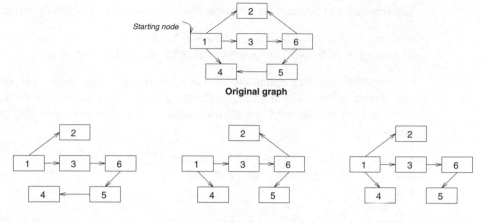

Figure 7.7 Examples of depth-first search trees of a graph.

```
dfst::(Ix n,Num w) => Graph n w -> (Set n , [Tree n]) -> n
                            -> (Set n , [Tree n])
dfst g (vs,ts) n
    | inSet n vs  = (vs,ts)
    | otherwise   = (vs',(NodeGT n ts'):ts)
    where (vs',ts') = foldl (dfst g)
                            (addSet n vs, [])
                            (adjacent g n)
```

We have made here the assumption that a depth-first traversal will only involve the nodes reachable from the starting node. If we want to reach all nodes, a traversal must produce a *depth-first search forest* where every node will appear in one of the trees of the forest. The corresponding program involves finding trees for each starting node; if a node of g already appears in a previous tree, it will not be considered because it will appear in the resulting set of previous calls to dfst.

```
dfsforest :: (Num w,Ix n) => Graph n w -> [Tree n]
dfsforest g = snd (foldl (dfst g) (emptySet,[]) (nodes g))
```

7.6.2 Lazy depth-first search

The previous dfst function carries out two functions at once: generating the depth-first search tree and cutting branches according to nodes that have been visited. King and Launchbury [71] proposed the following lazy implementation of depth-first search where these two functions are computed separately:

● generating an infinite depth-first search tree for every node;
● pruning unwanted branches.

The function that generates the infinite depth-first search tree is simply written as:

```
generate :: Ix a => Graph a -> a -> Tree a
generate g v = NodeGT v (map (generate g) (adjacent g v))
```

Pruning is achieved by examining each depth-first search tree in the sequence produced, recording the nodes in a tree, then cutting all the descendants of visited nodes. As before, a set will be used to hold the visited nodes. The corresponding pruning function is:

```
prune    :: Ix a => [Tree a] -> [Tree a]
prune ts = snd (prune' emptySet ts)
  where
    prune' m []      = (m,[])
    prune' m ((NodeGT v ts):us)
       | inSet v m  = prune' m us
       | otherwise  = let (m',as) = prune' (addSet v m) ts
                          (m'',bs)= prune' m' us
                      in
                          (m'',(NodeGT v as):bs)
```

Given these two functions, generating the depth-first forest is achieved as follows:

```
klDfsForest   :: Ix a => Graph a -> [Tree a]
klDfsForest g = prune (map (generate g) (nodes g))
```

The motivation behind this approach is that the two functions (generate and prune) constitute two separate modules which can be combined in several ways to generate several other graph algorithms. For example, the depth-first search path from any node can be obtained by flattening the corresponding depth-first tree according to a preorder traversal strategy. Therefore, an alternative definition of the depthFirstsearch function is:

```
klDfs         :: Ix a => a -> Graph a -> [a]
klDfs v g     = preorderT (head (prune (map (generate g) [v])))

preorderT     :: Tree a -> [a]
preorderT (NodeGT v l)
              = v:(concat (map preorderT l))
```

More graph algorithms, developed using this approach, are described in King and Launchbury's paper (King and Launchbury [71]).

7.7 Conclusion

This chapter presented an overview of graphs and provided examples of graph algorithms. Most of them were implemented simply by using one or several ADTs. For this

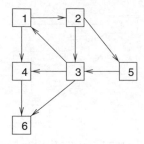

Figure 7.8 Example of a graph.

reason, it is very hard to reason about the time or space efficiency of these algorithms as it depends on how the underlying ADTs are implemented.

Most graph algorithms involve one sort of graph traversal strategy or another. More complex traversal strategies, such as *backtracking*, will be considered in the next chapter.

Exercises

7.1 Consider the graph in Figure 7.8. Starting from node 1, list all nodes in an order that corresponds to:

(a) a depth-first search,

(b) a breadth-first search.

7.2 Define a depth-first search function whose output is a list of the edges in the depth-first search tree.

7.3 (a) Define a function based on depth-first search which determines whether an undirected graph has a cycle.

(b) Define a function based on depth-first search which determines whether a directed graph has a cycle.

(c) Repeat (a) and (b) using breadth-first search. Is any strategy better than the other?

7.4 Show that a graph can have more than one minimum spanning tree.

7.5 Which graph ADT implementation yields the best performance in Kruskal's minimum spanning tree algorithm?

7.6 Modify Kruskal's and Prim's algorithms such that they can deal with a graph that is not connected.

7.7 Does the order of visiting vertices in Prim's minimum spanning algorithm corresponds to a depth-first search, breadth-first search or none of them?

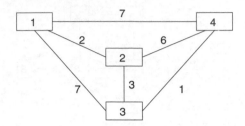

Figure 7.9 Computing the shortest paths starting from vertex 1.

7.8 Given a weighted graph $G = \langle V, E \rangle$, the cost of a path $v_1, v_2, \ldots, v_n$ is equal to the sum $\sum_{i=1}^{n-1} weight(v_i, v_{i+1})$ of the weights of all the edges that constitute it. Given a starting vertex v_1, the problem is finding the shortest path (that is, path with the lowest cost) from v_1 to all other vertices in the graph. For example, consider the graph displayed in Figure 7.9. The shortest paths from vertex 1 to all other vertices are: $1 \rightarrow 2$ (total cost 2), $1 \rightarrow 2 \rightarrow 3$ (total cost 5), $1 \rightarrow 2 \rightarrow 3 \rightarrow 4$ (total cost 6). The problem has numerous applications such as finding the minimum road distances from one city to all the other cities in the country.

Find an algorithm for computing all shortest paths based on Prim's minimum spanning algorithm. It should work by dividing vertices into 2 sets T and R. At each stage in the algorithm, among all the edges (u, v) where $u \in T$ and $v \in R$, the edge which causes the minimum distance between v_1 and v is selected.

7.9 Using lazy depth-first search, define a function that returns for every vertex in a non-connected graph two numbers: the first one indicates the component number of the vertex and the second one is a sequence number of the vertex in the corresponding depth-first search tree.

7.10 Define a topological sort function which operates on a directed acyclic graph in three stages. First, it builds the depth-first search forest, then it lists the nodes in the forest according to a postorder traversal, and finally, it reverses the list.

7.8 Bibliographical notes

Most standard algorithms textbooks include sections on graph algorithms (for example [3, 19, 111]). The application of depth-first search in a variety of problems has its roots in the work by Tarjan [114], Hopcroft and Tarjan [57]. The topological sort algorithm is due to Kahn [69]. Functional versions of topological sort are described by Harrison [50] and Paulson [93]. Prim's algorithm for the minimum spanning tree problem originates from [103] and Kruskal's algorithm from [75].

King's thesis [72] is devoted to the implementation of graph algorithms in Haskell. King and Launchbury's paper [71] provides the basis for our discussion on depth-first search trees and forests. Their paper also describes how to use the same framework for specifying other graph problems based on depth-first search.

Chapter 8

Top-down design techniques

So far, algorithms have always been designed around a particular application. We now consider some fundamental techniques that can be used to design a collection or a *class* of algorithms.

In this chapter, we start by presenting a set of design techniques that follow a *top-down* approach: given an initial problem specification, we work our way down to the solution by considering alternatives.

8.1 Divide-and-conquer

Divide-and-conquer is the first fundamental technique (or *paradigm*) for designing algorithms we consider in this chapter. Given a problem specification, it can be informally described as follows:

● divide the problem into smaller subproblems;

● solve each of the subproblems separately; if the subproblem is large enough, use the same technique recursively; otherwise solve the subproblem directly;

● combine all the solutions of the subproblems into a single solution.

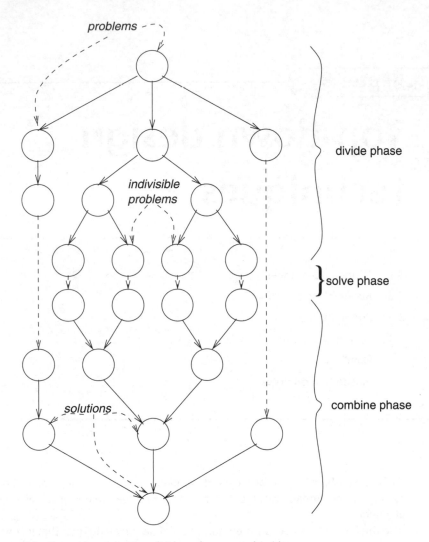

Figure 8.1 Successive stages in a divide-and-conquer algorithm.

As the diagram in Figure 8.1 illustrates, the general pattern of execution is that of a tree that first expands (divide phase), then contracts (combine phase). In the first phase, the nodes of the tree correspond to problems whereas in the second phase, the nodes correspond to solutions. The leaves at the bottom of the tree in the first phase correspond to *indivisible* problems which are turned into *basic* solutions.

The rest of this section describes a function (we call it divideAndConquer) which captures the divide-and-conquer computational pattern, followed by some applications of this function to known problems. This function must be a higher-order function since some of the parameters of the problem (such as how the division of problems is performed) are themselves functions.

8.1.1 The divide-and-conquer higher-order function

Assuming a type p that denotes problems and a type s that denotes solutions, the divideAndConquer higher-order function takes the following arguments:

ind :: p -> Bool This function returns True if an instance of the problem is indivisible and False otherwise.

solve :: p -> s This function solves an indivisible problem instance.

divide :: p -> [p] This function divides a problem into a list of subproblems.

combine :: p -> [s] -> s Given the original problem and the solution of its subproblems, this function combines them into a single solution.

Consequently, the definition of the divideAndConquer function is as follows:

```
divideAndConquer :: ( p -> Bool) -> (p -> s) -> (p -> [p]) ->
                    (p -> [s] -> s) -> p -> s
divideAndConquer ind solve divide combine initPb
    = dc' initPb
    where dc' pb
            | ind pb  = solve pb
            | otherwise = combine pb (map dc' (divide pb))
```

The same approach will be adopted for each of the fundamental techniques presented in this chapter: we first define a higher-order function that illustrates its computational behavior then show some example algorithms expressed using this function. Such higher-order functions are by no means representative of all algorithms within their class. Often, they are only selected because they give a clear idea about the technique in action, and also, because they are sufficient for expressing the instance algorithms selected as case studies.

8.1.2 Mergesort

The mergesort algorithm presented in Section 6.3.4 is essentially a divide-and-conquer algorithm where problem and solution instances consist of unsorted and sorted lists respectively. A problem instance is indivisible when the length of the corresponding list is 0 or 1. Solving an indivisible instance just returns the corresponding list. Dividing a problem splits the list into two equal halves and combining solutions consists of merging the corresponding lists. The merge function has already been described in Section 6.3.4. So the mergesort function can now be expressed as an instance of the divide-and-conquer higher-order function as follows:

```
msort xs = divideAndConquer ind id divide combine xs
    where ind xs          = length xs <= 1
          divide xs       = let n = length xs 'div' 2
                            in [take n xs , drop n xs]
          combine _ [l1,l2] = merge l1 l2
```

> **Table 8.1** Time efficiency of divide-and-conquer algorithms.

Assumption	Time complexity	
$T_{\text{divide}}(n) + T_{\text{combine}}(n) \in O(n)$	$T_{\text{dc}'}(n) \in O(n),$	if $k < b$
	$T_{\text{dc}'}(n) \in O(n \log n),$	if $k = b$
	$T_{\text{dc}'}(n) \in O(n^{\log_b k}),$	if $k > b$
$T_{\text{divide}}(n) + T_{\text{combine}}(n) \in O(1)$	$T_{\text{dc}'}(n) \in O(n)$	

8.1.3   Quicksort

The quicksort algorithm is another example of a divide-and-conquer algorithm, very similar to mergesort except that the divide operation splits the list according to a pivot and the combine operation appends the two sorted sublists with the pivot in the middle (see the basic description in Section 6.3.3). Using the divide-and-conquer function, we thus get the following definition for quicksort.

```
qsort xs = divideAndConquer ind id divide combine xs
    where ind xs               = length xs <= 1
          divide (x:xs)        = [[ y | y<-xs, y<=x],
                                  [ y | y<-xs, y>x] ]
          combine (x:_) [11,12] = 11 ++ [x] ++ 12
```

Notice that this version is less efficient than the one presented in Section 6.3.3 because it involves more than one traversal to split the list and also because it uses the append operator (++). This is usually the case with algorithms expressed using a higher-order function because we are constrained in the way the program is described.

8.1.4   Efficiency of divide-and-conquer algorithms

Divide-and-conquer is used to design algorithms in a variety of applications areas such as numerical analysis, cryptography, and image processing. The main motivation for using it is that it often leads to very efficient algorithms. Supposing that a problem of size n is divided into k problems of size n/b, and supposing that an indivisible instance is always of size 1, analyzing the time efficiency of the dc' function leads to the following recurrence relations:

$$T_{\text{dc}'}(n) = \begin{cases} 1 + T_{\text{ind}}(n) + T_{\text{solve}}(n) & , n = 1 \\ 1 + T_{\text{ind}} + k\,T_{\text{dc}'}(\frac{n}{b}) + T_{\text{divide}}(n) + T_{\text{combine}}(n) & , n > 1 \end{cases}$$

Assuming that both the indivisible and the solve functions operate in constant time (that is, $T_{\text{ind}}(n)$ and $T_{\text{solve}}(n) \in O(1)$), Table 8.1 shows some formulas for determining the time efficiency of divide-and-conquer problems in general. We can see that quicksort and mergesort both have an $O(n \log n)$ efficiency since $k = b = 2$. These figures usually compare favorably against those of more intuitive but less efficient algorithms (called *basic* algorithms). An important factor in designing a divide-and-conquer algorithm is deciding when to stop the division of problems, since applying the algorithm recursively for sizes below a certain threshold may cost more than solving them using a basic algorithm. To determine the optimal threshold, an empirical approach, often based on execution profile information, can be used.

8.2 Backtracking search

The next design strategy considered involves searching for a particular solution to a problem by systematic trial and error. The main characteristics of such problems are:

- a set of all possible situations or nodes which constitute the *node space*; these are the potential solutions that need to be explored;
- a set of legal moves from a node to other nodes, called the *successors* of that node;
- an initial node;
- a goal node, that is, the solution.

This type of problem arises in a variety of applications such as finding an object in a room, diagnosis of a fault in some equipment or of a disease, proving theorems, etc. In the rest of this section, we give a more precise definition of a search space and present a higher-order function for conducting a search, followed by some applications of this function.

8.2.1 Implicit graphs

Since searching takes place over a large graph, it is not desirable to store this entire data structure in memory. For efficiency reasons, it is better to examine one node at a time, then generate adjacent nodes from the value of that node. Therefore, we differentiate between an *explicit* graph as described in the previous chapter, where nodes and edges are defined in advance, and an *implicit* graph which is generated as the computation proceeds. To handle an implicit graph, all we need is the following information:

- an appropriate type node which represents node information;
- a successor function of type node -> [node] which generates the list of successors of a particular node.

As an example, consider the *eight-tile game* which consists of a three-by-three tray that contains eight square tiles, one of the nine spaces being left unoccupied. The board configuration may be changed by moving into the space any of the tiles adjacent to it. Figure 8.2 shows a portion of the implicit graph generated by the various board configurations. The purpose of the game is to reach the goal configuration (shown in the figure) from any initial configuration.

Each configuration is represented as an array of tile positions. This array contains the row-column coordinates of each tile such that an entry i in the array contains the position of the ith tile and entry 0 contains the position of the space. The corresponding type definitions are:

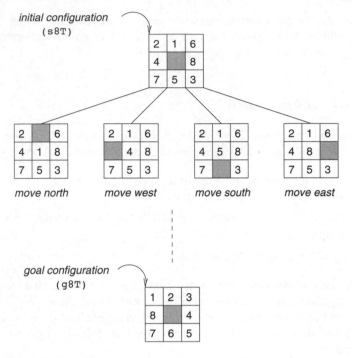

Figure 8.2 The eight-tile problem.

```
type Position          = (Int,Int)
type Board             = Array Int Position
```

For example the goal node and the start node (see Figure 8.2) are both represented as:

```
g8T :: Board
g8T = array (0,8) [(0,(2,2)),(1,(1,1)),(2,(1,2)),
                   (3,(1,3)),(4,(2,3)),(5,(3,3)),
                   (6,(3,2)),(7,(3,1)),(8,(2,1))]
s8T :: Board
s8T = array (0,8) [(0,(2,2)),(1,(1,2)),(2,(1,1)),
                   (3,(3,3)),(4,(2,1)),(5,(3,2)),
                   (6,(1,3)),(7,(3,1)),(8,(2,3))]
```

A simple move takes a tile and moves it to the space position. The legality test must check that the new position of the space is adjacent to the original tile position. We use the notion of *Manhattan distance*, horizontal plus vertical distance, to identify those tiles that are adjacent to the space. The Manhattan distance of two points is given by the following function:

```
mandist                    :: Position -> Position -> Int
mandist (x1,y1) (x2,y2) = abs (x1-x2) + abs (y1-y2)
```

Two tiles are adjacent if and only if their Manhattan distance is equal to one. For a given configuration, the list of configurations that can be reached in one move is obtained by placing the space at position i and indicating that tile i is now where the space was. These configurations can be generated using the following function:

```
allMoves   :: Board -> [Board]
allMoves b = [ b//[(0,b!i),(i,b!0)]
                | i<-[1..8], mandist (b!0) (b!i) == 1]
```

We are now in a position to define what constitutes a node in the search graph and the corresponding successor function. For reasons that will become clearer later, a node is represented by an algebraic type containing a list of board configurations. This list corresponds to the intermediate configurations from the initial configuration to the current configuration in reverse order.

```
data Boards        = BDS [Board]
```

The successor function generates the successors of a node by augmenting this list with all configurations that correspond to one move from the last board configuration. In addition, all successor nodes must be nodes that have not been encountered before. This involves checking all intermediate configurations against the proposed one (using a function notIn).

```
succ8Tile    :: Boards -> [Boards]
succ8Tile (BDS(n@(b:bs)))
              = filter (notIn bs) [ BDS(b':n) | b' <- allMoves b]
   where
     notIn bs (BDS(b:_)) = not (elem (elems b) (map elems bs))
```

A more efficient method would be to associate a unique number to each configuration so that checking equality between configurations just involves a comparison between their numbers.

8.2.2 The backtracking search higher-order function

When exploring the graph, each visited path can lead to the goal node with an equal chance. However, there could be a situation in which we know that the current path will not lead to the solution. In this case, we *backtrack* to the next level up the tree and try a different alternative. This process, similar to a depth-first graph traversal, is illustrated in Figure 8.3. Not all backtracking applications stop when the first goal node is reached; others work by selecting all valid solutions in the search space.

The following shows a backtracking search higher-order function which assumes an acyclic implicit graph. It has the same structure as the depthFirstSearch function presented in Section 7.3.2, except that since we are dealing with an implicit tree, successor nodes are now generated from the current node. Another difference is that there is no need to keep track of the traversed nodes nor test for cycles since we have assumed that the search graph is acyclic. This function returns all valid goal nodes, that is it continues to search for more goal nodes even after one goal node has been found.

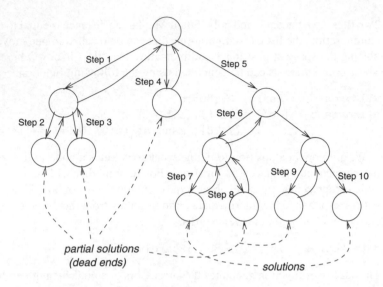

Figure 8.3 General stages in a backtracking algorithm.

The search can be made to terminate either when the first solution is found or when all alternatives have been explored. Lazy evaluation ensures that only the goal nodes which are required are computed.

```
searchDfs:: (Eq node) => (node -> [node]) -> (node -> Bool)
                                          -> node -> [node]
searchDfs succ goal x = search' (push x emptyStack)
 where
    search' s
      | stackEmpty s = []
      | goal (top s) = top s : search' (pop s)
      | otherwise    = let x = top s
                       in search' (foldr push (pop s) (succ x))
```

The rest of this section presents some applications of the backtracking search higher-order function.

8.2.3 The eight-tile problem

As an application of backtracking search, we consider the eight-tile game again. The representation of a node in the search tree and the successor function have already been described in Section 8.2.1, as well as the start and the goal node. To conduct a search, we need to define a goal function:

```
goal8Tile              :: Boards -> Bool
goal8Tile (BDS (n:_)) = elems n == elems g8T
```

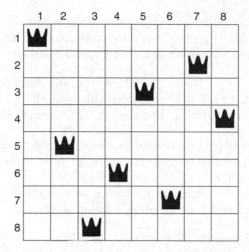

Figure 8.4 An example solution for the eight-queens problem.

Using the function succ8Tile defined earlier, a depth-first search that produces the first sequence of moves (in reverse order) that leads to the goal configuration can simply be expressed as:

```
dfs8Tile  :: [[Position]]
dfs8Tile  = map elems ls
 where ((BDS ls):_) = searchDfs succ8Tile goal8Tile (BDS [s8T])
```

Such a search is likely to take too much time because of the huge size of the graph. A more efficient version will be presented in Section 8.3.2.

8.2.4 The *n*-queens problem

This is another classic application of backtracking. The problem consists of finding an arrangement of n queens on an $n \times n$ chessboard, such that no queen threatens the other. Figure 8.4 shows one of such arrangements on an 8×8 chessboard.

A queen's placement on the chessboard is represented as a pair of column–row coordinates. A partial solution for $(i - 1)$ queens consists of a list containing the positions of these queens in the first $(i - 1)$ columns. To find a solution using backtracking search, a node in the search tree consists of the column number where the queen is to be put next, the size of the chessboard, and the partial solution:

```
type Column    = Int
type Row       = Int
type SolNq     = [(Column,Row)]

type NodeNq    = (Column,Column,SolNq)
```

We need an auxiliary function which, given a partial solution psol and a proposed assignment (c,r) returns True if the proposed assignment is valid (that is, the queen will not threaten any other queen in the partial solution):

```
valid               :: SolNQ -> (Column,Row) -> Bool
valid psol (c,r)    = and (map test psol)
    where test (c',r') = and [c'+r'/=c+r,c'-r'/=c-r,r'/=r]
```

There is no need to check if the proposed queen is on the same column as another queen because the proposed assignment will always be on a different column than all those in the partial solution.

Computing the successors of a node is achieved by generating all valid placements on the new column from the partial solution as follows:

```
succNq :: NodeNQ -> [NodeNQ]
succNq (c,n,psol)
    = [(c+1,n,psol++[(c,r)]) | r<-[1..n] , valid psol (c,r)]
```

Finally, the goal is reached when all columns have been placed:

```
goalNq :: NodeNQ -> Bool
goalNq (c,n,psol) = c > n
```

We are now in a position to define a function that returns the first valid placement of n queens:

```
firstNq    :: Column -> SolNQ
firstNq n = s
    where ((_,_,s):_) = searchDfs succNq goalNq (1,n,[])
```

The solution is contained in the first goal node found in the graph. As an example, consider the following execution for an 8×8 chessboard:

```
firstNq 8  ⇒  [(1,1),(2,5),(3,8),(4,6),(5,3),(6,7),(7,2),(8,4)]
```

Quite often in the n-queens problem, we are more interested in the number of solutions. In this case, the search proceeds until all alternatives have been explored. This is a variant of search called *exhaustive search*. The solution to this problem is expressed as follows:

```
countNq    :: Column -> Int
countNq n = length (searchDfs succNq goalNq (1,n,[]))
```

As an example, consider the number of solutions to the eight-queens problem:

```
countNq 8  ⇒  92
```

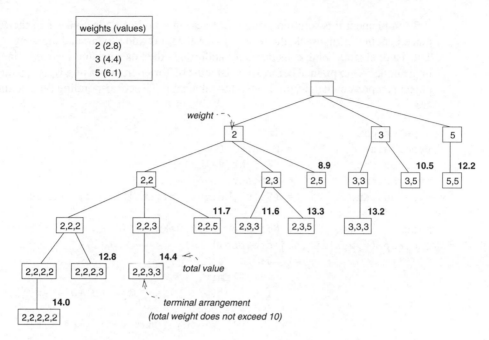

Figure 8.5   Example of building a search tree for the knapsack problem.

8.2.5   The knapsack problem†

This is another classic problem which can be solved using backtracking search. We suppose a knapsack with a fixed weight capacity w and a list of n objects to be placed in this knapsack. Each object i has a weight w_i and a value v_i ($1 \le i \le n$). Given the possibility of placing the same object more than once in the knapsack, the problem is to maximize the value of all the objects in the knapsack while not exceeding its capacity.

Solving the problem consists of building a search tree, where each node corresponds to a list of the objects already placed in the knapsack and the corresponding weight. From each node, the set of successor nodes contains those whose additional weight will not make the total weight exceed its capacity.

For example, consider a knapsack of capacity 10 and 3 objects of weight 2, 3, and 5, and of value 2.8, 4.4, and 6.1 respectively. Figure 8.5 shows a tree depicting all possible arrangements of the objects that lead to a weight equal or just below the maximum capacity. Starting from an empty knapsack, we have the choice of adding the objects of weights 2, 3, or 5. Having added the object 2, we have the choice between adding the object 2 again, or the object 3 or the object 5. Once an object has been included in the knapsack, we do not consider any object with a lesser weight for inclusion. For example, having added the object 3, we can only add the object 3 again or the object 5. The reason is to avoid repeated combinations such as {2,2,3} and {3,2,2}.

The leaves of the tree correspond to terminal arrangements where it is not possible to add any object without exceeding the maximum weight. We can see from the figure that the best arrangement is {2,2,3,3} with a combined value of 14.4.

To implement this solution using backtracking search, a node consists of the current placement in the knapsack, the weight so far, the total value so far, and the weight limit. The list of objects being considered for addition in the knapsack has also to be included in the node. As explained before, this list must be sorted in increasing weight value. An object is represented as a simple weight–value pair. The corresponding type definitions are:

```
type Weight        = Int
type Value         = Float
type Object        = (Weight,Value)
type SolKnp        = [Object]
type NodeKnp       = (Value,Weight,Weight,[Object],SolKnp)


succKnp            :: NodeKnp -> [NodeKnp]
succKnp (v,w,limit,objects,psol)
                   =[( v+v',
                       w+w',limit,
                       [ o | o@(w'',_) <- objects,(w''>=w')],
                       (w',v'):psol )
                     | (w',v') <- objects , w+w' <= limit]


goalKnp (_,w,limit,((w',_):_),_)
                   = (w+w'>limit)


knapsack           :: [Object] -> Weight -> (SolKnp,Value)
knapsack objects limit
                   = (sol,v)
  where
    (v,_,_,_,sol) = maximum (searchDfs succKnp goalKnp
                             (0,0,limit,qsort objects,[]))
```

As with counting the number of queens placements, the problem requires exhaustive search. Here is an example of executing the knapsack function:

```
knapsack [(2,2.8),(3,4.4),(5,6.1)] 10
   ⇒   ([(3,4.4),(3,4.4),(2,2.8),(2,2.8)] , 14.4)
```

8.2.6   Conclusion

Backtracking search is very demanding in time and space, especially when the search tree is very large. Determining the size of the tree in advance is difficult and has to be carried out on a case-by-case basis. For example, in the n-queens problem, there is a choice of n potential successors at every level in the search tree, the maximum depth of the tree being n, resulting in an $O(n^n)$ search tree. Simple backtracking search may terminate early if the solution is found quickly but in the worst case, it has the same complexity as exhaustive search which may be exponential.

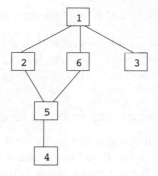

Figure 8.6 Example of a graph.

Backtracking search is particularly useful when designing game strategies. To model a game-playing situation, each level in the tree represents all possible moves a player can make and each node has some value denoting the goodness of the position reached. The strategy for a player is finding the path that leads to the best position. If the search tree is too large, which is often the case in games like chess, the search can stop at some predefined level.

There are other variations of the backtracking mechanism which aim at limiting the size of the search tree. One of them uses information to order candidate nodes according to the most promising node (priority-first search) and another limits the search to the immediate successors of a node (greedy search). Both will be considered in the rest of this chapter.

8.3 **Priority-first search**

Backtracking search as described so far can be referred to as *unguided* or *blind* search because there are no clues as to where the goal node is. Because of depth-first search, candidate nodes were examined in a last-in-first-out (LIFO) order but they could equally have been examined in a first-in-first-out (FIFO) order, that is breadth-first manner. Since the candidate nodes are examined in arbitrary order, the fastest solution occurs when the goal node very quickly finds its way to the front of the queue. If this happens, it will be a matter of luck rather than design. To arrange for the goal node to be examined as soon as possible, we can sort candidate nodes with the aim of placing the best candidate node, that is the candidate node that will lead soonest to the goal node, at the front of the queue.

This leads to a generalization of both depth-first and breadth-first search that consists of arranging candidate nodes into a *priority queue* instead of a stack or queue. This means that nodes are ordered according to some comparison operation, and the node with the highest priority or lowest cost is selected. This technique is called *priority-first search* or *best-first search*.

For example, supposing that nodes in the graph displayed in Figure 8.6 are ordered according to their own values, here are the various traversal orders starting from node 1:

depth-first search	$\Rightarrow$	`[1,2,5,4,6,3]`
breadth-first search	$\Rightarrow$	`[1,2,6,3,5,4]`
priority-first search	$\Rightarrow$	`[1,2,3,5,4,6]`

8.3.1   The priority-first search higher-order function

A priority-first search function can easily be derived from the function `searchDfs` given in Section 8.2.2 by replacing each stack ADT operation by its counterpart in the priority queue ADT. The resultant function is then:

```
searchPfs              :: (Ord node) => (node -> [node])
                          -> (node -> Bool) -> node -> [node]
searchPfs succ goal x = search' (enPQ x emptyPQ)
 where
   search' q
    | (pqEmpty q)      = []
    | goal (frontPQ q) = frontPQ q : search' (dePQ q)
    | otherwise        = let x = frontPQ q
                         in search' (foldr enPQ (dePQ q) (succ x))
```

This function assumes that there is an ordering between nodes such that the most promising node (that is, the 'smallest node') is placed at the front of the queue. Often, this means that an overloaded comparison operation (usually (`<=`)) must be defined over nodes. If there is no exact measure for ordering nodes, we might for a given problem be able to make a reasonable estimate. A procedure which gives us such an estimate is called a *heuristic*. A priority-first search program that uses a heuristic to order nodes in the priority queue is called a *heuristic search* program. A heuristic is a rule which does not guarantee to be correct but is nonetheless worth using if there is nothing better. We use a heuristic to estimate the cost of a given node: the lower the cost, the 'most promising' is the node.

Since the heuristic must be able to compare two nodes in the whole search space, this type of heuristic is called a global heuristic. Notice that the list of nodes to test may become quite large. We thus encounter a memory and time overhead for maintaining the priority queue.

Priority-first search, combined with the need to reduce the memory and time overhead, leads us to greedy or hill-climbing algorithms (see next section). These algorithms have a much lower memory and time overhead because they maintain a much smaller priority queue.

8.3.2   The eight-tile problem revisited

Section 8.2.3 presented a solution to the eight-tile problem using backtracking search. This section considers two heuristics for developing a more efficient solution based on priority-first search.

First heuristic

We can use Manhattan distance as the basis of a first heuristic for ordering the priority queue. To evaluate the cost of a path from the current node to the goal node we need to estimate how many moves will be required to transform the current node into the goal node. This is related to the distance each tile must travel to arrive at its destination, hence we sum the Manhattan distance of each square from its home position using the function heur1 defined below:

```
heur1    :: Board  -> Int
heur1 b = sum [ mandist (b!i) (g8T!i) | i<-[0..8]]
```

An overloaded comparison operation between nodes, based on this first heuristic, can now be defined as follows:

```
instance Ord Boards
   where BDS (b1:_) <= BDS (b2:_) = heur1 b1 <= heur1 b2
```

Since the Ord class is a subclass of the Eq class, we also need to define the equality operator over nodes:

```
instance Eq Boards
   where BDS(b1:_) == BDS(b2:_) = heur1 b1 == heur1 b2
```

Priority-first search can now be expressed in the same way as backtracking search but using searchPfs instead of searchDfs:

```
pfs8Tile  :: [[Position]]
pfs8Tile  = map elems ls
 where ((BDS ls):_) = searchPfs succ8Tile goal8Tile (BDS [s8T])
```

   Using this first heuristic, the goal node is reached after exploring 36 nodes. The solution returned solves the eight-tile puzzle in 25 moves.

Second heuristic

The first heuristic does not consider the fact that some tiles can be far from their final positions yet they are arranged in the right order. Therefore, an alternative heuristic should consider the number of tiles that are 'out-of-sequence'. An out of sequence score can be computed as follows:

- a tile in the center counts 1,
- a tile not in the center counts 0 if it is followed by its proper successor as defined by the goal arrangement,
- otherwise, a tile counts 2.

This can be implemented as follows:

```
outseq    :: Board -> Int
outseq b = sum [score (b!i) ((b!(i+1))) | i<-[1..7]]
             + score (b!8) (b!1)
```

```
score :: Position -> Position -> Int
score (2,2) _      = 1

score (1,3) (2,3)  = 0
score (2,3) (3,3)  = 0
score (3,3) (3,2)  = 0
score (3,2) (3,1)  = 0
score (3,1) (2,1)  = 0
score (2,1) (1,1)  = 0
score (1,1) (1,2)  = 0
score (1,2) (1,3)  = 0

score _ _          = 2
```

We can now combine this out-of-sequence score with the previous heuristic to produce a new heuristic function as described by Bratko [20]:

```
heur2 :: Board -> Int
heur2 l = (heur1 l)  + 3 * (outseq l)
```

To use this heuristic function, all we need is to change the overloaded definition of the comparison operator for nodes:

```
instance Eq Boards
   where BDS(b1:_) == BDS(b2:_) = heur2 b1 == heur2 b2
instance Ord Boards
   where BDS(b1:_) <= BDS(b2:_) = heur2 b1 <= heur2 b2
```

The search is invoked in exactly the same way as before. This time, the goal node is reached after 68 nodes have been explored but the corresponding solution solves the eight-tile puzzle in only 19 moves.

8.4 Greedy algorithms

We now move on to a variant of priority-first search. Instead of ordering all candidate nodes in the priority-queue, a *greedy* search always chooses what appears to be the best candidate node from the immediate successors of the current node, as illustrated in Figure 8.7. The crucial feature of a greedy algorithm, the thing that makes it greedy in fact, is that we commit ourselves to each step we take during the search.

Since only one path is explored during the search, greedy algorithms are very efficient. The greedy approach is also known as 'hill climbing', although a more accurate term would be 'hill descending'. Since at each stage we consider only the adjacent nodes to the current node, 'hill climbing' is rather like the limited vision available when descending a hill in fog. Always choosing the path which is locally down hill is no guarantee that you will reach the bottom of the hill. The search may get stuck at a local minimum. To find the optimal solution, it is necessary to climb out of the local minimum and explore new descents.

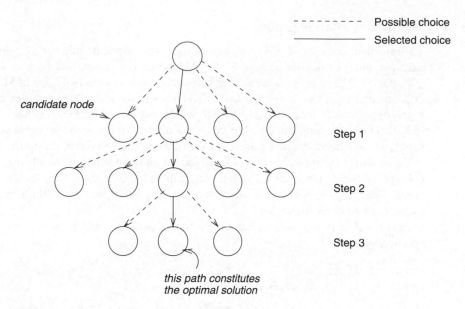

Figure 8.7   Successive stages in a greedy algorithm.

Only certain problems can be solved using the greedy or hill climbing approach. These are the problems where there is a representation that provides a search space in which there are no local minima. For some problems, it is difficult to find such a representation, for others, it is impossible. In such cases, a representation in which the local minima are almost as low and the absolute minimum may be adequate in the sense that any local minimum is a good approximate solution. In such a situation we have a heuristic algorithm.

8.4.1   The greedy higher-order function

A greedy search function can be easily adapted from the function searchPfs (see Section 8.3.1). All that is needed is to replace the expression (dePQ q) by emptyPQ in the recursive call to search' to 'flush out' old candidate nodes from the priority queue. The resultant function is then:

```
searchGreedy :: (Ord node) => (node -> [node]) -> (node -> Bool)
                                 -> node -> [node]
searchGreedy succ goal x     = (search' (enPQ x emptyPQ) )
   where search' q
            | pqEmpty q       = []
            | goal (frontPQ q) = [frontPQ q]
            | otherwise = let x = frontPQ q
                          in search' (foldr enPQ emptyPQ (succ x))
```

Note that in this case, at most one goal node is returned. The rest of this section examines some examples of greedy search.

8.4.2   The money change problem

This problem consists of giving money change with the least number of coins. For example, suppose that the amount $2.33 (233 cents) is to be handed back in $1, 50c, 20c, 10c, 5c, 2c and 1c coins, most of us can easily work it out as two coins of $1, one of 20c, one of 10c, one of 2c and one of 1c. The basis of the algorithm used is essentially a greedy approach because at every step, we choose the largest coin whose value is less than the remaining amount. For this particular set of coins and given an adequate supply of each denomination, the greedy approach always produces the optimal result.

Cases where the algorithm does not produce an optimal solution include the English coinage system before decimalization which included 30p, 24p, 12p, 6p, 3p and 1p coins. Changing 48p for instance leads to a solution with three coins (30p, 12p and 6p) instead of two coins (twice 24p).

In the rest of this section, we assume a list of coins for which there is an optimal solution such as:

```
coins :: [Int]
coins = [1,2,5,10,20,50,100]
```

A node in this case consists of the remaining amount of money and the partial solution (the coins that have been used so far).

```
type SolChange      = [Int]
type NodeChange     = (Int , SolChange)
```

The successor function generates all amounts by removing every possible coin from the remaining amount. An example of changing the amount 199 using the previously defined list of coins is illustrated in Figure 8.8.

The corresponding succCoins function is:

```
succCoins       :: NodeChange -> [NodeChange]
succCoins (r,p) = [ (r-c,c:p) | c <- coins , r - c >=0 ]
```

Finally the goal function is:

```
goalCoins       :: NodeChange -> Bool
goalCoins (v,_) = v==0
```

Nodes (of type NodeChange) are already ordered according to the first number in the tuple so there is no need to use overloading. Given an amount to be changed, the problem is solved as follows:

```
change         :: Int -> SolChange
change amount = snd (head (searchGreedy succCoins goalCoins
                                        (amount,[])))
```

The execution of the previous example proceeds as follows:

```
    change 199   ⇒   [2,2,5,20,20,50,100]
```

coins = [1,2,5,10,20,50,100]

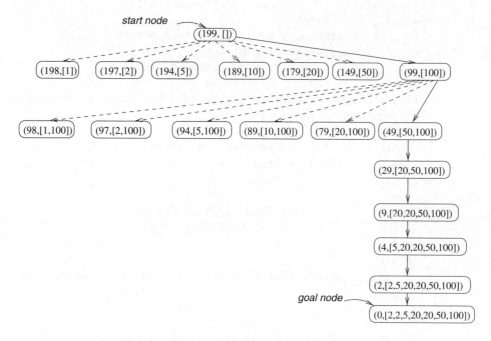

Figure 8.8 Computing money change using a greedy approach.

8.4.3 Prim's minimum spanning tree algorithm†

Some graph algorithms are also based on a greedy approach. As an example, Prim's minimum spanning tree algorithm can be expressed as a greedy search where nodes in the search tree contain the following information:

- the set T representing vertices included in the tree and the set R representing remaining vertices;
- the weight of the selected edge uv with $u \in T$ and $v \in R$;
- the partial solution, represented as a list of edges.

A node can thus be represented by the following type:

```
type NodeMst a b = (b , [a] ,[a], [(a,a,b)])
```

As before (see Section 7.5.2), we choose to represent the sets as lists. Nodes are ordered according to the weight of the selected edge which is the first component in the tuple. This way, the edge uv with the lowest cost is selected at every stage in the search. The successor function is defined as follows:

```
succMst :: (Ix a,Num b) => (Graph a b) -> (NodeMst a b)
                                      -> [(NodeMst a b)]
succMst g (_,t,r,mst)
      = [(weight x y g, (y:t), delete y r,
          (x,y,weight x y g):mst)
          | x <- t , y <- r, edgeIn g (x,y)]
```

The goal is reached when the list of remaining nodes is empty. Therefore, the problem can be expressed as follows:

```
goalMst            :: NodeMst a b -> Bool
goalMst (_,_,[],_) = True
goalMst _          = False

prim               :: (Num b, Ix a, Ord b)
                       => Graph a b -> [(a,a,b)]
prim g             = sol
   where
       [(_,_,_,sol)] = searchGreedy (succMst g) goalMst
                                   (0,[n],ns,[])

       (n:ns)        = nodes g
```

Note that the successor function takes an additional parameter (the graph) through the use of currying.

As an example, consider the following execution on the graph in Figure 7.4:

```
prim g  =>  [(2,4,55),(1,3,34),(2,5,32),(1,2,12)]
```

Exercises

8.1 Given a range of integers [1..h] and a predicate p of type Int -> Bool, the problem is finding the smallest integer within the specified range that satisfies the predicate p. We assume that p is a *monotonic* predicate, that is once it has become true for a value x, it stays true for all values y>x in the interval [1..h].

Solve this problem using the divide-and-conquer higher-order function.

8.2 Design a divide-and-conquer algorithm which, given a sorted list of numbers, builds a balanced binary search tree containing these numbers.

8.3 Repeat Exercise 5 in Chapter 6, which consists of defining a quicksort function with a threshold, using the divideAndConquer higher-order function.

8.4 Analyze and compare the efficiency of the version of the *n*-queens problem which returns the first solution (function firstNq) with the efficiency of the version which returns the number of solutions (function countNq).

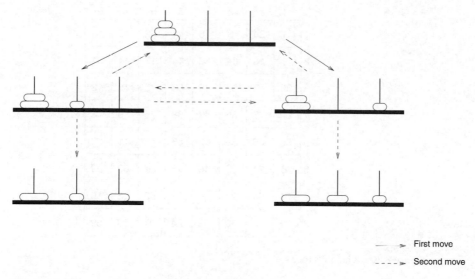

First move

Second move

Figure 8.9 Towers of Hanoi configurations after two moves.

8.5 The Towers of Hanoi problem can be expressed as follows: initially, three rings of different sizes are piled on a peg in order of size, with the largest at the bottom (see top of Figure 8.9). Given two empty pegs, the problem is moving all the rings to the third peg by moving one ring at a time and never placing a ring on top of a smaller one. Figure 8.9 shows all possible configurations after two moves.

Using backtracking search, develop a program that produces a sequence of moves that solves the problem.

8.6 Three missionaries and three cannibals are on the left side of the river and want to get to the other side. Crossing from one side of the river to another is achieved using a boat which can take one or two people only. The constraint is that the number of cannibals should never exceed the number of missionaries on either side of the river.

Using backtracking search, develop a program that produces a safe sequence of river crossings.

8.7 A knight's tour is a succession of knight's moves on a chessboard that starts and ends from the same position, visiting each position on the chessboard only once. For example, Figure 8.10 shows a sequence of moves that starts and ends from the top-left corner of the chessboard. Write a program that gives one valid solution to the knight's tour problem. A solution only exists if the size of the chessboard is even. There is a set of rules which can be used to find the solution faster. These rules are:

(a) At any point in the tour, if it is possible to move to the initial square and be in a dead-end situation, then the current tour should be abandoned because we will never be able to go back to the initial square.

	1	2	3	4	5	6	7	8
1	1	34	3	18	41	32	13	16
2	4	19	64	33	14	17	44	31
3	32	2	37	40	63	42	15	12
4	20	5	56	47	38	45	30	43
5	55	36	39	62	57	48	11	26
6	6	21	52	49	46	27	60	29
7	51	54	23	8	61	58	25	10
8	22	7	50	53	24	9	28	59

Figure 8.10   A knight's tour.

(b) If any of the successor squares leads to a position with one descendant only, we must move to that square, otherwise it would be cut off for a subsequent tour in the tour.

(c) At any point in the tour, if there is more than one move with one descendant, the current tour is abandoned because at least one descendant would become unreachable.

(d) If all successor moves have more than one descendant, the next move should correspond to the move with the smallest number of descendants.

The descendant of a move consists of subsequent moves to valid positions within the chessboard and positions that have not been traversed before.

8.8 Find a simple heuristic and give an approximate solution to the knapsack problem using a greedy search function. Under which conditions is the solution optimal?

8.9 Compute the shortest path from one vertex to all other vertices in the graph (see Exercise 8 of Chapter 7) using the greedy search function.

8.10 A simple topological sort algorithm, based on a greedy technique, works by associating a cost to each vertex, where this cost corresponds to the in-degree of that vertex such that vertices are included in the solution in increasing cost numbers. After selecting the vertex with the lowest cost, the in-degree of all its adjacent vertices must be decreased. Express this problem using the greedy search function.

8.5 Bibliographical notes

The idea of grouping classes of algorithms using higher-order functions is inspired from Cole's concept of *algorithmic skeletons* [28]. Divide-and-conquer applications are described in most algorithm textbooks [3, 5, 111]. For most efficiency, there is a technique to determine the optimal threshold (see Section 8.1.4) which is attributable to Brassard and Bratley [18].

Backtracking search and several of its variations are well-established methods in artificial intelligence and have been traditionally tackled with languages such as Lisp and Prolog [20, 25, 87, 89]. The eight-tile problem and its solutions are described by Bratko [20]. The exercise on the knight's tour is based on an algorithm described by Bornat [16] and implemented in Haskell by Hill [54].

There are numerous other examples of backtracking in the functional programming literature. Holyer [56] describes an expert system with a searching module which works using backtracking. Major, Lapalme and Cedergren [84] describe a class of problems called *constraint satisfaction problems* which can also be solved using several variations of the backtracking search mechanism. Two other notable references include Wadler [121] who describes a general implementation of backtracking similar to ours and Fokkinga [39] who presents a scheme for formal derivation of backtracking and branch-and-bound programs using transformations. Building parsers for grammars using a combination of higher-order functions is also a popular application of backtracking [35, 40, 64, 79, 97].

Edmonds introduced the idea of a greedy algorithm [34]. This type of algorithm is described in most algorithm textbooks (such as Horowitz and Sahni [58]). Thompson's textbook [115] expresses some greedy algorithms in a functional language.

Dynamic programming

The previous chapter described some top-down fundamental design techniques in which a problem was solved by breaking it down to smaller problems. This chapter now examines an alternative approach called *dynamic programming* which works in a 'bottom-up' fashion.

9.1 Introduction

First, we explain the motivation behind the dynamic programming approach. The main problem with top-down algorithms is that they may generate a large number of identical problem sub-instances. If these problems are solved separately, this can lead to a significant replication of work. A 'bottom-up' way to proceed would solve the smaller instances first, save their results and then use these intermediate results to solve the larger instances. This is the principle behind the *dynamic programming* approach.

As an example, consider the computation of the nth Fibonacci number expressed as a simple divide-and-conquer problem:

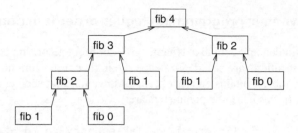

Figure 9.1   Divide-and-conquer computation of the Fibonacci numbers.

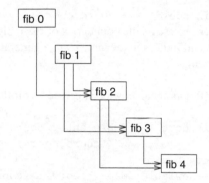

Figure 9.2   Dynamic programming computation of the Fibonacci numbers.

```
fib 0 = 0
fib 1 = 1
fib n = fib (n-1) + fib (n-2)
```

Figure 9.1 shows the recursive calls generated by the expression (fib 4) and the dependencies between them. We can see that the computation of (fib 2) is carried out twice, (fib 1) three times, and (fib 0) twice. Figure 9.2 shows a dynamic programming solution for computing the Fibonacci numbers where previously calculated numbers are reused in subsequent computations. The corresponding program will be described later.

A recurrence relation, which describes how to compute large problem instances from smaller ones, will be associated with every application. This relation must rely on a principle called the *principle of optimality* [19]. Informally, this principle states that a solution is optimal if it can be constructed using optimal subsolutions. Therefore, as with greedy algorithms (see Section 8.4), it is not always possible to formulate an optimal solution using the dynamic programming approach. Proofs that recurrence relations are determined according to the principle of optimality will be omitted.

The rest of this chapter describes a framework for defining dynamic programming algorithms. As with top-down algorithms, we define a higher-order function (we call it dynamic) which expects some problem-dependent parameters. Then, some dynamic programming applications are expressed using this function.

9.2 The dynamic programming higher-order function

The main concept behind a dynamic programming algorithm is that of a table in which partial solutions are saved. To define the higher-order function `dynamic`, we assume that this table contains entries of type `entry`, and that each entry has an index of type `coord`. In this case, the parameters are:

- `compute ::  (Ix coord) => Table entry coord -> coord -> entry`
  Given a table and an index, this function computes the corresponding entry in the table (possibly using other entries in the table).
- `bnds ::  (Ix coord) => (coord,coord)`
  This parameter represents the boundaries of the table. Since the type of the index is in the class `Ix`, all indices in the table can be generated from these boundaries using the function `range`.

The `dynamic` function can now be expressed as follows:

```
dynamic :: Ix coord => (Table entry coord -> coord -> entry)
                          -> (coord,coord) -> (Table entry coord)
dynamic compute bnds = t
    where t = newTable (map (\coord ->(coord,compute t coord))
                            (range bnds))
```

In this definition, we use the table ADT defined in Section 5.6. The `dynamic` function generates a table in which each entry consists of a closure containing a call to the `compute` function for all possible indices between the boundaries. Usually, there is one entry in the table which contains the solution. When this entry is requested, it triggers the evaluation of other entries which correspond to subsolutions. Once a subsolution has been computed, it is available in the table for other inspections. Because of lazy evaluation, only entries requested by the demanded solution will be computed.

For example, to compute the nth Fibonacci number, the following definitions are needed:

```
bndsFib :: Int -> (Int,Int)
bndsFib n = (0,n)

compFib                  :: Table Int Int -> Int -> Int
compFib t i | i<=1     = i
            |otherwise = findTable t (i-1) + findTable t (i-2)

fib :: Int -> Int
fib n = findTable t n
    where t = dynamic compFib (bndsFib n)
```

Note that currying has been used to make the second parameter of the `dynamic` function take an additional parameter.

Table 9.1   Number of multiplications required for every ordering.

Ordering	Number of multiplications required			
$((A_1A_2)A_3)A_4$	$30 \times 1 \times 40$	$+$ $\quad 30 \times 40 \times 10$	$+$ $\quad 30 \times 10 \times 25$	$= 20\,700$
$A_1(A_2(A_3A_4))$	$40 \times 10 \times 25$	$+$ $\quad 1 \times 40 \times 25$	$+$ $\quad 30 \times 1 \times 25$	$= 11\,750$
$(A_1A_2)(A_3A_4)$	$30 \times 1 \times 40$	$+$ $\quad 40 \times 10 \times 25$	$+$ $\quad 30 \times 40 \times 25$	$= 41\,200$
$A_1((A_2A_3)A_4)$	$1 \times 40 \times 10$	$+$ $\quad 1 \times 10 \times 25$	$+$ $\quad 30 \times 1 \times 25$	$= 1\,400$
$(A_1(A_2A_3))A_4$	$1 \times 40 \times 10$	$+$ $\quad 30 \times 1 \times 10$	$+$ $\quad 30 \times 10 \times 25$	$= 8\,200$

9.3 Chained matrix multiplications

This section describes our first problem which is finding the optimal ordering of chained matrix multiplications.

9.3.1 Description of the problem

Given an $m \times p$ matrix A and a $p \times n$ matrix B, their product AB is an $m \times n$ matrix P defined as:

$$p_{ij} = \sum_{k=1}^{p} a_{ik}b_{kj} \quad 1 \le i \le m, \ 1 \le j \le n$$

In total, this operation involves carrying out pnm multiplications. Suppose now that we have to multiply a sequence of matrices $A_1 A_2 \ldots A_n$ to get a matrix A. This operation can be carried out in several ways such as:

$$A = (\ldots ((A_1A_2)A_3) \ldots A_n)$$
$$A = (A_1(A_2(A_3 \ldots (A_{n-1}A_n) \ldots)))$$
$$A = ((A_1A_2)(A_3A_4)) \ldots ((A_{n-3}A_{n-2})(A_{n-1}A_n))$$

Two observations can be made. Firstly, we would obtain the same result regardless of the order in which the multiplications are done since matrix multiplication is associative. Secondly, the order of multiplying matrices can make an enormous difference to the amount of work to be done.

For example, consider the following matrices to be multiplied:

$$A_1 \ (30 \times 1), \ A_2 \ (1 \times 40), \ A_3 \ (40 \times 10), \ A_4 \ (10 \times 25)$$

Table 9.1 shows the number of multiplications needed for every possible ordering. We can see that the most efficient ordering $(A_1((A_2A_3)A_4))$ is almost 30 times faster than the slowest ordering $(A_1A_2)(A_3A_4)$. Therefore, the chained matrix multiplications problem consists of finding the optimal way of ordering matrix multiplications which minimizes the total number of multiplications required.

9.3.2 The algorithm

First, we try to develop a divide-and-conquer algorithm to solve the problem. We define $c_{i,j}$ as the minimum number of multiplications required for multiplying the sequence

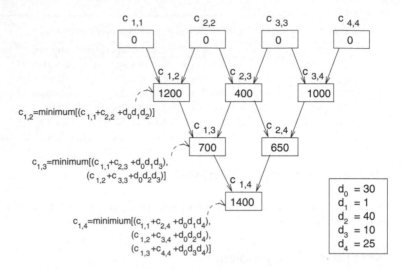

Figure 9.3 Chained matrix multiplication using dynamic programming.

of matrices $A_i \ldots A_j$ (where $1 \leq i \leq j \leq n$) so that $c_{1,n}$ represents the solution of the problem. Assuming that each matrix A_i has dimensions $d_{i-1} \times d_i$, the recurrence relation for finding the value of $c_{i,j}$ is:

$$
\begin{aligned}
c_{i,i} &= 0 \\
c_{i,j} &= \min_{i \leq k \leq j-1} (c_{i,k} + c_{k+1,j} + d_{i-1}d_k d_j)
\end{aligned}
\tag{9.1}
$$

The first case simply states that the cost of multiplying the sequence A_i is 0 since no multiplications take place. In the general case (that is, a sequence $A_i \ldots A_j$ of more than one matrix), we operate an arbitrary split at every possible position k (that is, from i to $j-1$) and select the minimum cost. Each cost is obtained by adding three terms: the first one is the cost of multiplying the sequence $A_i \ldots A_k$ (returning a matrix of dimension $d_{i-1} \times d_k$) which is $c_{i,k}$; the second one is the cost of multiplying $A_{k+1} \ldots A_j$ (returning a matrix of dimension $d_k \times d_j$) which is $c_{k+1,j}$; the third one is the cost of multiplying the two matrices together which involves of $d_{i-1}d_k d_j$ multiplications.

Writing a recursive function to compute the values of c using Relation (9.1) would be extremely inefficient and would involve redundant computations since subproblems 'overlap'. The complexity of such a function would be exponential. It would be better to store the values of c for small intervals and reuse them for computing the values of c for large intervals.

For the previous example with $d_0 = 30, d_1 = 1, d_2 = 40, d_3 = 10, d_4 = 25$, the calculation will proceed as shown in Figure 9.3.

9.3.3 The program

In this implementation, each table entry of index (i, j) contains a tuple where the first component is the value $c_{i,j}$, and where the second component is the optimal value of the split *k* which needs to be remembered so that the optimal ordering can be displayed. The corresponding type definitions are:

```
type CmmCoord   = (Int,Int)
type CmmEntry   = (Int,Int)
```

Given a table t, the function that computes an entry of coordinates (i,j) can be directly derived from Relation (9.1):

```
compCmm           :: [Int] -> Table CmmEntry CmmCoord -> CmmCoord
                     -> CmmEntry
compCmm d t (i,j)
  | (i==j)       = (0,i)
  | otherwise    = minimum [( fst(findTable t (i,k))
                            + fst(findTable t (k+1,j))
                            + d!!(i-1) * d!!k * d!!j   ,   k)
                            | k <- [i..j-1]]
```

Here we have again assumed that the minimum function operates on tuples by ordering them according to the first component.

Given the final table t and an interval (i,j), one way of displaying the ordering of multiplications $A_i \ldots A_j$ is to use the following function:

```
solCmm :: Table CmmEntry CmmCoord -> CmmCoord -> ShowS
solCmm :: Table CmmEntry CmmCoord -> CmmCoord -> ShowS
solCmm t (i,j) str =
    let (_,k) = findTable t (i,j)
    in if i==j
        then showChar 'A' (shows i str)
        else showChar '('
               (solCmm t (i,k)
               (showChar ','
                (solCmm t (k+1,j)
                (showChar ')' str))))
```

We use here the showChar function (see Section 5.2) to efficiently build a string describing the ordering of multiplications. The remaining definitions for computing the optimal ordering of chained matrix multiplications are:

```
bndsCmm           :: Int -> ((Int,Int),(Int,Int))
bndsCmm n         = ((1,1),(n,n))


cmm    :: [Int] -> (String , Int)
cmm p = (solCmm t (1,n) "" , fst (findTable t (1,n)))
    where n = (length p) - 1
          t = dynamic (compCmm p) (bndsCmm n)
```

For example, executing this function on the example described earlier gives the following result:

```
cmm [30,1,40,10,25]
    ⇒   ("(A1,((A2,A3),A4))",1400)
```

9.3.4   Efficiency of the program

First, the efficiency depends on the table ADT implementation. If we assume an efficient implementation with a constant $O(1)$ access time, we need to know precisely how many times the compCmm function is called. Considering the table as an $n \times n$ matrix, we can observe that entries are computed diagonal by diagonal. At any diagonal d, there are $(n - d)$ entries that need to be computed. Each entry requires $O(d)$ steps to be computed because there are d entries inspected by the minimum function. Therefore, the time required for the entire problem is in $O(n^3)$. Although this is a cubic order of efficiency, it is still an improvement over the top-down approach which leads to an exponential execution time.

As for space efficiency, the accumulated space usage is in $O(n^3)$ and the largest space is in $O(n^2)$ which corresponds to the size of the table.

9.4   Optimal binary search trees

The next problem consists of finding the best arrangement for a list of keys in a binary search tree.

9.4.1   Description of the problem

Binary search trees have been described in Chapter 5 (see Section 5.7). One of their particular characteristics is that there are many ways of organizing the keys in the tree. Figure 9.4 shows three ways in which to arrange the keys 1, 3, 4, 8, 10, 11, 15 in a binary search tree.

We suppose that a probability of access $p(i)$ is associated with each key K_i, as the example in Table 9.2 illustrates. We define t_i as the number of comparisons needed to find a particular key K_i in a given tree. Returning to Figure 9.4, we can see that in the first tree, the key with the highest probability of being accessed is placed in the root node. The second one is a balanced search tree. The third one is just another way of arranging the keys. To find the key 4 for example, we need to perform three comparisons in the first tree, three comparisons in the second tree and one comparison in the third tree.

We define the average number of comparisons for all keys in a tree T as:

$$a(T) = \sum_{i=1}^{n} p_i t_i$$

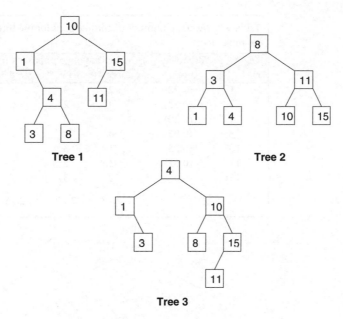

Figure 9.4 Three possible binary search trees from the same set of keys.

Table 9.2 A list of keys and their probabilities of access.

Key (K_i)	Probability (p_i)
1	0.22
3	0.18
4	0.20
8	0.05
10	0.25
11	0.02
15	0.08

The problem is finding the optimal binary search tree which corresponds to the smallest value of a. For example, the values of the function a for the three trees in Figure 9.4 are displayed in Table 9.3. It can be seen that tree 3 is an optimal binary search tree because it has the minimum average number of comparisons.

9.4.2 The algorithm

Using the same approach as in the previous problem, the dynamic programming solution to this problem is derived from its divide-and-conquer equivalent.

Let $c_{i,j}$ be the minimum value of $a(T)$ where T contains the sorted sequence of keys $K_i \ldots K_j$. To determine $c_{i,j}$, the sequence $K_i \ldots K_j$ is split into a binary tree whose root is K_k, whose left subtree contains $K_i \ldots K_{k-1}$ and right subtree contains

Table 9.3 Average number of comparisons for the three example trees.

| Key K_i | (Probability p_i) | Number of comparisons (t_i) | | |
		Tree 1	Tree 2	Tree 3
1	(0.22)	2	3	2
3	(0.18)	4	2	3
4	(0.20)	3	3	1
8	(0.05)	4	1	3
10	(0.25)	1	3	2
11	(0.02)	3	2	4
15	(0.08)	2	3	3
	a(T)	2.43	2.70	2.15

Figure 9.5 Building a binary search tree for the sorted sequence $K_i \ldots K_j$.

$K_{k+1} \ldots K_j$ (see Figure 9.5). The recurrence relation for computing $c_{i,j}$ is:

$$
\begin{aligned}
c_{i,j} &= 0 & ,i > j \\
c_{i,j} &= p_i & ,i = j \\
c_{i,j} &= \min_{i \leq k \leq j} \left[(c_{i,k-1} + \textstyle\sum_{l=i}^{k-1} p_l) + (c_{k+1,j} + \sum_{l=k+1}^{j} p_l) + p_k \right] & ,i < j
\end{aligned}
$$

The first line shows that the searching time for empty subtrees is 0. The second line states that the searching time for a tree with one node containing K_i is $1 \times p_i$ since the number of comparisons is always 1. The third line states that the searching time of a binary search tree containing keys $K_i \ldots K_j$ is the minimum searching time of all possible binary search trees obtained by moving the splitting point k from i to j. The value of $c_{i,j}$ is obtained by increasing the access time for all keys in the left tree and in the right tree by 1, then adding $1 \times p_k$ which corresponds to the root node.

The third line can be simplified by summing all the probabilities together and moving them out of the minimum function since they represent a constant value. Therefore, the new set of recurrence relations is:

$$
\begin{aligned}
c_{i,j} &= 0 & ,i > j \\
c_{i,j} &= p_i & ,i = j \\
c_{i,j} &= \min_{i \leq k \leq j} \left(c_{i,k-1} + c_{k+1,j} \right) + \textstyle\sum_{l=i}^{j} p_l & ,i < j
\end{aligned}
\qquad (9.2)
$$

As in the previous problem, using a recursive function to compute the values of c would take an exponential time. A better approach, which uses dynamic programming, stores values of c in a table and reuses them in subsequent computations.

9.4.3   The program

In this implementation, the keys are of type Int and their probabilities are of type Float. An entry in the table consists of the cost $c_{i,j}$ as defined previously and the optimal value of k. The corresponding definitions are:

```
type ObstCoord  = (Int,Int)
type ObstEntry  = (Float,Int)
```

Once again, the function that computes an entry in the table can be directly derived from Relation (9.2):

```
sumfromto        :: Int -> Int-> Array Int Float -> Float
sumfromto i j p = sum [p!l | l<-[i..j]]


compObst :: Array Int Float -> Table ObstEntry ObstCoord
            -> ObstCoord -> ObstEntry
compObst p c (i,j)
   | i > j     = (0.0,0)
   | i==j      = (p!i,i)
   | otherwise = addfst (minimum [(fst(findTable c (i,k-1))
                                    + fst(findTable c (k+1,j)) , k)
                                   | k <- [i..j]] )
                        (sumfromto i j p)
                    where addfst (x,y) z = (x+z,y)
```

The final solution is a tuple where the first component is the optimal tree T and the second component is the optimal value $a(T)$. The function that determines the optimal tree from the table can be expressed as:

```
data BinTree a = EmptyBT
               | NodeBT a (BinTree a) (BinTree a) deriving Show

solObst :: Array Int Int -> Table ObstEntry ObstCoord
           -> ObstCoord -> BinTree Int
solObst keys c (i,j)
         | i > j     = EmptyBT
         | i == j    = NodeBT key EmptyBT EmptyBT
         | otherwise = NodeBT key (solObst keys c (i,k-1))
                                  (solObst keys c (k+1,j))
         where (_,k) = findTable c (i,j)
               key   = keys ! k
```

Finally, the remaining definitions are:

```
bndsObst   :: Int -> ((Int,Int),(Int,Int))
-- these range should be ((1,n),(1,n)) but in compObst
-- indices (i,k-1) and (k+1,j) are needed i<= k <= j
```

```
-- adding a supplementary a row and column simplifies
-- testing for the boundary conditions
bndsObst n     = ((1,0),(n+1,n))


obst           :: [Int] -> [Float]  -> (BinTree Int,Float)
obst keys ps = (solObst keysA t (1,n) , fst (findTable t (1,n)))
    where n    = length ps
          keysA= listArray (1,n) keys
          psA  = listArray (1,n) ps
          t    = dynamic (compObst psA) (bndsObst n)
```

The (pretty-printed) result of applying the function to the example of Table 9.2 is:

```
obst [ 1, 3, 4, 8, 10, 11, 15]
       [0.22,0.18,0.20,0.05,0.25,0.02,0.08]
   ⇒   (Node 4 (Node 1 Empty
                      (Node 3 Empty Empty))
             (Node 10 (Node 8 Empty Empty)
                      (Node 15 (Node 11 Empty Empty)
                               Empty)),
       2.15)
```

This corresponds to Tree 3 in Table 9.3 and Figure 9.4.

9.4.4   Efficiency of the program

The table is built in exactly the same fashion as in the previous problem (diagonal by diagonal). The number of steps required is also in $O(n^3)$ which is also an improvement over the exponential complexity of the divide-and-conquer algorithm. The accumulated space is also in $O(n^3)$ and the largest space in $O(n^2)$.

9.5 All-pairs shortest path

9.5.1   Description of the problem and the algorithm

Given an undirected graph, the problem is to compute all shortest paths from any vertex i to any vertex j. In other words, we need to compute a two-dimensional matrix where an entry of index (i, j) represents the shortest path from vertex i to vertex j. For example, Figure 9.6 shows a graph and its shortest paths matrix. Since the graph is undirected, only half of the matrix is computed (the shortest path from i to j is the same as the shortest path from j to i).

To develop the dynamic programming solution, we assume that $c_{i,j}$ represents the minimum cost between vertices i and j. We also assume that the weight function (denoted $w_{i,j}$) is defined for every pair of vertices i and j. This can be easily achieved by considering the equalities $w_{i,j} = 0$ if $(i = j)$ and $w_{i,j} = \infty$ if the edge ij does not exist. The solution of the problem can now be expressed using the following recurrence

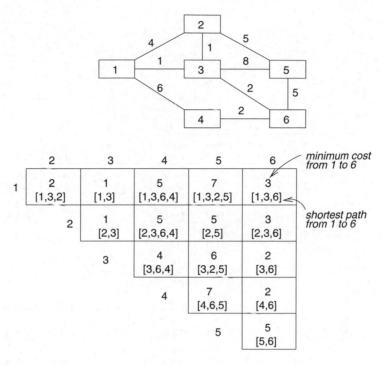

Figure 9.6 Computing all-pairs shortest paths in a graph.

relation:

$$c_{i,j}^{0} = w_{i,j}$$
$$c_{i,j}^{k} = \min c_{i,j}^{k-1}\left(c_{i,k}^{k-1} + c_{k,j}^{k-1}\right) \tag{9.3}$$

This algorithm is known as *Floyd's algorithm*. Starting from the weights of the edges, the values c are built progressively through a series of iteration steps, each step being referred to by an index k. We can see that computing the values at the kth iteration depends on values computed at the $(k-1)^{th}$ iteration. The final result is obtained at iteration n where n is the number of vertices in the graph. Figure 9.7 shows some of the intermediate values of the c matrix during the execution of the algorithm.

9.5.2   The program

A simple implementation of Floyd's algorithm uses a three-dimensional table to store the values of c for the indices i, j, and k. An entry at position (i, j, k) is a tuple consisting of the cost of the shortest path $c_{i,j}^{k}$ (an integer) and a list containing the shortest path from i to j at this iteration. The corresponding type definitions are:

```
type AspCoord   = (Int,Int,Int)
type AspEntry   = (Int,[Int])
```

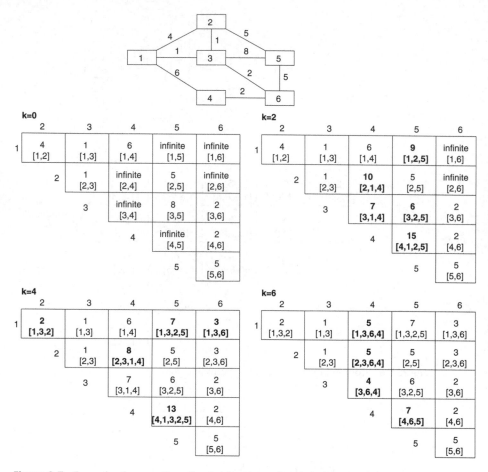

Figure 9.7 Example of computing all-pairs shortest paths through successive steps.

The function that computes an entry in the table according to Relation (9.3) is:

```
compAsp          :: (Graph Int Int) -> Table AspEntry AspCoord
                    -> AspCoord -> AspEntry
compAsp g c (i,j,k)
    | k==0    = (weight i j g , if i==j then [i] else [i,j])
    | otherwise = let (v1,p)   = findTable c (i,j,k-1)
                      (a,p1)   = findTable c (i,k,k-1)
                      (b,_:p2) = findTable c (k,j,k-1)
                      v2 = a+b
                  in if v1<=v2 then (v1,p) else (v2,p1++p2)
```

In this definition, we have made use of the `weight` graph ADT operation (see Section 7.2). The rest of the program is similar to all other problems, the result being a list of the form `((i,j),(c,l))` where `c` is the cost of the shortest path `l` between `i` and `j`:

```
bndsAsp    :: Int -> ((Int,Int,Int),(Int,Int,Int))
bndsAsp n = ((1,1,0),(n,n,n))


asp    :: (Graph Int Int) -> [ ((Int,Int) , AspEntry) ]
asp g = [ ((i,j) , findTable t (i,j,n)) | i<-[1..n], j<-[i+1..n]]
   where n = length (nodes g)
         t = dynamic (compAsp g) (bndsAsp n)
```

Assuming that the graph displayed in Figure 9.6 is referred to as graphEx, here is an example of executing this program:

```
asp graphEx
  ⇒   [((1,2),(2,[1,3,2])),  ((1,3),(1,[1,3])),
        ((1,4),(5,[1,3,6,4])),  ((1,5),(7,[1,3,2,5])),
        ((1,6),(3,[1,3,6])),  ((2,3),(1,[2,3])),
        ((2,4),(5,[2,3,6,4])),  ((2,5),(5,[2,5])),
        ((2,6),(3,[2,3,6])),  ((3,4),(4,[3,6,4])),
        ((3,5),(6,[3,2,5])),  ((3,6),(2,[3,6])),
        ((4,5),(7,[4,6,5])),  ((4,6),(2,[4,6])),
        ((5,6),(5,[5,6]))]
```

9.5.3 Efficiency of the program

In this problem, the time efficiency is also in $O(n^3)$. Since a three-dimensional structure is used, the accumulated as well as the largest space efficiency are both in $O(n^3)$. This is very space inefficient since entries at dimension k only require entries at dimension $(k-1)$ to be computed. A version, based on destructive updating, can perform all the computations in a two-dimensional table reducing the largest space to $O(n^2)$.

9.6 The traveling salesperson

9.6.1 Description of the problem and the algorithm

This is a classic graph theory problem where, given a weighted graph in which vertices represent cities and edges represent distances between cities, a traveling salesperson has to visit each city exactly once and come back to the starting town. The problem is finding the shortest route, that is the route whose cost is minimum. Figure 9.8 shows an example of a graph and its shortest route starting and ending in vertex 6. This problem arises naturally in a number of important applications and has been studied quite intensively.

We assume that the graph is denoted $G = \langle V, E \rangle$ where V is the set of vertices $1, 2, \ldots, n$ and that the weight of an edge connecting i to j is denoted $w_{i,j}$. As in the previous problem, we assume that $w_{i,j} = 0$ if $(i = j)$ and $w_{i,j} = \infty$ if the edge ij does not exist. Finally, we assume that the starting and ending vertex is always the last vertex n.

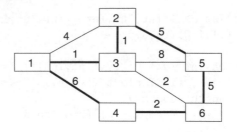

shortest tour starting from 6 = [6,4,1,3,2,5,6]
(cost=20)

Figure 9.8   Example of a shortest tour.

The algorithm for solving the traveling salesperson problem is derived from the following argument: assume that the cost $c_{i,S}$ is associated with the shortest route starting from i, going through all vertices in the set S and ending up in n, the recurrence relation to determine the values of c is:

$$c_{i,\emptyset} = w_{i,n} \qquad\qquad\qquad i \neq n$$
$$c_{i,S} = min_{j \in S}\, [w_{i,j} + c_{j,S\setminus\{j\}}] \quad i \neq n,\ i \notin S$$

(9.4)

where $\emptyset$ denotes the empty set and $\setminus$ the set difference operator.

The shortest path $c_{i,S}$ is constructed by computing the minimum of the shortest path $c_{j,S\setminus\{j\}}$ plus the weight $w_{i,j}$ of the edge ij. The shortest distance between a vertex i and the final vertex n without passing through any intermediate vertex is simply $w_{i,n}$.

Therefore, the solution of the problem is simply $c_{n,A\setminus\{n\}}$ since it is the shortest distance starting from n, going through all remaining vertices in A and ending up in n.

9.6.2   The program

To construct the program, each entry in the table is indexed by both a vertex (which we assume is an integer) and a set of vertices. Therefore, we need a set representation in which each set would be associated with a unique index. To this effect, we can use the same algorithms as the ones used in the bit representation of the set ADT (see Section 5.5.3). We cannot use this ADT directly because this would violate the fundamental assumption that an ADT be independent of its concrete representation. This is why we give here a new and simplified implementation of a set that can also be used as an integer for indexing in the table.

```
type Set = Int

emptySet = 0

setEmpty n = n==0
```

```
fullSet n | (n>=0) && (n<=maxSet) = 2^(n+1)-2
                                   -- element 0 is not there...
          | otherwise = error ("fullset:illegal set =" ++ show n)


addSet i s = d'*e+m
    where (d,m) = divMod s e
          e  = 2^i
          d' = if odd d then d else d+1

delSet i s = d'*e+m
    where (d,m) = divMod s e
          e  = 2^i
          d' = if odd d then d-1 else d

set2List s = s2l s 0
    where s2l 0 _              = []
          s2l n i | odd n      = i : s2l (n 'div' 2) (i+1)
                  | otherwise  = s2l (n 'div' 2) (i+1)

maxSet = truncate (logBase 2 (fromInt (maxBound::Int))) - 1
```

An entry in the table is a tuple which consists of the value *c* (of type Int) and the corresponding shortest path (a list of vertices). We are now in a position to define the types required for our problem:

```
type TspCoord      = (Int,Set Int)
type TspEntry      = (Int,[Int])
```

Assuming a graph g and a starting vertex n, the function that computes an entry in the table is derived from Relation (9.4):

```
compTsp :: Graph Int Int -> Int -> Table TspEntry TspCoord
                         -> TspCoord -> TspEntry
compTsp g n a (i,k)
    | setEmpty k = (weight i n g,[i,n])
    | otherwise = minimum [ addFst (findTable a (j, delSet j k))
                                   (weight i j g)
                          | j <- set2List k]
    where addFst (c,p) w = (w+c,i:p)
compTsp        :: Graph Int Int -> Int -> Table TspEntry TspCoord
```

The remaining definitions are:

```
bndsTsp    :: Int -> ((Int,Set),(Int,Set))
bndsTsp n  =  ((1,emptySet),(n,fullSet n))

tsp    :: Graph Int Int -> (Int,[Int])
```

```
tsp g = findTable t (n,fullSet (n-1))
    where n = length (nodes g)
          t = dynamic (compTsp g n) (bndsTsp n)
```

If the graph displayed in Figure 9.8 is referred to as `graphEx`, here is an example of executing the program:

```
tsp graphEx  ⇒  (20,[6, 4, 1, 3, 2, 5, 6])
```

9.6.3   Efficiency of the program

Since we need 2^n values to represent all sets of up to n items, the size of the table is in $O(n2^n)$. Each entry requires up to n steps to be computed so the algorithm's efficiency is in $O(n^2 2^n)$ which seems considerable. However, there is no other efficient algorithm to solve this problem and the dynamic programming approach leads to a reasonably good performance for small graphs.

9.7 Conclusion

This chapter examined a class of algorithms which use a bottom-up approach to solve problems that generate several identical subproblem instances. By saving the subsolutions into a table, this technique can result in a significant improvement in efficiency, usually from an exponential time to a polynomial time. The main limitation of this approach is that it does not always lead to the optimal solution. We have not discussed optimality conditions, limiting ourselves to presenting the appropriate recurrence relations and deriving programs from them.

Compared to imperative solutions, functional versions have two distinct advantages. First, they can be expressed in a very simple framework, where the recurrence relation can be directly translated into a parameter function (the function that computes an entry in the table). Second, there is no need to specify the order in which entries in the table are specified: lazy evaluation allows each entry to be defined and only computed if it is needed. Imperative versions usually involve finding a suitable ordering of the indices to make sure an entry in the table is only accessed after it has been defined and possibly updated.

Exercises

9.1 Develop a program based on the dynamic programming technique to compute binomial coefficients. The binomial coefficient $c_{n,k}$ is defined by the following recurrence relation:

$$
\begin{array}{lll}
c_{n,k} & = & 1 & , \; k = 0 \text{ or } k = n \\
c_{n,k} & = & c_{n-1,k-1} + c_{n-1,k} & , \; 0 < k < n \\
c_{n,k} & = & 0 & , \; \text{otherwise}
\end{array}
$$

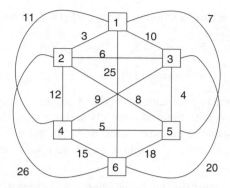

Figure 9.9 Example graph.

9.2 In the chained matrix multiplication problem, show that a divide-and-conquer implementation based on Relation (9.1) has an exponential complexity.

9.3 Given a graph of n vertices, all-pairs shortest paths can also be computed using an algorithm that computes the shortest path from one vertex to all other vertices in the graph (see Exercise 8 of Chapter 7) repeated n times.

Compare the efficiency of this algorithm with Floyd's algorithm for dense and sparse graphs.

9.4 Using the function `tsp` developed in Section 9.6.2, find the shortest tour of the graph displayed in Figure 9.9.

9.5 The traveling salesperson problem can be tackled using a greedy approach. At each step, we choose the smallest edge providing:

(a) it does not form a cycle with the edges already selected, except for the very last edge which completes the salesperson's tour;

(b) it will not be the third selected edge incident on some node.

Using a counter-example, show that this approach does not lead to the optimal solution.

9.6 Given a sequence of n distinct integers, the problem is to find the longest increasing subsequence of integers (not necessarily consecutive). For example, if the sequence is $[21,27,15,18,16,14,17,22,13]$, the longest subsequence is $[15,16,17,22]$.

Develop a dynamic programming solution for this problem and implement it using the `dynamic` higher-order function.

9.7 Consider a slightly modified version of the knapsack problem (see Section 8.2.5) where an object cannot be inserted in the knapsack more than once. Given a list of objects of values v_i and weights w_i ($1 \le i \le n$) and a weight limit w, we define a cost function $c_{i,j}$ where $(0 \leq i \leq n)$ and $(-w < j < w)$ as follows:

$$
\begin{aligned}
c_{i,j} &= -\infty && , j < 0 \\
c_{0,j} &= 0 && , j \geq 0 \\
c_{i,j} &= \max_{i,j}(c_{i-1,j-w_i} + v_i)\, c_{i-1,j} && , \text{otherwise}
\end{aligned}
$$

The term $c_{i,j}$ corresponds to the maximum value obtained if we had to solve the problem with the first i objects and a weight limit j. The first two equations correspond to boundary conditions. In the third equation, we choose between adding i and not adding i in the knapsack depending on the highest value obtained.

The optimal value in the knapsack corresponds to $c_{n,w}$. Develop a function, based on the dynamic programming technique, that returns this optimal value as well as the corresponding list of objects to be included in the knapsack. Contrast the efficiency of this function with the backtracking search version.

9.8 Bibliographical notes

Dynamic programming has its origins in the work of Bellman [8] and Bellman and Dreyfus [9]. Chained matrix multiplication is described in Godbole [43], the optimal search trees solution comes from Gilbert and Moore [41], the all-pairs-shortest-paths algorithm and the traveling salesperson are respectively from Floyd [38] and Held and Karp [53]. All these problems and their imperative implementation are described in most algorithms textbooks, notably by Brassard and Bratley [19]. In the context of functional languages, Hartel and Glaser [51] describe a dynamic programming implementation of a particular problem based on a technique similar to the one presented in this chapter.

Advanced topics

This last chapter examines some advanced concepts related to the development of complex applications using functional languages. The first section introduces *process networks* which allow the definition of concurrent systems. The next section describes the concept of *monads* and demonstrates their usefulness on some of the algorithms described in previous chapters. Finally, the last section introduces *parallel algorithms* and shows how some fundamental design techniques are 'naturally' parallel. Some Haskell extensions, which allow a better support for these concepts, are also discussed.

10.1 Process networks

10.1.1 Description

We first consider a class of algorithms in which the computation is divided into several independent entities that are (at least conceptually) running concurrently or simultaneously. We call such entities *processes*. As these processes usually communicate by exchanging messages through *channels*, the resulting program is often referred to as a *process network*. Another way of looking at these systems is as a graph of nodes, each node being a process and each edge representing data flowing between the nodes, hence the name *data flow graphs*.

As an example, consider a sorting process network, based on the mergesort algorithm (see Section 6.3.4), which consists of a tree of processes. Each process in the network implements a merge operation (see Section 6.3.4). A leaf process merges two lists each containing a single element from the original list and the last process produces the

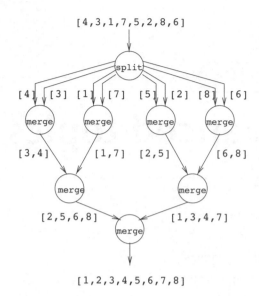

Figure 10.1   Sorting with a tree of merge operations.

sorted list. An example of sorting a list of eight items is illustrated in Figure 10.1. The figure also shows that an additional process is needed to split the input list into single lists.

Although these problems can easily be defined as (sequential) functional programs, the main reasons for showing their process network nature are:

- In more complex applications, the use of concurrency allows a *modular* approach in the design of the algorithm. Such applications include graphical user interfaces and real-time embedded systems, where it is often easier to design the processes separately, then provide the interaction between the processes later.
- Identifying distinct processes gives the opportunity to execute every process on a separate processor, thus the program can be made to run faster.

The rest of this section discusses the implementation of process networks in a functional programming context.

10.1.2   A higher-order function for arbitrary process networks

A simple implementation of process networks uses a list processing function to simulate each process and a lazy list (called a *stream*) to implement each channel. The network is defined by giving a name to every channel and defining a set of local definitions in which output channels are expressed as a result of applying process functions on the input channels. Feedback loops are possible because streams are lazy lists, computing their elements on demand.

We now consider a higher-order function for an arbitrary static process network, attributed to Kelly and his group [29, 70]. We assume that each process reads its input from a list of channels and delivers its outputs to another list of channels. All channels carry items of the same type denoted a. The corresponding type declarations are:

```
type Channel a = [a]
type Process a = [Channel a] -> [Channel a]
```

The processNetwork higher-order function, which defines arbitrary process networks, requires the following parameters:

```
ps ::  [Process a]
```
This is the list of processes in the network.

```
ct ::  Table [(Int,Int)] Int
```
This is a *connection table* which records the connections between the processes. The Table ADT was defined in Section 5.6.

The connection table has one entry for every process p_i ($1 \leq i \leq n$). This entry contains a list of pairs of integers. A pair of the form (p_j, o_j) means that process p_i reads from the o_jth output of process p_j. For a given process p_i, the list of pairs must be presented in the same order as in the list of input streams in the definition of p_i. Similarly, the list of output streams produced by a process must follow the same order as the numbering of the output channels.

Given a connection table and a list of processes, the processNetwork function, which builds an arbitrary static network, can now be defined:

```
processNetworks :: [Process a] -> Table [(Int,Int)] Int
                   -> (Channel a) -> (Channel a)
processNetworks ps ct input   = (outputs!n)!!0
  where outputs          = array (0,n)
                             ([(0,[input])]
                              ++[ (m,((ps!!(m-1))(parameters m)))
                                  | m <-[1..n]])
        parameters i  = [(outputs!p)!!o | (p,o) <- findTable ct i]
        n             = length ps
```

This function uses an array outputs which holds output streams for every process. Each process is supplied with its appropriate input streams, selected from this array according to the connections defined in the table ct. We have supposed that the input to the entire process network is the 0th output of (a fictional) process 0 and that the output of the entire process network is the 0th output of the last process.

10.1.3 The mergesort network

The mergesort network is now used as an example of using the processNetwork function. To implement this algorithm, the processes and the output channels need to be numbered as shown in Figure 10.2. The corresponding connection table is defined as follows:

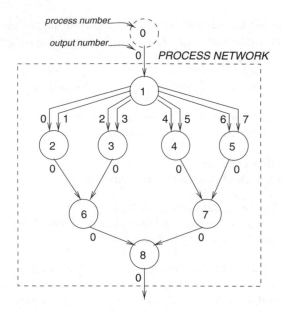

Figure 10.2 Numbering processes and connections in a mergesort network.

```
ct8 :: Table [(Int,Int)] Int
ct8 = newTable
           [(1,[(0,0)]),(2,[(1,0),(1,1)]),(3,[(1,2),(1,3)]),
            (4,[(1,4),(1,5)]),(5,[(1,6),(1,7)]),(6,[(2,0),(3,0)]),
            (7,[(4,0),(5,0)]),(8,[(6,0),(7,0)])]
```

The remaining definitions for the mergesort network are:

```
ps8 :: [Process Int]
ps8 = split:[merge' | i<-[1..7]]
    where split [xs]      = (map (\x -> [x]) xs)
          merge'[xs1,xs2] = [merge xs1 xs2]

sort8    :: Channel Int -> Channel Int
sort8 xs = processNetworks ps8 ct8 xs
```

Note that the program is very much similar to bottom-up mergesort (see Section 6.3.4) with the same `merge` and `split` functions. This network can only sort eight numbers but it is possible to extend it to any number of items by constructing a new connection table before calling the `processNetwork` function.

10.1.4   Other types of process networks

It is possible to define more complex process networks. First, if the number of processes is not always the same (that is, not *static*), the process network is referred to as *dynamic*.

A *pipeline* is a simple process network containing n processes linked into a chain, each process p_i receiving its input from process p_{i-1} and delivering its output to process p_{i+1}. For regular process networks (such as a pipeline), it is also possible to define some special higher-order functions that 'capture' the corresponding communication pattern. To define a simple pipeline, we assume that each process reads its input from a channel and delivers its outputs to another channel. As before, all channels carry items of the same type denoted a:

```
type PipeProcess a = Channel a -> Channel a
```

A pipeline can be expressed using a higher-order function called pipe which expects a list of pipe processes ps and an input stream input:

```
pipe          :: [PipeProcess a] -> Channel a -> Channel a
pipe ps input = (foldr (.) id ps) input
```

An insertion sorting (see Section 6.3.2) network can then be built with the following:

```
sorting xs = pipe [(\l -> insert(xs!!i)l) | i<-[0..length xs-1]]
                  []
```

Similarly, it is also possible to define higher-order functions for other regular communication patterns such as grids and trees. Such networks can also be expressed using the processNetwork higher-order function by constructing the appropriate connection table but the regularity of communication will be somehow 'lost'.

10.1.5 Conclusion

This section introduced the concept of a process network and presented a simple implementation using lazy lists or streams to simulate inter-process communication. Just as with other algorithm design techniques, it is also possible to define higher-order functions that capture specific or general communication patterns.

All the process networks that have been presented are *deterministic*. Determinism means that the program executes the same actions in the same order every time it is executed. This is a direct consequence of the referential transparency property discussed in the first chapter (see Section 1.2.4). Usually, non-determinism is not desirable because the results of a non-deterministic program not only depend on the program but also on accidental timings of events in the system.

In some situations, it is useful to have non-determinism. For example, an embedded control system might wait on several input sources at the same time, then take some action when the first input arrives. Other examples of non-deterministic waiting arise in interactive and client–server applications. As this is impossible to model within a purely functional context, many language extensions have been proposed, among them the *monadic* approach described in the next section. Non-determinism might also be useful in the context of other classes of algorithms.

Another limitation of the functional programming style is that processes often contain a certain amount of state information which should be regularly updated. We will also address this problem in the next section.

10.2 Monads

The first chapter mentioned as being among the advantages of functional languages the absence of side-effects, which was a consequence of the referential transparency property and the fact that all flow of data is made explicit. As a program in a functional language is written as a set of equations, explicit data flow ensures that the value of an expression depends only on its free variables and that the order of evaluation of computation is irrelevant. But in some cases, having to make all data in and out explicit can be cumbersome and inefficient. It is often more convenient to have a global state that is updated as the computation is carried out. But passing this state around can bury the basic computation under 'the plumbing' necessary to carry data from the point of creation to its point of use. Another use is in the updating of a large data structure, in which case there is no need to replicate this data structure if the old version is never to be used again. There are other situations where side-effects are needed such as dealing with input–output and file handling.

Haskell provides a way of dealing with side-effects by using the mathematical notion of *monad* [68, 86, 127, 128]. This concept arises from category theory but it can be expressed and understood without any reference to categorical *things*. Monads represent computations: if m is a monad then an object of type m a represents a computation producing a result of type a. A particular monad reflects the use of a specific programming language feature during the computation: for example, a computation implying the modification of a state for keeping track of the number of evaluation steps might be described by a monad which takes the state as input parameter and returns the new state as part of its result. Computations raising exceptions or performing input–output can also be described by monads.

10.2.1 Monad definition

In Haskell a computation described by a monad is defined using a data type for which two fundamental operations are given in an instance declaration of the predefined Monad class.

The Monad class provides two operations:

- return to give back a value without other effect;
- (>>=) to combine computations when a value is passed from one computation to another (this infix operator is often called bind).

The Standard Prelude defines the Monad class with these three operations as follows:

```
class Monad m where
    (>>=)  :: m a -> (a -> m b) -> m b
    return :: a -> m a

    (>>)   :: m a -> m b -> m b
    p >> q = p >>= \ _ -> q

    fail   :: String -> m a
    fail S = error s
```

(>>) is defined in terms of (>>=) to combine two computations when the second computation does not need the value of the first one.

The rest of this section discusses state manipulation as well as interactive programming using monads.

10.2.2 Using a monad for representing a state

Side-effect operations rely on the notion of an 'invisible' state which is available for inspection as well as modification all along the execution of the program. The main idea behind a monad is that the state is passed around functions in a *single-threaded way*, that is, the state cannot be shared. Therefore, it is possible to perform destructive updating safely (behind the scene).

Following [68], we model programs that make use of an internal state using a *state transformer* which is a function of type s -> (a,s), mapping an initial state of type s to a result value of type a paired with the final possibly modified state also of type s. So we define the following data type; we will first show how to use it in a small example before giving the implementation of the monad:

```
data State s a = ST(s -> (a,s))
```

As an example of using a state monad, we define the numTree function that transforms an arbitrary binary tree into a binary tree of integers in which the original elements are replaced by natural integers starting from 0. All occurrences of equal elements must be replaced by the same integer at every occurrence (this function is reminiscent of the numbervar predicate in Prolog). A binary tree is defined as in Section 2.6.5. Given the following trees:

```
test:: BinTree Int
test  = NodeBT 45
            (NodeBT 54
                (NodeBT 67 (NodeBT (27*2) Empty Empty)
                        Empty)
                (NodeBT 45 (NodeBT 67 (NodeBT (15*3) Empty Empty)
                                    Empty)
                        Empty))
            Empty

test':: BinTree String
test' = NodeBT "Guy" (NodeBT "Fethi" Empty
                                    (NodeBT "Guy" Empty Empty))
                    (NodeBT "Fethi" Empty Empty)
```

we can renumber them by the following calls. We give here the (properly indented) corresponding resulting tree:

```
    numTree test
  ⇒
        NodeBT 0
            (NodeBT 1 (NodeBT 2 (NodeBT 1 Empty Empty)
                                 Empty)
                      (NodeBT 0 (NodeBT 2 (NodeBT 0 Empty Empty)
                                          Empty)
                                Empty))
            Empty

    numTree test'
  ⇒
        NodeBT 0 (NodeBT 1 Empty (NodeBT 0 Empty Empty))
                 (NodeBT 1 Empty Empty)
```

These results are obtained by traversing the tree while keeping track of the numbers associated with previously encountered values in the binary tree. These associations are kept in a list that is updated while going through each node.

```
data BinTree a = Empty | NodeBT a (BinTree a) (BinTree a)
    deriving Show

type Table t = [t]

search :: Eq t => t -> Table t -> Int
search x t = head [i| (i,x')<-zip [0..] t,x==x']
```

search returns the index of element x in table t; we will always check that the element is in the list before calling search to avoid causing an error.

This table is used by the numberNode function that returns a monad which assigns a number to a node of a binary tree: the monad receives as input state the original table; if element x is already in the table it returns a pair comprising the index of x in the table and the original table; if x is not in the table it returns a pair comprising the length of the table (which is one more than the value of the last index) and the new table obtained by adding x at the end of the initial table.

```
numberNode :: Eq t => t -> State (Table t) Int
numberNode x  = ST (\table -> if elem x table
                              then (search x table,table)
                              else (length table,table++[x]))
```

We now define the numberTree function that returns a monad which renumbers each node of the tree by first numbering its node and then combining the result with the numbering of its subtrees.

```
numberTree :: Eq t => BinTree t -> State (Table t) (BinTree Int)
numberTree Empty = return Empty
numberTree (NodeBT x t1 t2)
```

```
   = numberNode x >>= \n ->
     numberTree t1 >>= \nt1 ->
     numberTree t2 >>= \nt2 ->
     return (NodeBT n nt1 nt2)
```

To hide the manipulation of the state monad we create a function which calls numberTree on its arguments with an empty table as initial state and then returns only the resulting binary tree of integers.

```
numTree :: Eq t => BinTree t -> BinTree Int
numTree t = extract (numberTree t)
  where extract::Eq t => State(Table t)(BinTree Int)->BinTree Int
        extract (ST m) = fst (m [])
```

The only thing missing is the definition of the monad which defines the return and >>= functions for our type State.

```
instance Monad (State s) where
    return x = ST (\s -> (x,s))
    (ST m) >>= f = ST (\s -> let (x,s1) = m s
                                 ST f' = f x
                             in f' s1)
```

return merely returns its parameter paired with the original state. m >>= f is a computation which runs m on the initial state producing a result x and a new state s1, then f is applied to the result x and the new state s1. Some care is needed to remove and put back the ST constructor of the monad.

Haskell provides a more readable syntax for monadic programming with the following rewriting rules defined in more detail in Section 3.14 of the Haskell report.

$$e >>= \backslash p \text{-> do } \{ \text{ stmts } \} = \text{do } \{ p \text{ <- } e \text{; stmts } \}$$
$$\text{do } \{e\} \qquad \qquad = e$$

Applying these rules, we can thus rewrite numberTree in the following way which is more convenient: the do keyword indicates a monad context for the following more indented and thus dependent expressions.

```
numberTree :: Eq t => BinTree t -> State (Table t) (BinTree Int)
numberTree Empty = return Empty
numberTree (NodeBT x t1 t2)
    = do n   <- numberNode x
         nt1 <- numberTree t1
         nt2 <- numberTree t2
         return (NodeBT n nt1 nt2)
```

We thus clearly see the steps of the algorithm and that the state manipulation is hidden from the algorithm. Should we decide to change the representation of the state, we would only need to change the monad definition.

10.2.3   List monad

While list comprehensions are commonly used to generate lists, Haskell makes the list type an instance of the Monad class for dealing with multiple values. Monadic binding takes a list of values and applies a function to each of them, collecting all generated values together. The return function creates a singleton list. So the following three expressions:

```
l1 = [(x,y) | x <- [1,2,3], y <- ['a','b']]

l2 = do x <- [1,2,3]
        y <- ['a','b']
        return (x,y)

l3 = [1,2,3] >>= (\x -> ['a','b'] >>= (\y -> return (x,y)))
```

all return the same value:

```
[(1, 'a'), (1, 'b'), (2, 'a'), (2, 'b'), (3, 'a'), (3, 'b')]
```

10.2.4   The input–output monad

Haskell defines a monad for input–output appropriately called the IO monad. The Haskell report does not describe the internals of the IO monad or its instances as the computation depends on the environment of the computer on which the Haskell program is executed. But the monad concept makes the encapsulation of the external environment explicit and allows an efficient and yet functional treatment of the input–output which are, in other functional languages, quite often loopholes where referential transparency can be lost.

All Haskell input–output functions are of type IO a where a depends on the operation; a is of type () in the case where the value returned by the IO computation is not relevant, as for the computation for displaying a String:

```
putStr:: String -> IO ()
```

In the case of getLine, which reads a line from the user, the returned value is of type IO String.

A very simple example of input–output is the following program that first asks a string from the user which is then returned in reverse order:

```
revinput  = putStr "String to reverse: " >>
            getLine >>= \l ->
            putStr (reverse l)
```

As IO is an instance of Monad, we can combine each IO computation with (>>=) and (>>). The evaluation of revinput results in the following interaction:

```
String to reverse:  deliver no evil
live on reviled
```

Where *deliver no evil* was typed by the user after the prompt string has been written as the result of the first call to putStr. Although this behavior seems simple, the fact that Haskell uses lazy evaluation could have the effect that the prompt is not issued before it is needed, that is, after getting the value from the user. In other lazy functional languages, this forces some extra synchronization steps in order to achieve the intended behavior. The monad approach allows a simple synchronization in this case and hides this complexity.

Again the rule described in Section 10.2.2 allows for a more readable version of revinput:

```
revinput = do putStr "String to reverse: "
              l <- getLine
              putStr (reverse l)
```

We only gave here two elementary functions for dealing with input–output; the reader should consult the Haskell report for the complete set of functions which allow a purely functional handling of complex interactive systems.

10.2.5   Conclusion

Although most algorithms can be expressed in a functional language, the basic evaluation model can lead to time or space deficiencies (for example, replication of data structures problem). In addition, the programming style might not allow some types of algorithms to be expressed naturally (for example, concurrency, non-determinism). For these reasons, there is an increasing tendency to separate the study of the semantics and the declarative meaning of a functional program from its operational behavior. The monadic approach described in this section expresses some algorithms in a purely functional context, but the implementation can be totally different from the one implied by the program, as long as it preserves the original semantics.

A similar approach is explored in the next section, where some algorithms are defined in a purely functional way, while they can be evaluated in parallel.

10.3 Parallel algorithms

This last section examines the notion of a parallel algorithm. The main motivation for designing such an algorithm is that of speed, that is solving a problem faster. It requires a special computer architecture, consisting of several processors, capable of executing several instructions simultaneously. Since we are using a functional language, whose evaluation was defined in a sequential manner in Chapter 3, we also need to rethink the way functional programs are evaluated. The design of languages, compilers and architectures for parallel functional programming is a vast research area. In this section, we will limit ourselves to:

● describing the concept of a parallel algorithm and presenting a brief overview of parallel architectures and their effect on the efficiency of algorithms;

- describing how the evaluation model presented in Chapter 3 can be extended to cope with parallel evaluation;

- showing how some fundamental design techniques, presented in earlier chapters, are naturally parallel and lead to parallel implementations.

Several pointers for further reading are provided at the end of this chapter.

10.3.1   General concepts

In the introductory chapter, an algorithm was defined as a *sequence* of actions to be performed by a (sequential) computer. A sequential computer is based on a simple model, called the *von Neumann* model, in which a single processor executes one instruction at a time.

There is a more general class of algorithms in which several actions are carried out simultaneously or *in parallel*. Consider for example the quicksort algorithm described in Section 6.3.3. This algorithm can be viewed as a parallel algorithm because the two sublists obtained by splitting the input list can be sorted simultaneously.

Parallel architectural models

As mentioned before, the main motivation for designing parallel algorithms is to solve problems faster but requires specialized hardware. Building a parallel machine is a costly option but in recent years it has become more viable because microprocessor technology has evolved considerably and the prices of electronic components have fallen dramatically. In addition, a network of PCs or workstations can be made to 'behave' like a parallel architecture.

Unfortunately, a unique model for parallel machines, which would play the same role as the von Neumann model in the sequential world, has yet not emerged. Proposed models vary in two fundamental aspects:

- **Control of the operations**   processors could be all executing the same instruction (on different data), or different instructions at any particular time (see Figure 10.3). The former is referred to as SIMD (single instruction multiple data) whereas the latter is called MIMD (multiple instruction multiple data).

- **Memory organization**   the memory could be shared among processors or each processor can have a *local* memory, and communicate with other processors via an *interconnection network* (see Figure 10.4). The former is referred to as the shared memory model and the latter the distributed memory model.

These models can be further refined. In shared-memory organizations, models are often differentiated by the strategy used to resolve memory conflicts; and in distributed memory models, models are usually differentiated by the topology used for inter-processor communication (for example, tree, grid, hypercube).

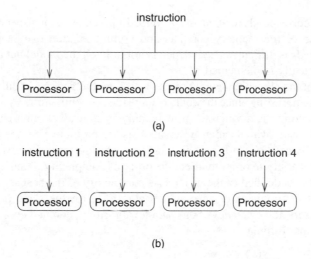

Figure 10.3 Models for the control of the operations. (a) SIMD; (b) MIMD.

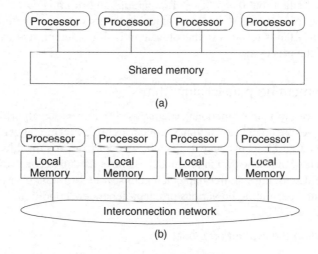

Figure 10.4 Memory organization models. (a) Shared memory; (b) distributed memory.

Efficiency of parallel algorithms

Due to the lack of a single model for parallel architectures, it is hard to estimate the (theoretical) execution time of a parallel algorithm. If n processors are accessing a single value in memory at the same time, it can take: $O(1)$ steps if the memory is shared and can be concurrently read, $O(\log n)$ steps if the value has to be broadcasted in a tree-like fashion to every processor, or $O(n)$ steps if it has to be read sequentially by every processor.

At best, if the sequential algorithm executes in $s(n)$ steps and if the number of processors used is p, the corresponding parallel algorithm executes in $O(s(n)/p)$ steps which corresponds to an *ideal speedup*. In practice, such a speedup cannot be attained because of the memory conflicts and communication overheads. Estimating these overheads is difficult since it depends not only on the model but also on how the model is physically implemented.

From the algorithmic point of view, architectures with a small number of processors are not interesting since they only change the sequential time by a constant factor which is ignored in the asymptotic growth analysis anyway. If an architecture has a number of processors which can grow as much as the problem size, the execution time can be reduced from $O(n^2)$ to $O(n)$, for example. This means that *massively parallel* machines are a necessity in order to affect the order of complexity of an algorithm.

If $s(n)$ is defined as the worst-case complexity of the best sequential algorithm, and $t(n)$ as the complexity of a parallel algorithm for the same problem that uses $p(n)$ processors, the *efficiency* of this parallel algorithm, denoted $e(n)$, is measured using the following formula:

$$e(n) = \frac{s(n)}{t(n) \times p(n)}$$

Given the fact that $0 < e(n) \leq 1$, a parallel algorithm is *cost optimal* if its efficiency is close to 1. In other words, no other algorithm can do (asymptotically) better. If its efficiency tends towards 0, this algorithm is not efficient, that is, it is not making full use of the processors.

10.3.2   Implementing parallel algorithms

Since we are using functional languages to express our algorithms, and since these languages are not tied to the von Neumann architectural model, it is possible to introduce parallel algorithms in a way that is independent from any machine model. This section shows how the basic evaluation model can be extended to cope with parallel evaluation, before discussing parallel implementations of algorithmic classes. Efficiency will be estimated depending on various problem-dependent conditions.

Extending the evaluation model

In our terminology, we call a *task* every independent sequence of action executing in parallel. Notice that a task is similar to a process (see Section 10.1) except that we use this term specifically in the context of parallel processing.

To implement parallel algorithms, the approach adopted in most imperative languages is to add special constructs to handle task creation, communication and synchronization. This approach, based on *explicit parallelism*, has been adopted in some proposals for parallel functional languages. There is an alternative approach called *implicit parallelism*. The rationale is that, as functional languages are declarative in nature, the compiler has some freedom in deciding the order of evaluation. Considering the expression a + b as an example, the expression a can be evaluated before b, or b before a, or both expressions a and b can be evaluated in parallel (by two tasks). This is a consequence of the referential transparency property: there are no side-effects in the evaluation of a or b which makes the order of evaluation important.

For the moment, we will ignore the explicit vs implicit issue and assume that the division into tasks has already been decided by the compiler and examine parallel evaluation in some detail. We will also consider an extension to the basic graph reduction model called *parallel graph reduction*. During normal (that is, sequential) execution, there is a single task reducing the graph to its normal form. In the parallel evaluation model, there are several tasks, each of which is reducing a separate portion of the graph. Therefore, the graph, which is shared among tasks, is accessed and modified concurrently. This model allows the possibility of a task becoming blocked if it needs the value of a node being evaluated by another task.

For example, let us go back to the example described in Section 3.1.1 where these two functions were defined:

```
add x y  = x + y
double x = add x x
```

Consider now the following expression:

```
add (double 4) (double 5)
```

Suppose that the compiler has decided to evaluate this expression using the following strategy: the parent task creates two child tasks to evaluate (double 4) and (double 5) in parallel then executes the function add. The corresponding execution is illustrated in Figure 10.5.

Obviously, this model contains several simplifications but the main idea has been exposed: the graph achieves complete synchronization between the tasks in a very simple and effective manner. This model can be implemented on a parallel architecture with a shared memory; each processor executes a set of tasks and the graph is concurrently manipulated in the shared memory. Alternatively, portions of the graph could be allocated to different local memories in a distributed memory architecture, taking into account the fact that most of the graph accesses are local. In our previous example, the child tasks create and manipulate their own sub-graphs; they only access their parent's graph to communicate the final result.

Efficiency considerations

For the parallel program to be efficient, the decisions concerning when to create a task, where to execute it, and how to distribute the graph are of crucial importance. The first problem faced by the compiler is that tasks must involve sufficient work so that they are worth the extra effort of dispatching them to other processors. In our example, it is hardly worth evaluating the function double on another processor since the work involved is very small. Another danger is that since tasks are dynamically created, there could be an overwhelming number of tasks swamping the resources of the machine.

The rest of this section shows that such decisions can be made depending on the *class* of algorithms being implemented. As this is still a research area, we will not go into the details of implementations.

HEAP

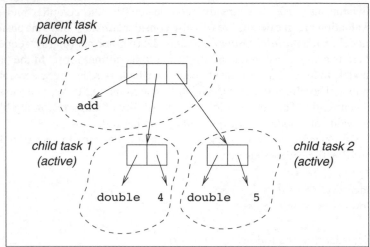

HEAP

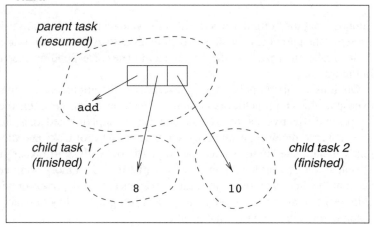

HEAP

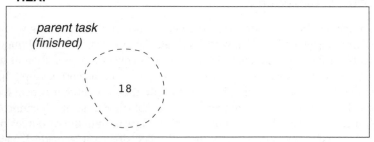

Figure 10.5   Executing a program under parallel evaluation.

10.3.3   Process networks

Process networks, described at the start of this chapter, represent one particular form of parallel algorithms. While in most cases they are designed purely for their expressive power in defining concurrent systems such as operating systems and distributed systems, they still represent our first class of parallel algorithms.

Static process networks are ideal for distributed memory architectures. In Section 10.1.2, we described a simple higher-order function processNetwork which, given a list of processes and a connection table, generates any static process network. For example, if the following expression denotes a process network specification:

```
processNetwork ps ct input
```

then the work of the compiler is simply to adopt the following strategy to achieve partitioning and scheduling:

● Create one parallel task for every process in the list ps. Tasks can be statically allocated to processors. If there are more tasks than processors, then we need to allocate groups of tasks on processors. Grouping may be decided on some analysis of the work performed by each task.

● The allocation of tasks to processors also depends on the communication requirements of each task. If the table ct shows that there is a connection between two processes, then it is desirable to allocate their corresponding tasks on processors that are physically connected to reduce communication overheads.

For dynamic process networks, such as pipelines, the compiler must choose the best match between the topology of the problem and the topology of the machine. For example, there are known techniques for embedding arbitrary trees onto hypercube topologies. This also depends on the specific parameters of the problem.

A fixed static network does not result in a significant improvement in time efficiency. A larger gain (in asymptotic terms) is usually obtained with dynamic networks, where the configuration depends on the problem size. Considering the mergesort network (see Section 10.1.1), ignoring the cost of the splitting operation, this algorithm performs in $\log n$ stages: at each stage i (starting from 0), all lists of length 2^i are merged. As the time to merge two lists of length l is $2l$ steps in the worst case, the total execution time is:

$$\sum_{i=0}^{\log n - 1} (2^{i+1}) \in O(n)$$

Since $O(n)$ processors have been used, the efficiency is in $O(\log n / n)$ so the algorithm is not cost optimal. This could have been predicted because only processors at one given depth are active at any given time.

10.3.4   Divide-and-conquer algorithms

Divide-and-conquer algorithms also lend themselves naturally to parallel evaluation. By breaking every problem into smaller subproblems, it does not matter in many cases the order in which these subproblems are solved. For example, given the following

Table 10.1 Parallel time complexity of divide-and-conquer algorithms.

Assumption		Parallel time complexity
$T_{\texttt{divide}}(n) + T_{\texttt{combine}}(n)$	$\in O(n)$	$T_{\text{dc}'}(n) \in O(n)$
$T_{\texttt{divide}}(n) + T_{\texttt{combine}}(n)$	$\in O(1)$	$T_{\text{dc}'}(n) \in O(\log_b n)$

divide-and-conquer specification using the `divideAndConquer` function (see Section 8.1.1):

```
divideAndConquer ind solve divide comb pb
```

the compiler may adopt the following strategy:

- the root processor, which executes the initial call to `dc'`, determines the list of subproblems;
- then it creates a parallel task for each of the recursive calls of the function `dc'`, except one which is evaluated by itself;
- the division into subproblems continues until indivisible problem instances are encountered, in which case they are solved directly; a task proceeds until it is eventually blocked, waiting for one of its child tasks to complete;
- in the combine phase, each task combines the subsolutions received from its children and passes on the combined solution to its parent;
- the root processor delivers the final result.

We can see that tasks are created dynamically and that the overall communication structure is that of a tree. For the purpose of the analysis, we assume that every task is executed by a separate processor. In Section 8.1.1, we presented a general table which gives the time complexity of any divide-and-conquer algorithm, depending on the complexity of its constituent functions `divide` and `combine`. Assuming a regular algorithm in which a problem of size n is always divided in k subproblems of size n/b, and assuming that the functions `ind` and `solve` operate in constant time, the parallel complexity of divide-and-conquer problems is displayed in Table 10.1.

For example, a divide-and-conquer sorting algorithm such as mergesort would execute in $O(n)$ steps since $T_{\texttt{combine}}(n) \in O(n)$. As this algorithm uses $O(n)$ processors, it is not cost-optimal. This is not surprising since we obtained the same result with the process network implementation of the mergesort algorithm which is very similar. In contrast, it is not possible to make accurate predictions for an algorithm such as quicksort since it is not regular; we cannot make the same assumption that subproblems are of size n/b since the division into subproblems is problem dependent.

It would appear that all divide-and-conquer problems are not cost-optimal, since there is only one particular level in the tree which is active at any particular time. In practice, we get a better efficiency as several tasks are grouped and executed by one processor. Several theoretical results suggest that, providing there is sufficient work to keep the processors busy (this is called *parallel slackness* [120]), these algorithms can be implemented in a cost-optimal manner. The main problem is in the difficulty of allocating tasks to processors, since tasks are generated dynamically. This problem is known as *dynamic load balancing* or *adaptive load sharing*. As a tree can grow very large and generate tasks well in excess of the number of processors available, some strategy for turning to sequential evaluation at some point to avoid the tiny tasks at the leaves of the tree must be employed.

10.3.5 Dynamic programming

It is possible to view a dynamic programming algorithm as the second phase (the combine phase) of a divide-and-conquer problem, except that the solution of a subproblem is returned to several tasks instead of one. For this reason, it more desirable to assume an architecture with a shared memory where the solutions table is stored.

Given the following dynamic programming specification using the `dynamic` function (see Section 9.2):

```
dynamic compute bnds
```

a parallel implementation can be derived as follows:

- a table is generated from the boundary information `bnds` in the shared memory;
- the root processor starts executing a task which requests the solution from the table;
- when a task calls the `compute` function for an entry e, a child task is created for every table entry required in the computation of e; a task proceeds until it is eventually blocked, waiting for one of its child tasks to complete;
- when all tasks have completed, the solution is returned by the root processor.

Since this implementation assumes a shared memory, a simple load balancing strategy is to maintain a central queue of tasks. Processors remove tasks from this queue for execution whenever they are idle. The queue contains newly created tasks as well as blocked tasks which have just become reactivated.

The efficiency of such a parallel implementation depends on the data dependencies between the entries in the table. Considering problems that use a table organized as half a matrix such as the chained matrix multiplication or the optimal binary search tree problems, these problems use $O(n^2)$ processors and execute in $O(n^2)$ steps under the same assumptions as with the sequential complexity analysis. Therefore, since the sequential time was in $O(n^3)$ they are not cost-optimal.

As with divide-and-conquer, grouping several tasks and executing them on the same processor will increase the efficiency. Tasks can be allocated to processors depending on the data dependencies between them. In the problems described above, the tasks which compute entries on the same diagonal should be allocated to different processors since there are no data dependencies between these entries.

10.3.6 Conclusion

This section showed that several fundamental design techniques for algorithms can also be used for designing parallel algorithms. Given an algorithm specification, expressed in a higher-order function which forms the *skeleton* of the corresponding design technique, it is possible to provide a generic implementation adapted to the characteristics of that skeleton. Such an implementation can be refined according to the characteristics of the parameters supplied to the skeleton function.

Another fundamental technique which is also candidate for parallel evaluation is backtracking search (see Section 8.2). Under various conditions, it is possible to visit several candidate nodes in parallel. Not every fundamental technique has a parallel implementation. For example, greedy algorithms (see Section 8.4) cannot be executed in parallel since only one successor node is explored at any time.

It is also possible to create some skeleton function adapted to a specific parallel architecture. Any algorithm that 'fits' into this function is guaranteed to have an efficient implementation on the corresponding architecture. Finally, it is also important to realize that skeletons are only one approach to the design and implementation of parallel algorithms using functional languages. The beauty of this approach is that no extra constructs are added to the language and most of the drawbacks of implicit parallelism are avoided.

10.4 Bibliographical notes

Most functional programming textbooks include a section on process networks and lazy lists. Kelly's book [70] is dedicated to process networks, and their implementation on both sequential and parallel computers. Modeling communication as streams requires some methods for reasoning about infinite lists [14].

The case that process networks (with functions and lazy lists) increase the modularity of programs is argued by Hughes [63]. A functional language extension that allows process networks to be expressed is Caliban [70] and its implementation is discussed by Cox et al. [29]. Extensions to functional languages to cope with GUIs include Gadgets (based on continuations) [88]. Other approaches at introducing non-determinism in functional languages include the *ambiguous merge* operator [63] and the use of *bags* instead of streams for inter-process communication [83].

Monads, described by Wadler [127, 129], were first introduced to computer science by Moggi [86]. They are gaining popularity in the Haskell community and are being used in several applications (see, for example, [65]). There is a comprehensive article on state manipulation in Haskell and state transformers, with several useful references, by Peyton Jones and Launchbury [98]. The Concurrent Haskell proposal can be found in [99]. This paper also contains a useful survey of current research in concurrent functional programming. A similar proposal, which includes a symmetrical fork, is described by Hudak and Jones [67].

There are numerous textbooks on parallel algorithms, most of them based on the PRAM model (such as [76]). Other models have been proposed, among them the BSP (Bulk Synchronous Parallel) model [82]. The concept of parallel slackness is discussed by Valiant [120].

Our extension of the evaluation model for functional languages is based on parallel graph reduction techniques [10, 94, 95]. Cole [28] established the term skeleton by defining *algorithmic classes* which have obvious parallel implementations and into which applications can be fitted. Skeletons were later defined through *higher-order functions* which capture the parallel structure of a class of algorithms. Any program can be specified by defining a set of parameters to be supplied to the corresponding higher-order function [104]. In recent times, skeletons have gained widespread popularity and are used in a variety of forms and projects such as Skel-ML [21], BMF [112], and others [17, 31, 110].

Bibliography

[1] The ACQUA Team, (1995) The Glorious Glasgow Haskell Compiler System, Department of Computing Science, University of Glasgow, (latest information available on WWW at http://www.dcs.gla.ac.uk/fp/software/ghc).

[2] G.M. Adelson-Velskii and E.M. Landis, (1962) 'An algorithm for the organisation of information', *Soviet Math. Doklady* (English translation), vol. 3, pp. 1259–1263.

[3] A.V. Aho, J.E. Hopcroft and J.D. Ullman, (1983) *Data Structures and Algorithms*, Addison-Wesley, Reading MA.

[4] L. Augustsson, (1987) *Compiling Lazy Functional Languages (Part II)*, PhD thesis, Chalmers University of Technology, Goteborg.

[5] M. Azmoodeh, (1988) *Abstract Data Types and Algorithms*, Macmillan Education, Houndsmills, Hampshire.

[6] J.W. Backus, (1978) 'Can programming be liberated from the von Neumann style? a functional style and its algebra of programs', *Communications of the ACM*, vol. 21, no. 8, pp. 613–641.

[7] H.P. Barendregt, (1984) *The λ-Calculus: its Syntax and Semantics*, North Holland, Amsterdam.

[8] R.E. Bellman, (1957) *Dynamic Programming*, Princeton University Press, Princeton NJ.

[9] R.E. Bellman and S.E. Dreyfus, (1957) *Applied Dynamic Programming*, Princeton University Press, Princeton NJ.

[10] D.I. Bevan, G.L. Burn, R.J. Karia and J.D. Robson, (1989) 'Design principles of a distributed memory architecture for parallel graph reduction', *The Computer Journal*, vol. 32, no. 5, pp. 461–469.

218

[11] R.S. Bird, (1984) 'Using circular programs to eliminate multiple traversals of data', *Acta Informatica*, vol. 21, pp. 239–250.

[12] R.S. Bird, (1984) 'The promotion and accumulation strategies in functional programming', *ACM Transactions on Programming Languages and Systems*, vol. 6, no. 4, pp. 487–504.

[13] R.S. Bird, (1987) 'An introduction to the theory of lists'. In M. Broy (ed.), *Logic of Programming and Calculi of Discrete Design*, NATO ASI Series, Series F: Computer and Systems Science, vol. 36, Springer Verlag, Heidelberg, pp. 3–42.

[14] R.S. Bird, (1998) *Introduction to Functional Programming using Haskell*, 2nd edn, Prentice Hall, Hemel Hempstead.

[15] A. Bloss and P. Hudak, (1988) 'Path semantics'. In M. Main, A. Melton, M. Mislove and D. Schmidt (eds), *Proc. Third Workshop on the Mathematical Foundations of Programming Language Semantics*, Lecture Notes in Computer Science 298, Springer Verlag, Heidelberg, pp. 476–489.

[16] R. Bornat, (1986) *Programming from First Principles*, Prentice Hall, Englewood Cliffs NJ.

[17] G.H. Botorog and H. Kuchen, (1996) 'Efficient parallel programming with algorithmic skeletons'. In L. Bougé, P. Fraigniaud, A. Mignotte and Y. Robert (eds), *Proc. EuroPar '96*, vol. 1, Lecture Notes in Computer Science 1123, Springer Verlag, Heidelberg, pp. 718–731.

[18] G. Brassard and P. Bratley, (1988) *Algorithmics: Theory and Practice*, Prentice Hall, Englewood Cliffs NJ.

[19] G. Brassard and P. Bratley, (1996) *Fundamentals of Algorithmics*, Prentice Hall, Englewood Cliffs NJ.

[20] I. Bratko, (1990) *Prolog Programming for Artificial Intelligence*, Addison-Wesley, Reading MA.

[21] T.A. Bratvold, (1993) 'A skeleton based parallelising compiler for ML'. In *Proc. 5th Int. Workshop on Implementation of Functional Languages*, TR 93-21, University of Nijmegen, September pp. 23–33.

[22] R.M. Burstall and J. Darlington, (1977) 'A transformation system for developing recursive programs', *Journal of the ACM*, vol. 24, pp. 44–67.

[23] R.M. Burstall, D.B. MacQueen and D.T. Sannella, (1980) 'HOPE, an experimental applicative language'. In *Proc. 1980 Lisp Conference*, Stanford CA, pp. 136–143.

[24] F.W. Burton, (1982) 'An efficient implementation of FIFO queues', *Information Processing Letters*, vol. 14, pp. 205–206.

[25] E. Charniak and D. McDermott, (1985) *Introduction to Artificial Intelligence*, Addison-Wesley, Reading MA.

[26] A. Church, (1941) *The Calculi of Lambda Conversions*, Princeton University Press, Princeton NJ.

[27] C. Clack, C. Myers and E. Poon, (1994) *Programming with Miranda*, Prentice Hall, Hemel Hempstead.

[28] M. Cole, (1989) *Algorithmic Skeletons: a Structured Approach to the Management of Parallel Computation*, Research Monographs in Parallel and Distributed Computing, Pitman, London.

[29] S. Cox, S.Y. Huang, P. Kelly, J. Liu and F. Taylor, (1992) 'An implementation of static functional process networks'. In D. Etiemble and J.C. Syre (eds), *Proc. Parallel Architectures and Languages Europe (PARLE'92)*, Lecture Notes in Computer Science 605, Springer Verlag, Heidelberg, pp. 497–512.

[30] H.B. Curry and R. Feys, (1958) *Combinatory Logic* vol. 1, North Holland, Amsterdam.

[31] J. Darlington, A.J. Field, P.G. Harrison, P.H.J. Kelly, R.L. White and Q. Wu, (1993) 'Parallel programming using skeleton functions'. In A. Bode, M. Reeve and G. Wolf (eds), *Proc. Parallel Architectures and Languages Europe (PARLE '93)*, Lecture Notes in Computer Science 694, Springer Verlag, Heidelberg.

[32] A.J.T. Davie, (1992) *An Introduction to Functional Programming Systems Using Haskell*, Cambridge University Press, Cambridge.

[33] E.W. Dijkstra, (1959) 'A note on two problems in connection with graphs', *Numerische Mathematik*, vol. 1, pp. 269–271.

[34] J. Edmonds, (1971) 'Matroids and the greedy algorithm', *Mathematical Programming*, vol. 1, pp. 127–136.

[35] J. Fairbairn, (1987) 'Making form follow function: an exercise in functional programming style', *Software Practice and Experience*, vol. 17, no. 6, pp. 379–386.

[36] J. Fairbairn and S. Wray, (1987) 'TIM: a simple, lazy abstract machine to execute supercombinators'. In G. Kahn (ed.), *Proc. Functional Programming Languages and Computer Architecture (FPCA'87)*, Lecture Notes in Computer Science 274, Springer Verlag, Heidelberg, pp. 34–46.

[37] A.J. Field and P.G. Harrison, (1988) *Functional Programming*, Addison-Wesley, Wokingham, Berkshire.

[38] R.W. Floyd, 'Algorithm 97: Shortest path', *Communications of the ACM*, vol. 5, no. 6, p. 345.

[39] M.M. Fokkinga, (1991) 'An exercise in transformational programming: backtracking and branch-and-bound', *Science of Computer Programming*, vol. 16, pp. 19–48.

[40] R.A. Frost and B. Szydlowski, (1996) 'Memoizing purely functional top-down backtracking language processors', *Science of Computer Programming*, vol. 27, pp. 263–288.

[41] E.N. Gilbert and E.F. Moore, (1959) 'Variable length encodings', *Bell System Technical Journal*, vol. 38, no. 4, pp. 933–968.

[42] A. Gill, J. Launchbury, and S.L. Peyton Jones, (1993) 'A short cut to deforestation'. In Arvind (ed.), *Functional Programming and Computer Architecture (FPCA'93)*, ACM Press, pp. 223–232

[43] S. Godbole, (1973) 'On efficient computation of matrix chain products', *IEEE Transactions on Computers*, vol. C-22, no. 9, pp. 864–866.

[44] G. H. Gonnet and R. Baeza-Yates, (1991) *Handbook of Algorithms and Data Structures*, 2nd edn, Addison-Wesley, Reading MA.

[45] M. Gordon, R. Milner, L. Morris, M. Newey and C. Wadsworth, (1978) 'A metalanguage for interactive proof in LCF', *Proc. 5th Symposium on Principles of Programming Languages (POPL'78)*, Tucson, AZ, ACM, pp. 119–130.

[46] J.V. Guttag, (1977) 'Abstract data types and the development of data structures', *Communications of the ACM*, vol. 20, pp. 397–404.

[47] J.V. Guttag, (1978) 'The algebraic specification of abstract data types', *Acta Informatica*, vol. 10, no. 1, pp. 27–52.

[48] C. Hankin, (1994) *Lambda Calculi, a Guide for Computer Scientists*, Clarendon Press, Oxford.

[49] D. Harel, (1987) *Algorithmics: the Spirit of Computing*, Addison-Wesley, Reading MA.

[50] R. Harrison, (1993) *Abstract Data Types in Standard ML*, J. Wiley, Chichester.

[51] P.H. Hartel and H. Glaser, (1996) 'The resource constrained shortest path problem', *Journal of Functional Programming*, vol. 6, no. 1, pp. 29–45.

[52] T.L. Heath, (1956) *The Thirteen Books of Euclid's Elements (Volume 2)*, 2nd edn, Dover Publications Inc., New York.

[53] M. Held and R. Karp, (1962) 'A dynamic programming approach to sequencing problems', *SIAM Journal on Applied Mathematics*, vol. 10, no. 1, pp. 196–210.

[54] J.M.D. Hill, (1992) 'The knights tour in Haskell' (unpublished paper), Computing Laboratory, University of Oxford.

[55] C.A.R. Hoare, (1962) 'Quicksort', *The Computer Journal*, vol. 5, pp. 10–15.

[56] I. Holyer, (1991) *Functional programming with Miranda*, UCL Press, London.

[57] J.E. Hopcroft and R.E. Tarjan, (1973) 'Efficient algorithms for graph manipulation', *Communications of the ACM*, vol. 16, no. 6, pp. 372–378.

[58] E. Horowitz and S. Sahni, (1978) *Fundamental of Computer Algorithms*, Computer Science Press.

[59] P. Hudak, (1986) 'Tables, non-determinism, side effects and parallelism: a functional perspective'. In J.H. Fasel and R.M. Keller (eds), *Graph Reduction*, Lecture Notes in Computer Science 279, Springer Verlag, Heidelberg, pp. 312–327.

[60] P. Hudak, (1989) 'Conception, evolution, and application of functional programming languages', *ACM Computing Surveys*, vol. 21, no. 3, pp. 359–411.

[61] P. Hudak, S.L. Peyton Jones and P. Wadler (eds), (1992) 'Report on the programming language Haskell', *ACM SIGPLAN Notices*, vol. 27, no. 5.

[62] P. Hudak, J. Peterson and J.H. Fasel, (1997) 'A Gentle Introduction to Haskell', Available at `http://haskell.cs.yale.edu/tutorial`.

[63] R.J.M. Hughes, (1984) *The Design and Implementation of Programming Languages*, PhD thesis, Oxford University.

[64] G. Hutton, (1992) 'Higher-order functions for parsing', *Journal of Functional Programming*, vol. 2, no. 3, pp. 323–343.

[65] G. Hutton and E. Meijer, (1996) 'Monadic parser combinators', *Report NOTTCS-TR-96-4*, Department of Computer Science, University of Nottingham.

[66] T. Johnsson, (1987) *Compiling Lazy Functional Languages*, PhD thesis, Chalmers University of Technology, Goteborg.

[67] M. P. Jones and P. Hudak, (1993) 'Implicit and explicit parallel programming in Haskell', *Research Report YALEU/DCS/RR-982*, Department of Computer Science, Yale University, August 1993.

[68] M. P. Jones, (1995) 'Functional programming with overloading and higher-order polymorphism'. In J. Jeuring and E. Meijer (eds), *Advanced Functional Programming*, Lecture Notes in Computer Science 925, Springer Verlag, Heidelberg, pp. 97–136.

[69] A.B. Kahn, (1962) 'Topological sorting of large networks', *Communications of the ACM*, vol. 5, pp. 558–562.

[70] P. Kelly, (1989) *Functional Programming for Loosely-coupled Multiprocessors*, Research Monographs in Parallel and Distributed Computing, Pitman, London.

[71] D.J. King and J. Launchbury, (1995) 'Structuring depth-first search algorithms in Haskell'. In *Proc. 22nd Symposium on Principles of Programming Languages (POPL'95)*, San Francisco, California, ACM, January 1995.

[72] D.J. King, (1996) *Functional Programming and Graph Algorithms*, PhD thesis, Department of Computing Science, University of Glasgow.

[73] D.E. Knuth, (1973) *The Art of Computer Programming; Volume 1: Fundamental Algorithms* 2nd edn, Addison-Wesley, Reading MA.

[74] D. E. Knuth, (1973) *The Art of Computer Programming; Volume 3: Searching and Sorting*, Addison-Wesley, Reading MA.

[75] J.B. Kruskal Jr, (1956) 'On the shortest spanning subtree of a graph and the traveling salesman problem', *Proc. of the American Mathematical Society*, vol. 7, pp. 48–50.

[76] V. Kumar, A. Grama, A. Gupta and G. Karypis, (1994) *Introduction to Parallel Computing*, Benjamin Cummings, Redwood City CA.

[77] P.J. Landin, (1964) 'The mechanical evaluation of expressions', *The Computer Journal*, vol. 6, pp. 308–328.

[78] P.J. Landin, (1967) 'The next 700 programming languages', *Communications of the ACM*, vol. 9, no. 3, pp. 157–166.

[79] G. Lapalme and F. Lavier, (1993) 'Using a functional language for parsing and semantic processing', *Computational Intelligence*, vol. 9, no. 2, pp. 111–131.

[80] J. McCarthy, (1960) 'Recursive functions of symbolic expressions and their computation by machine (part I)', *Communications of the ACM*, vol. 3, no. 4, pp. 184–195.

[81] J. McCarthy, P.W. Abrahams, D.J. Edwards, T.P. Hart, T.P. and M.I. Levin, (1965) *Lisp 1.5 Programmer's Manual*, 2nd edn, MIT Press.

[82] W.F. McColl, (1995) 'Bulk synchronous parallel computing'. In J.R. Davy and P.M. Dew (eds), *Abstract Machine Models for Highly Parallel Computers*, Oxford University Press, pp. 41–63.

[83] G. Marino and G. Succi, (1989) 'Data structures for parallel execution of functional languages'. In E. Odijk, M. Rem and J.C. Syre (eds), *Parallel Architectures and Languages Europe (PARLE'89)*, Lecture Notes in Computer Science 365, Springer Verlag, Heidelberg, pp. 346–356.

[84] F. Major, G. Lapalme and R. Cedergren, (1991) 'Domain generating functions for solving constraint satisfaction problems', *Journal of Functional Programming*, vol. 1, no. 2, pp. 213–227.

[85] R. Milner, (1978) 'A theory of type polymorphism in programming', *Journal of Computer and System Sciences*, vol. 17, no. 3, pp. 349–375.

[86] E. Moggi, (1989) 'Computational lambda calculus and monads'. In *IEEE Symposium on Logic in Computer Science*, Asilomar, California, IEEE, June 1989.

[87] N. Nilsson, (1971) *Problem Solving Methods in Artificial Intelligence*, McGraw-Hill, New York.

[88] R.J. Noble and C. Runciman, (1995) 'Gadgets: lazy functional components for graphical user interfaces'. In E.M. Hermenegildo and S.D. Swierstra (eds), *Proc. 7th International Symposium on Programming Languages: Implementations, Logics and Programs (PLILP'95)*, Lecture Notes in Computer Science 982, Springer Verlag, Heidelberg, pp. 321–340.

[89] J.L. Noyes, (1992) *Artificial Intelligence with Common Lisp*, D.C. Heath, Lexington MA.

[90] C. Okasaki, (1995) 'Simple and efficient purely functional queues and dequeues', *Journal of Functional Programming*, vol. 5, no. 4, pp. 583–592.

[91] C. Okasaki, (1998) *Purely Functional Data Structures*, Cambridge University Press, Cambridge.

[92] R. A. O'Keefe, (1982) 'A smooth applicative merge sort', *Research Paper 182*, Department of Artificial Intelligence, University of Edinburgh, Edinburgh.

[93] L. C. Paulson, (1991) *ML for the Working Programmer*, Cambridge University Press, Cambridge.

[94] S.L. Peyton Jones, (1987) *The Implementation of Functional Programming Languages*, Prentice Hall, Hemel Hempstead.

[95] S.L. Peyton Jones, C. Clack and J. Salkild, (1989) 'High performance parallel graph reduction'. In E. Odijk, M. Rem and J.C. Syre (eds), *Proc. Parallel Architectures and Languages Europe (PARLE '89)*, Lecture Notes in Computer Science 365, Springer Verlag, pp. 193–207.

[96] S.L. Peyton Jones, (1992) 'Implementing lazy functional languages on stock hardware: the spineless tagless G-machine', *Journal of Functional Programming*, vol. 2, no. 2, pp. 127–202.

[97] S.L. Peyton Jones and D. Lester, (1992) *Implementing Functional Languages: a Tutorial*, Prentice Hall, Hemel Hempstead.

[98] S.L. Peyton Jones and J. Launchbury, (1995) 'State in Haskell'. In *Lisp and Symbolic Computation*, vol. 8, no. 4, December 1995, pp. 293–341.

[99] S.L. Peyton Jones, A. Gordon, and S. Finne, (1996) 'Concurrent Haskell'. In *Proc. 23rd Symposium on Principles of Programming Languages (POPL'96)*, St Petersburg Beach, Florida, January 1996, ACM, pp. 295–308.

[100] S.L. Peyton-Jones and R.J.M. Hughes (eds), (1999) Report on the programming Language Haskell 98, February 1999. Available at `http://www.haskell.org`.

[101] S.L. Peyton-Jones and R.J.M. Hughes (eds), (1999) Standard Labraries for the Haskell 98 Programming Language, February 1999. Available at `http://www.haskell.org`.

[102] R. Plasmeijer and M. van Eekelen, (1993) *Functional Programming and Parallel Graph Rewriting*, Addison-Wesley, Wokingham, Berkshire.

[103] R.C. Prim, (1957) 'Shortest connection networks and some generalizations', *Bell System Technical Journal*, vol. 36, pp. 1389–1401.

[104] F.A. Rabhi, (1995) 'Exploiting parallelism in functional languages: a paradigm oriented approach'. In J.R. Davy and P.M. Dew (eds), *Abstract Machine Models for Highly Parallel Computers*, Oxford University Press, Oxford, pp. 118–139.

[105] Research Software Limited, (1987)*Miranda System Manual*.

[106] M. Rosendahl, (1989) 'Automatic complexity analysis'. In *Proc. Functional Programming Languages and Computer Architecture (FPCA'89)*, ACM, pp. 144–156.

[107] C. Runciman and D. Wakeling, (1993) 'Heap profiling of lazy functional programs', *Journal of Functional Programming*, vol. 3, no. 2, pp. 217–245.

[108] C. Runciman and N. Rojemo, (1996) 'New dimensions in heap profiling', *Journal of Functional Programming*, vol. 6, no. 4, pp. 587–620.

[109] D. Sands, (1995) 'A naive time analysis and its theory of cost equivalence', *The Journal of Logic and Computation*, vol. 5, no. 40, Oxford University Press, Oxford, pp. 495–541.

[110] J. Schwarz and F.A. Rabhi, (1996) 'A skeleton-based implementation of iterative transformation algorithms using functional languages'. In M. Kara, J.R. Davy, D. Goodeve and J. Nash (eds), *Abstract Machine Models for Parallel and Distributed Computing*, IOS Press, Amsterdam, pp. 119–134.

[111] R. Sedgewick, (1992) *Algorithms in C++*, Addison-Wesley, Reading MA.

[112] D.B. Skillicorn, (1992) 'The Bird-Meertens Formalism as a parallel model'. In J.S. Kowalik and L. Grandinetti (eds), *Software for Parallel Computation*, Springer Verlag, Heidelberg.

[113] J.D. Smith, (1989) *Design and Analysis of Algorithms*, PWS-KENT Publishing Company, Boston MA.

[114] R.E. Tarjan, (1972) 'Depth-first search and linear graph algorithms', *SIAM Journal on Computing*, vol. 1, no. 2, pp. 146–160.

[115] S. Thompson, (1995) *Miranda: The Craft of Functional Programming*, Addison-Wesley, Harlow.

[116] S. Thompson, (1996) *Haskell: The Craft of Functional Programming*, Addison-Wesley, Harlow.

[117] D.A. Turner, (1982) 'Recursion equations as a programming language'. In J. Darlington, P. Henderson and D.A. Turner (eds), *Functional Programming and its Applications*, Cambridge University Press, Cambridge, pp. 1–28.

[118] D.A. Turner, (1983) 'SASL language manual (revised version)', *Technical Report*, University of Canterbury, Kent.

[119] D.A. Turner, (1985) 'Miranda – a non strict functional language with polymorphic types'. In P. Jouannaud (ed.), *Proc. Functional Programming and Computer Architecture (FPCA'85)*, Lecture Notes in Computer Science 201, Springer Verlag, Heidelberg, pp. 1–16.

[120] L.G. Valiant, (1990) 'General purpose parallel architectures'. In J. van Leeuwen (ed.), *Handbook of Theoretical Computer Science: Volume A, Algorithms and Complexity*, North Holland, Amsterdam, pp. 943–971.

[121] P. Wadler, (1985) 'How to replace failure by a list of successes'. In P. Jouannaud (ed.), *Proc. Functional Programming and Computer Architecture (FPCA'85)*, Lecture Notes in Computer Science 201, Springer Verlag, Heidelberg, pp. 113–128.

[122] P. Wadler, (1986) 'A new array operation'. In J.H. Fasel and R.M. Keller (eds), *Graph Reduction*, Lecture Notes in Computer Science 279, Springer Verlag, Heidelberg, pp. 328–335.

[123] P. Wadler, (1989) 'The concatenate vanishes' (unpublished paper), Department of Computing, University of Glasgow, November 1989.

[124] P. Wadler, (1988) 'Strictness analysis aids time analysis'. In *Proc. 15th Symposium on the Principles of Programming Languages (POPL'88)*, San Diego, California, ACM, January 1988.

[125] P. Wadler and Q. Miller, (1988) 'An introduction to Orwell', *Technical Report*, Programming Research Group, Oxford University.

[126] P. Wadler, (1990) 'Deforestation: transforming programs to eliminate trees', *Theoretical Computer Science*, vol. 73, pp. 231–248.

[127] P. Wadler, (1992) 'Comprehending monads', *Mathematical Structures in Computer Science*, vol. 2, pp. 461–493.

[128] P. Wadler, (1995) 'Monads for functional programming'. In J. Jeuring and E. Meijer (eds), *Advanced Functional Programming*, Lecture Notes in Computer Science 925, Springer Verlag, Heidelberg, pp. 24–52.

[129] P. Wadler, (1997) 'How to declare an imperative', *ACM Computing Surveys*, vol. 29, no. 3, September 1997, pp. 240–263.

[130] M.A. Weiss, (1992) *Data Structures and Algorithm Analysis*, Benjamin Cummings, Redwood City CA.

[131] A. Wikstrom, (1987) *Functional programming using Standard ML*, Prentice Hall, Hemel Hempstead.

[132] J.W.J. Williams, (1964) 'Algorithm 232: Heapsort', *Communications of the ACM*, vol. 7, pp. 347–348.

[133] D. Wise, (1987) 'Matrix algebra and applicative programming'. In G. Kahn (ed.), *Proc. Functional Programming Languages and Computer Architecture (FPCA'87)*, Lecture Notes in Computer Science 274, Springer Verlag, Heidelberg, pp. 134–153.

Haskell implementations

The official World Wide Web site for information about Haskell is:

```
http://www.haskell.org
```

where all kinds of information can be found such as the Haskell Report and the Haskell Library Report and links to Haskell compilers and interpreters.

The most popular interpreter for Haskell is Hugs, developed by Mark Jones at the University of Nottingham and Yale University. This implementation is small, easy to use and is available under various platforms including UNIX, Windows, DOS and Macintosh environments. The programs given in this book have been tested under version 98 of Hugs. Information on Hugs is available on the WWW at:

```
http://www.haskell.org/hugs
```

For producing executable machine code, Haskell compilers have been developed at Chalmers and Glasgow Universities. These compilers (which run best under Unix) can be obtained by ftp at:

Chalmers: `http://www.cs.chalmers.se/~augustss/hbc.html`

Glasgow: `http://www.dcs.gla.ac.uk/fp/software/ghc/`

The functional programming FAQ is located at:

```
http://www.cs.nott.ac.uk/Department/Staff/gmh/faq.html
```

Further supporting material for this book, including all the programs in the text, is available on the World Wide Web at the following address:

```
http://www.iro.umontreal.ca/~lapalme/Algorithms-functional.html
```

All programs are completely implemented in Haskell. Some functions, such as Abstract Data Type (ADT) operations, are used in many parts of the book. To provide easy access to their definitions, these functions are indexed by their name. They are included in a Haskell module, so their definitions must be imported before they are used.

Mathematical background

This appendix presents some mathematical notions that are essential for the analysis of programs.

B.1 Notation

The notation $\lfloor x \rfloor$ means the largest integer at most x. Similarly, $\lceil x \rceil$ denotes the smallest integer at least x. For example, $\lfloor 3.8 \rfloor$ is 3 and $\lceil 2.1 \rceil$ is 3.

B.2 Logarithms

The fundamental property of a logarithm (base b) is:

$$y = b^x \iff x = \log_b y$$

The conditions are $b > 1$ and $y > 0$. All the logarithms used in this book are to base 2 so the notation $\log x$ really means $\log_2 x$. Here are some of the logarithms properties:

1. $\log xy = \log x + \log y$

2. $\log \frac{x}{y} = \log x - \log y$

3. $\log x^y = y \log x$

4. $\log 1 = 0$

5. $\log 2 = 1$

B.3 Summation formulas

Summations occur frequently in the analysis of algorithms. The solutions of the most popular ones are listed in the table below:

Name	Summation	Solution
Sum of consecutive integers	$\sum_{i=1}^{n} i$	$\frac{n(n+1)}{2}$
Sum of squares	$\sum_{i=1}^{n} i^2$	$\frac{2n^3+3n^2+n}{6}$
Sum of the powers of 2	$\sum_{i=0}^{k} 2^i$	$2^{k+1} - 1$
Geometric sum	$\sum_{i=0}^{k} a^i$	$\frac{a^{k+1}-1}{a-1}$
Miscellaneous	$\sum_{i=1}^{k} i2^i$	$(k-1)2^{k+1} + 2$
Ceilings and logarithms	$\sum_{i=1}^{n} \lceil \log(i+1) \rceil$	$(n+1)\log(n+1) - n$
Floors and logarithms	$\sum_{i=1}^{n} \lfloor \log i \rfloor$	$(n+1)\log(n+1) - 2n$

B.4 Solving recurrence equations

A *recurrence relation* is a recursive function that often arises when analyzing the complexity of a recursive algorithm. Recurrence relations are defined using two equations, one representing the *base case* and the another representing the *general case*. The following table gives some common recurrence relations and their solution:

Recurrence relation	Solution
$f(n) = \begin{cases} d & ,n=0 \\ f(n-1)+bn+c & ,n>0 \end{cases}$	$\frac{b}{2}n^2 + \left[c + \frac{b}{2}\right]n + d$
$f(n) = \begin{cases} d & ,n=1 \\ f(n-1)+bn+c & ,n>1 \end{cases}$	$\frac{b}{2}n^2 + \left[c + \frac{b}{2}\right]n + (d-c-b)$
$f(n) = \begin{cases} d & ,n=1 \\ af(\frac{n}{a})+bn+c & ,n>1 \end{cases}$	$bn\log_a n + \left[\frac{c}{a-1} + d\right]n - \frac{c}{a-1}$ (assuming $n = a^k$)

As an example, consider the following recurrence relation:

$$f(n) = \begin{cases} 1 & ,n=0 \\ f(n-1)+2n+4 & ,n>0 \end{cases}$$

This is an instance of the first recurrence relation in the table with $b = 2$, $c = 4$ and $d = 1$ so the solution is $n^2 + 5n + 1$.

More details and advanced concepts related to solving recurrence relations can be found in Section 4.7 of the book by Brassard and Bratley [19].

Index